CASES IN PUBLIC RELATIONS STRATEGY

CASES IN PUBLIC RELATIONS STRATEGY

Editors

Burton St. John III
University of Colorado–Boulder

Diana Knott Martinelli
West Virginia University

Robert S. Pritchard
University of Oklahoma

Cylor Spaulding
Georgetown University

Los Angeles | London | New Delhi
Singapore | Washington DC | Melbourne

FOR INFORMATION:

SAGE Publications, Inc.
2455 Teller Road
Thousand Oaks, California 91320
E-mail: order@sagepub.com

SAGE Publications Ltd.
1 Oliver's Yard
55 City Road
London EC1Y 1SP
United Kingdom

SAGE Publications India Pvt. Ltd.
B 1/I 1 Mohan Cooperative Industrial Area
Mathura Road, New Delhi 110 044
India

SAGE Publications Asia-Pacific Pte. Ltd.
3 Church Street
#10-04 Samsung Hub
Singapore 049483

Acquisitions Editor: Terri Accomazzo
Content Development Editor: Anna Villarruel
Editorial Assistant: Sarah Wilson
Production Editor: Bennie Clark Allen
Copy Editor: Melinda Masson
Typesetter: C&M Digitals (P) Ltd.
Proofreader: Sarah J. Duffy
Indexer: Molly Hall
Cover Designer: Anupama Krishman
Marketing Manager: Staci Wittek

Copyright © 2019 by SAGE Publications, Inc.

Printed in the United States of America

Library of Congress Cataloging-in-Publication Data

Names: St. John, Burton, 1957- editor.

Title: Cases in public relations strategy / editors, Burton St. John, III, University of Colorado-Boulder, Diana K. Martinelli, West Virginia University, Robert S. Pritchard, University of Oklahoma, Cylor Spaulding, Georgetown University.

Description: Thousand Oaks, California : SAGE, [2019] | Includes bibliographical references and index.

Identifiers: LCCN 2018013001 | ISBN 9781506349152 (pbk. : acid-free paper)

Subjects: LCSH: Public relations—Case studies. | Public relations—Study and teaching.

Classification: LCC HM1221 .C375 2019 | DDC 659.2—dc23
LC record available at https://lccn.loc.gov/2018013001

This book is printed on acid-free paper.

18 19 20 21 22 10 9 8 7 6 5 4 3 2 1

BRIEF CONTENTS

DETAILED CONTENTS

ACKNOWLEDGMENTS

This case study book began, conceptually, seven years ago. It took time to develop for numerous reasons: changes in publishers, changes in editors, and, more simply, new case contributors coming forward with more recent and compelling case studies. There are numerous individuals whom the editors wish to acknowledge for helping make this book possible.

Burton St. John III expresses particular gratitude to Alma Caldwell and Susan Malandrino, who provided extensive support, feedback, and "leg work" that led to conceiving a different kind of public relations case study book. Some of their work informed the book you now hold in your hands. There have also been at least two sets of anonymous reviewers for original proposals involving this book; their work is greatly appreciated. Michael Rosenberg and Megan Garvey were also original proponents of this book's approach and deserve many thanks. Finally, Burt thanks his family for their consistent, patient support.

Diana Knott Martinelli offers that, at the conclusion of any large project, there is a sense of satisfaction at seeing it realized. During times like these, she reflects on those whose love and support spurred both initiative and sound perspective: her amazing husband, David; her wise and witty father, Harold; and her lovely late mother, Elanda Lee. She is also grateful to all of her students over the years for their creativity, dedication, scholarship, energy, work ethic, and curiosity. She says, "You are why we do what we do."

Robert S. Pritchard thanks his bride, Brenda, for all her support and encouragement throughout this project. He also dedicates his efforts in bringing this project to fruition to the memory of his father, Harmon O. Pritchard Jr.

Cylor Spaulding thanks his family for their patience.

All the editors thank the contributors to this volume—without their constant and reliable partnership, this book would not have been possible. We also thank Terri Accomazzo, Matt Byrnie, Sarah Wilson, Bennie Clark Allen, Melinda Masson, Sarah Duffy, and the entire SAGE team for their enthusiastic support of this project.

ABOUT THE EDITORS

Burton St. John III, PhD, APR, is professor of public relations within the College of Media, Communication, and Information at the University of Colorado-Boulder. In 2017, he co-authored, with Yvette Pearson, *Crisis Communication and Crisis Management: An Ethical Approach* (SAGE), authored *Public Relations and the Corporate Persona: The Rise of the Affinitive Organization* (Routledge), and edited the previously unpublished Ivy Lee book manuscript *Mr. Lee's Publicity Book: A Citizen's Guide to Public Relations* (PRMuseum Press). He has 28 years of experience as a practitioner and educator in public relations.

Diana Knott Martinelli, PhD, serves as associate dean and is the Widmeyer Professor in Public Relations at the West Virginia University Reed College of Media. She is a member of the Arthur W. Page Society, the Public Relations Society of America, the Association for Education in Journalism and Mass Communication, and Kappa Tau Alpha, and serves on the advisory board of the Plank Center for Leadership in Public Relations at the University of Alabama. She also serves on a variety of editorial review boards, including those for the *Journal of Public Relations Research*, *Mass Communication and Society*, and *Communication Research Reports*. She regularly gives seminars to government, professional, and academic audiences and is an active member of Rotary International.

Robert S. Pritchard, MA, Captain, U.S. Navy (Ret.), APR, Fellow PRSA, is a member of the public relations faculty in the Gaylord College at the University of Oklahoma (OU). With more than 40 years of experience in public relations as a practitioner and educator, he serves as partner and chief strategic counsel for the Golding Group in Oklahoma City, Oklahoma. He is a member of the Public Relations Society of America National Board of Directors, the 2013 PRSA Outstanding Educator, the 2011–2015 PRSSA National Faculty Adviser, and a past chair of the PRSA Educators Academy. He serves as the faculty adviser for the Stewart Harral chapter of the OU Public Relations Student Society of America and advises Lindsey + Asp, the nationally affiliated student-run advertising and public relations firm at Gaylord College. His teaching and research expertise includes student leadership development, student-run firms, strategic public relations planning, crisis communications, and media relations.

Cylor Spaulding, PhD, is the faculty director and an assistant professor of practice for the public relations and corporate communications program at Georgetown University School of Continuing Studies, responsible for overseeing curriculum and faculty and teaching several courses within the program. Prior to going into academia, he spent 10 years in the public relations industry, working for several agencies, including Rogers &

Cowan and Weber Shandwick. In his role with these agencies, Spaulding managed analyst relations, media relations, and consumer relations campaigns on a regional, national, and international scale for clients across multiple industries. He holds a PhD in communication from the University of Miami, an MA in strategic public relations from the University of Southern California, and a BA in journalism from Arizona State University.

PREFACE

An Introduction to Public Relations Case Studies and Strategy

Burton St. John III and Diana Knott Martinelli

If you were to Google "public relations," scores of definitions and ideas about the profession and practice would likely appear. The *Merriam-Webster* dictionary, for example, defines it as "the business of inducing the public to have understanding for and goodwill toward a person, firm, or institution." BusinessDictionary.com says public relations is "the profession or practice of creating and maintaining goodwill of an organization's various publics (customers, employees, investors, suppliers, etc.), usually through publicity and other nonpaid forms of communication." It goes on to say "these efforts may also include support of arts, charitable causes, education, sporting events and other civic engagements."

A public relations textbook by Wilcox and Cameron[1] notes that Rex Harlow, a founder of what would become the Public Relations Society of America (PRSA), once compiled more than 500 definitions of public relations and distilled them into an 86-word sentence/definition! Because of the myriad ways public relations has been described and defined, PRSA, which is the largest professional society of public relations practitioners in the United States, initiated an international crowdsourcing campaign in 2011–2012 to settle on a definition. As a result, the organization describes public relations as "a strategic communication process that builds mutually beneficial relationships between organizations and their publics."[2]

Part of the difficulty in defining public relations is likely due to the many different communication roles public relations professionals can assume. The PRSA website[3] lists many of the following roles as professional areas of emphasis within the profession, although numerous other areas, including investor relations, public affairs, corporate social responsibility, research, nonprofit communications, fundraising/development, and advocacy, also could be included:

- Brand Journalism/Content Marketing
- Corporate Communications
- Digital and Interactive Media

- Employee Communications

- Executive Communications

- Marketing Communications

- Media Relations

- Social Media

- Special Events

- Speechwriting

Although this variety may make the profession seem ambiguous, the breadth of public relations also makes it an exciting and dynamic profession to be part of, and one that offers a plethora of professional opportunities. As you will see from the cases in this book, every organization and cause needs someone to help tell its story and engage others to act. This ubiquitous need for strong communications gives public relations professionals the opportunity to help make a difference for industries and causes about which they are passionate.

WHAT IS STRATEGY?

Beginning public relations students often use the terms *strategy* and *tactics* interchangeably. When asked to develop a communication plan, they tend to jump into the specific ways in which they will communicate: use Snapchat, hold an event, issue a news release, post flyers, and so on. However, if you reexamine the PRSA public relations definition above, you will see the words "*strategic* [emphasis added] communication process." This means the communication process is planned, deliberate, and overarching; it begins with a desired end in mind.

PRSA's website[4] explains, "Today's communicators are responsible for developing strategies and implementing integrated tactics across a wide variety of platforms to create differentiated positioning and align business objectives to further amplify the organization's message." Based on the desired results—be they, for example, greater donations and volunteers for a nonprofit or more engagement with and brand loyalty from consumers—public relations professionals learn all they can about the organization's specific problem or opportunity and the audiences they need to reach to achieve the organization's goals. They begin with research to help define the situation and to better understand the environments that incorporate the organization and its stakeholders.

Communication strategies are approaches that public relations professionals employ to help achieve the desired outcomes and to drive the communication tools needed to do so. These strategies include **defining the audiences** that will best help the organization achieve its goals. The better communication professionals can specify the stakeholders that are most apt to act, the better they can craft messages and approaches that resonate with these stakeholders. Therefore, identifying the audiences you *most need to reach* to achieve your communication goals and objectives—getting a picture of, for example, their demographics, psychographics, geographics, knowledge, attitudes, and behaviors—is a critical strategy for public relations professionals.

Tailoring messages, then, is also an important strategy. Mass "shotgun"-style messages often are not cost-efficient or effective; therefore, more nuanced messages can be developed when you understand your key audiences. For example, messages that include a benefit for your audience are more likely to gain attention, as we are typically motivated by self-interest. Unique selling propositions (USPs) also might be communicated; in other words, what is distinctive or different about your organization or client or its products/services that would interest your target audience?

Emotional and logical appeals also are useful in gaining audiences' attention and persuading them to act. Most of us do not, upon hearing a new message, decide to suddenly act on it. Instead, there tends to be a continuum of action that ranges from simple awareness of something to knowledge about it to a perceived positive (or perhaps negative) attitude toward it, and only then, after much repetition, may we be moved to act. Therefore, messages should be designed to meet target audiences where they are on the continuum, with the ultimate goal of motivating them to act on something (e.g., to donate, volunteer, make a purchase, vote, attend an event, recycle, exercise, or get a physical) or to *not* do something (e.g., smoke, eat junk food, or take drugs). The research we conduct in the beginning can help us identify the audiences we need to reach and what they already know, think/feel, and do or do *not* do.

To gain awareness, emotional appeals often work well. For example, think of a humorous public service announcement that got your attention or a tweeted photo from the local animal shelter that touched your heart. For low-stakes decisions—meaning those that do not take much effort, time, or money—emotional appeals alone may spur someone to act. But, usually, to get people to act, not only is repetition of messages—visually/verbally/aurally—needed, but so are appeals that go beyond touching your funny bone or heartstrings. In these cases, logical appeals also need to be included. For example, there may be facts, statistics, sale prices, research findings, or other types of compelling evidence and/or logical information that support your campaign's call to action.

PUTTING STRATEGY INTO ACTION

As mentioned earlier, students aspiring to a career in public relations, junior public relations professionals, and sometimes even more senior professionals customarily have little difficulty in articulating ways to put public relations strategies into action. Still, we need to acknowledge some particularly important tactical considerations. Examples include using credible **spokespersons** who are authentic, charismatic, and perceived to be similar to the audience you want to reach (i.e., who provide a sense of *homophily*), and/or have some expertise on the issue/topic at hand. Employing **interpersonal communication**, when possible, also is important. Research tells us we are more greatly persuaded by personal communication than by mediated messages. Therefore, if there are opportunities to chat personally through presentations, trade shows, product demonstrations, or events, or to use mediated interpersonal communication such as Skype or chat when real-world face-to-face is not possible, our messaging is likely to be more persuasive to our audience.

Interactivity—giving our audiences a chance to be personally engaged, such as through special events, games, and contests—also can help build trust and positive relationships. **Third-party endorsements** and **testimonials**, such as positive word of mouth on social media from respected bloggers, celebrities, and experts, also are persuasive message delivery tactics. **Partnering** with other respected organizations also can help enlarge our organizations' communications reach and influence.

Even the **timing and length** of campaigns should be considered carefully. For example, the different seasons or specially designated days or months (e.g., Breast Cancer Awareness Month) can be used as "hooks" for news coverage or special events if they are relevant to your organization, client, or brand goals. New services, programs, ideas, or products likely will need a rapid-fire or heavily concentrated/saturated communications schedule to help establish new name recognition among target audiences. These initial campaigns are typically intense, but shorter in duration. Already established or ongoing services, products, or causes might instead use a "slow drip" approach, which serves to remind audiences of the client's/organization's key messages over a longer period of time.

Understanding the many strategic and tactical options available and selecting those that best fit the situation within our allotted budgets and time frames will help you and your communications team be more successful. Furthermore, understanding and employing what we know from communication theory also helps us to be more strategic—and more effective—communicators.

MAJOR THEORIES RELATED TO PUBLIC RELATIONS

There are a number of theories that inform public relations practice, particularly as they relate to segmenting and communicating with audiences, and all offer potential insights for savvy communicators. Some of the better known theories are briefly summarized below:

Stakeholder theory focuses on (a) identifying various audience segments that have something at stake with the organization, (b) determining the level of importance of each of these audiences, and (c) shaping public relations strategies and tactics so as to establish beneficial relationships with them.[5] *Symmetrical communication*, articulated by Grunig and Hunt, maintains that public relations, ideally, acts as a mediator between an organization and its many stakeholders. Therefore, in an attempt to build mutual understanding, an organization should not only disseminate information, but actively seek and receive feedback from its audiences.[6]

Related to both stakeholder theory and symmetrical communication is *systems theory*, an approach that allows for discerning how entities thrive (or become imperiled) within a broader environment. With obvious parallels to natural ecology, a systems theory approach to organizations is concerned with how an organization attempts to stay in balance (or in equilibrium) with changes in the environment so it may persist toward reaching its goals.[7]

Other theories prominent in communications are relevant to public relations. *Agenda-setting theory*, as originally articulated, explains how the news media (and now, increasingly, social media) determine what issues audiences think are important, but not necessarily how they should think about those issues.[8] Increasingly, however, theorists who study *framing* articulate that media forms also tell us how to think about what they present—especially through how message creators select, emphasize, and elaborate on items, while excluding or de-emphasizing others.[9]

Furthermore, how audiences receive and process new information is also explained through the *diffusion of innovations* theory.[10] Depending on the idea, technology, product, or service being launched, individuals will consistently fall into one of five specific audience types: innovators, early adopters, early majority, late majority, or laggards. Understanding these audience segments is crucial, for innovators must accept and use/ buy the new concept first, before the idea or product will be accepted by the early adopters, who then must accept it before it is adopted by the early majority, and so on. Each of these audiences proceeds through five stages to accept or adopt the new information, ideas, and approaches: (1) acquire *knowledge* about the innovation, (2) seek out more information about the innovation, opening themselves up to *persuasion*, (3) make a *decision* to accept or reject the innovation, (4) *implement* the innovation, and (5) *confirm* to themselves whether to persist in the innovation or revise their course.[11]

Cognitive dissonance theory provides further insights into individual processing of information. Individuals who perceive that a message is incompatible with their beliefs can engage in selective exposure (the avoidance of that information) or selective retention (the recall of only information that is compatible with one's beliefs).[12] Introducing new facts, information, or research into messages designed for these selective audiences, and/or using an unexpected spokesperson, can help break through their self-defense mechanisms. Similarly, the *narrative paradigm theory* states that individuals process their world through stories that appear to be internally consistent (narrative coherence) and appear to ring true (narrative fidelity).[13] Collectively, all these theories provide grounding and the basis for further insights into how audiences may be disposed or resistant to strategic messages and tactical actions offered by an organization's communications team.

The *situational theory of publics*, developed by Grunig[14] and evolved over time, explores why people communicate about an organization or issue and when they are most likely to do so. It is often used to explore levels of activism or issues of crisis by dividing audiences into active publics, passive publics, and inactive publics for a given situation or issue. In doing so, it incorporates audience perceptions, which include *problem recognition*, where people believe something should be done about a situation and are thus active in seeking out information about it; *constraint recognition*, where people believe there are obstacles that limit their ability to act; and *level of involvement*, which indicates the extent to which people believe an issue is relevant to them.

There are other theories that explain how public relations has an important role in the prevention and/or management of crises. *Corporate apologia* addresses how organizations take several different defensive rhetorical approaches in the face of a crisis—often displayed through such strategies as denial, apology, minimization, or counterattack.[15] *Image repair theory* (once referred to as image restoration theory), while similar to apologia, focuses more on attempting to repair the image of the actor accused of promulgating the crisis, without necessarily acting on the organization's role in the root cause. This may involve some actions that are similar to apologia methods such as denial and attacking the accuser.[16]

Coombs's *Situational Crisis Communication Theory* (SCCT) is primarily concerned with how stakeholders understand and assign responsibility for a crisis. It states that organizations in the midst of crisis will need to provide two types of information to their audiences: (a) material that helps audiences take steps to protect themselves (informing information) and (b) expressions of concern by the responsible organization and what that organization is doing to address the crisis (adjusting information).[17]

Finally, a more optimistic, future-oriented approach to crisis is the *discourse of renewal theory*.[18] Rather than protecting or repairing the organization's image, this theory emphasizes learning from the crisis, growing as an organization, and employing an ethical approach to prospective communication. The theory moves beyond determining legal liability or responsibility for the crisis and provides a vision to overcome the crisis and transform the organization to mobilize stakeholder support.

The above descriptions provide simple summaries of theories that can help public relations professionals be more thoughtful, strategic, and effective in their communication approaches. There is a vast amount of research literature that explores and tests the theoretical concepts above, as well as theories that help define and predict successful organization–public relationships (OPRs), health communications, stewardship, and persuasion, among others. Through open access research journals and college library databases, a wealth of communications and public relations scholarship can be explored and applied.

THE IMPORTANCE OF THE RACE APPROACH

Understanding key theories that relate to the practice of public relations is valuable, but how does one best visualize how public relations strategy appears in the world around us? In 1963, John Marston said that the flow of public relations campaigns offer important insights. For a campaign to be successful, he said, events should progress in this order: (1) gathering of **research**, (2) determination of strategic **action** plans, (3) rollout of **communication** tactics, and (4) **evaluation** of outcomes. Using the acronym RACE (research, action planning, communication, and evaluation), he said that this approach facilitated an "orderly pattern of thought" that could allow one to "face the truth squarely," and to focus not on "what you would want to hear," but on "what others would find interesting."[19] Since 1963, there have been other similar acronyms for studying the pattern of public relations campaigns, including ROPE (research, objectives, programming, and evaluation) and GRACE (goal-setting, research, assessment, communication, and evaluation). This book, however, emphasizes the RACE model.

The RACE approach is particularly useful because it guides both the client and the public relations professional toward focusing first on priorities before discussing actions. For example, clients may maintain they have a clear idea of an opportunity or problem that needs to be addressed, but research should be methodically conducted nonetheless to identify the environmental factors affecting both clients and their stakeholders (the *R* element). Beginning with appropriate and useful research, the campaign can then

- pursue action-oriented discussion with clients about strategies that are aligned with their goals and objectives (the *A* element);

- effectively program communication activities for the client (the *C* element); and

- appropriately assess throughout the campaign and after its completion how well the campaign met the needs of the client (the *E* element).

As mentioned earlier, developing strategy is crucial. Furthermore, RACE is an ideal foundation for public relations practitioners to better realize that strategy is, in large part, carefully understanding and conceiving (a) the organization's vision, mission, values, and story lines (what the client is about, its culture, its value/importance to others, what it intends to achieve, etc.), and (b) how its story lines can best connect with the needs, desires, and wants of the stakeholders it relies on to survive and thrive. In a fast-paced world, where organizations and public relations practitioners often encounter pressures to act promptly, it is important to realize first the compelling needs displayed by both the client and its stakeholders. When one couples that aim with an understanding of the RACE process, the odds of helping an organization successfully meet its goals are greatly enhanced.

HOW TO USE THIS BOOK

This textbook uses real-life communication cases, submitted by a variety of professionals directing public relations efforts across the United States and, in some cases, around the world. As you read through the cases, note the problem or opportunity each communication campaign aims to solve or embrace, the research conducted to inform the effort, the overall communication goals, the various strategies and tactics employed, the calls to action used, and how theoretical approaches may have been—or could have been—applied. Also pay special attention to the objectives: Were they SMART (specific, measurable, achievable, relevant, and time-sensitive)? How were the objectives assessed? What did campaign "success" mean in each case? To encourage such critical questions, each full case study in Chapters 1–8 has two ending sections—called "RACE Pit Stop" and "Trendlines"—designed to help the reader pause and reflect on public relations' contributions. Additionally, some chapters feature shorter pieces called "A Strategic View," providing the reader with important firsthand observations about using public relations and strategy in real-world scenarios. The latter sections of this book also offer Chapter 8's shorter pieces on a range of different strategic public relations approaches, and the Appendix offers insights into the challenges public relations practitioners face when they offer strategic counsel to their clients.

While individual case studies are unique, they provide opportunities to learn through the decisions and work of current public relations professionals. While many cases within this text reflect today's modern communications landscape, others demonstrate timeless foundational principles and provide fodder for communicating within new contexts. In addition, many of the cases describe successful campaigns, but others fell short of their goals. The cases that appear to fall short are just as valuable (if not more so) than the cases that appear to be flawless. Failures can provide ideal opportunities to reflect, learn, and plan for better outcomes. In contrast, successes may lead to unimaginative, rote repetition of past activities—a risky approach in today's fast-paced and often discordant world. We hope all of the case studies contained herein serve to inspire creativity, critical thinking, rich reflection, and passion and enthusiasm for the public relations profession.

DIGITAL RESOURCES

SAGE edge content is open access and available on demand at **edge.sagepub.com/stjohn**.

SAGE edge for Students provides a personalized approach to help students accomplish their coursework goals in an easy-to-use learning environment.

- Mobile-friendly practice **quizzes** allow for independent assessment by students of their mastery of course material.

- **Chapter and Case summaries** reinforce the most important material.

SAGE edge for Instructors supports your teaching by making it easy to integrate quality content and create a rich learning environment for students.

- **Test banks** provide a diverse range of pre-written options as well as the opportunity to edit any question and/or insert your own personalized questions to effectively assess students' progress and understanding.

- Editable, chapter-specific **PowerPoint® slides** offer complete flexibility for creating a multimedia presentation for your course.

- **Sample course syllabi** for semester and quarter courses provide suggested models for structuring your courses.

- **Multimedia content** includes third-party video, audio, and web links that appeal to diverse learners.

- **Chapter and Case Summaries** summarize key concepts and cases by chapter to help you prepare for lectures and class discussions.

- **Case Study Resources** includes a resource guide for instructors teaching the case course the first time, links to award-winning cases, chapter activities, and sample long-term projects students can undertake to facilitate a deeper exploration of public relations.

1. Wilcox, D. L., & Cameron, G. T. (2010). *Public relations strategies and tactics* (9th ed.). Boston, MA: Allyn & Bacon.

2. PRSA. (2017). About public relations. *All About PR*. Retrieved from https://www.prsa.org/all-about-pr/

3. Ibid.

4. Ibid.

5. Freeman, R. (2010). *Strategic management: A stakeholder approach*. New York, NY: Cambridge University Press; Grunig, J., & Repper, F. (1992). Strategic management, publics, and issues. In J. Grunig (Ed.), *Excellence in public relations and communication management* (pp. 117–157). Hillsdale, NJ: Erlbaum.

6. Grunig, J. E., & Hunt, T. (1984). *Managing public relations*. New York, NY: Holt, Rinehart, and Winston; Register, M., & Larkin, J. (2005). *Risk issues and crisis management: A casebook of best practice* (3rd ed.) London, England: Kogan Page.

7. Miller, J. G. (1978). *Living systems*. New York, NY: McGraw-Hill; Katz, D., & Kahn, R. L. (1966). *The social psychology of organizations*. New York, NY: Wiley; Greenwood, C. A. (2010). Evolutionary theory: The missing link for conceptualizing public relations. *Journal of Public Relations Research, 22*(4), 456–476.

8. McComb, M., & Shaw, D. (1972). The agenda-setting function of the mass media. *Public Opinion Quarterly, 36*, 176–187; Waters, R. D. (2013). Tracing the impact of media relations and television coverage on U.S. charitable relief fundraising: An application of agenda-setting theory across three national disasters. *Journal of Public Relations Research, 25*(4), 329–346.

9. Entman, R. (1993). Framing: Toward clarification of a fractured paradigm. *Journal of Communication, 43*(3), 51–58; Shir-Rax, Y., & Avraham, E. (2017). "Under the regulation radar": PR strategies of pharmaceutical companies in countries where direct advertising of prescription drugs is banned—the Israeli case. *Public Relations Review, 43*(2), 382–391.

10. Rogers, E. (1995). *Diffusion of innovations* (4th ed.). New York, NY: Free Press.

11. Ibid. See also Avery, E., Lariscy, R., Amador, E., Icowitz, T., Primm, C., & Taylor, A. (2010). Diffusion of social media among public relations practitioners in health departments across various community population sizes. *Journal of Public Relations Research, 22*(3), 336–358.

12. Festinger, L. (1957). *A theory of cognitive dissonance*. Stanford, CA: Stanford University Press; Seiffert-Brockmann, J., & Thummes, K. (2017). Self-deception in public relations: A psychological and sociological approach to the challenge of conflicting expectations. *Public Relations Review, 43*(1), 133–144.

13. Fisher, W. (1987). *Human communication as narration: Toward a philosophy of reason*. Columbia: University of South Carolina; St. John, B. (2014). The good reason of public relations: *PR News* and the selling of a field. In B. St. John, M. O. Lamme, & J. L'Etang (Eds.), *Pathways to public relations: Histories of practice and profession* (pp. 321–339). New York, NY: Routledge.

14. Grunig, J. E. (1968). *Information, entrepreneurship, and economic development: A study of the decision-making processes of Colombian latifundistas*. Unpublished doctoral dissertation, University of Wisconsin, Madison; Kim, J., & Sung, M. (2017). The value of public relations: Different impacts of communal and exchange relationships on perceptions and communicative behavior. *Journal of Public Relations Research, 28*(2), 87–101.

15. Ware, B. L., & Linkugel, W. A. (1973). They spoke in defense of themselves: On the generic criticism of apologia. *Quarterly Journal of Speech, 59*(3), 273–283; Hearita, K. M., & Brown, J. (2004). Merrill Lynch: Corporate apologia and business fraud. *Public Relations Review, 30*(4), 459–466.

16. Benoit, W. L. (2015). *Accounts, excuses, and apologies: Image repair theory and research* (2nd ed.). Albany: State University of New York Press; Benoit, W. L. (1997). Image repair discourse and crisis communication. *Public Relations Review, 23*(2), 177–186.

17. Coombs, W. T. (2012). *Ongoing crisis communications* (3rd ed.). Thousand Oaks, CA: SAGE, p. 2.

18. Seeger, M. W., Sellnow, T. L., & Ulmer, R. R. (2002). A post-crisis discourse of renewal: The cases of Malden Mills and Cole Hardwoods. *Journal of Applied Communication Research, 30*, 126–142; Ulmer, R., Sellnow, T., & Seeger, M. (2015). *Effective crisis communication: Moving from crisis to opportunity*. Thousand Oaks, CA: SAGE, p. 234.

19. Marston, J. (1963). *The nature of public relations*. New York, NY: McGraw-Hill, p. 173.

BRANDING

A brand is essentially a reflection of an organization's identity, which means that branding is a crucial part of crafting a good public relations strategy. A strong, effective brand should communicate an organization's purpose and values to the public and all its stakeholders, is easily identifiable, and fosters positive associations in the mind of stakeholders long after a public relations campaign has ended.

The cases in this chapter, executed on behalf of the University of West Georgia, the United States Conference of Catholic Bishops, and the state of Mississippi, all illustrate how important branding is to an organization and how effective brands can be for communicating with audiences and key stakeholders.

"AMAZING THINGS HAPPEN WHEN YOU GO WEST": RAISING VISIBILITY, INTEREST, AND ENROLLMENT

Jami Payne Bower, Associate Vice President, University Communications and Marketing, University of West Georgia

Amber M. K. Smallwood, Associate Professor of Mass Communications, University of West Georgia

SITUATION

The University of West Georgia (UWG) is the state's seventh-largest public university, with a fall of 2017 enrollment of approximately 13,520. The university is located 45 minutes from Atlanta and draws students from 44 states and 75 countries. As UWG evolved, it developed a track record of growth in academic programs and in student enrollment. More recently, however, enrollment growth rates were slowing. Total enrollment growth slowed at some points from 2003 (10,255) to 2006 (10,163) and again from 2008 (11,252) to 2010 (11,283). In sum, the university saw the opportunity to increase its brand recognition among key constituencies including faculty, staff, alumni, students, prospective students, and parents. It needed to find ways to differentiate, and stand out, from peer universities.

RESEARCH

To better define the institutional challenge, UWG commissioned the university's Survey Research Center to gauge key constituencies' awareness, attitudes, and perceptions of the university.

Four focus groups were held with students, faculty, staff, alumni, and community audiences, comprising 7–10 individuals per group. Common themes heard in focus groups included the following:

> You could be a marginal student, an average student, or an exceptional student. No matter where you came from, you're going to leave better. There's a niche for everyone here.

> We provide a lot of opportunities. We're just the right size for that. There are opportunities for faculty interaction and involvement that you'd never have at a huge school.

> We're not your father's West Georgia. We've grown in research, in academics, in admissions. But we've done it quietly.

Phone surveys were conducted within a 10-county area surrounding the university and stretching to the Atlanta metro area. A total of 282 surveys were completed with prospective students, parents, and influencers. Additionally, a total of 585 web surveys were completed by undergraduate and graduate students, faculty, staff, and alumni. A key finding of this research was low awareness of the university; about 42% of respondents were not familiar with UWG. Among the various groups surveyed (including within metro Atlanta), there was considerable confusion about the difference between UWG and other institutions that include *Georgia* as part of their name. In addition to surveys, agency partner Mindpower Inc., a communications and marketing firm in Atlanta, conducted several weeks of intensive campaign interviews with campus leadership (administrators, deans, department chairs, etc.), campus directors (admissions, enrollment management, student affairs, athletics, alumni, development, etc.), civic and community groups, alumni groups, UWG board and foundation members, and student, faculty, and staff groups. This qualitative research revealed those who were familiar with UWG described it as up-and-coming, cool, understated, right-sized, a place for involvement and personal discovery, open-minded, proud, engaged, non-elite, first-choice, and ambitious. Through the focus groups, surveys, and interviews, it became clear that the university did not suffer from a negative perception. Rather, there was a bewildering non-perception. Survey participants noted a lack of tradition or legacy as the university was not known for specific traditions. They noted that UWG was not top-of-mind or in the "considered" category for many prospective students. It seemed many of the state's brightest students might not have UWG on their radars.

ACTION PLANNING

In 2010, university leadership, with a $2 million campaign budget, designated developing and investing in a brand identity as a top priority with the following goals in mind:

- Raise and improve the university's regional profile.

- Become a first-choice destination for more students.

The overall message for the campaign was that UWG was ready to show the world what it meant to "Go West." That phrase expressed not only where UWG was, but where it was going—becoming a forward-looking, future-oriented institution.

For students, UWG emphasized that to Go West was to explore, discover, and learn, both about oneself and about the world around one. Go West was a symbol of the academic community UWG had built and how that atmosphere could help students attain their goals and aspirations.

For prospective students (10th–12th graders) and parents (particularly mothers ages 45–54), Go West provided the opportunity for students who did not want to follow the crowd to be inspired by the virtually unlimited ways to *make their mark* through leadership opportunities, discovering potential career paths, and finding new ways to make a difference.

Faculty and staff could make their mark in the programs and courses they developed to support students—through research, mentoring, and transforming student lives.

Alumni went west and beyond to make their mark in successful lives and careers. Since they had blazed their own trails, they were in an excellent position to inspire and support the independent, adventurous spirit of the students who would follow.

Local communities and the general public could be inspired by the Go West spirit to connect to, and show support for, the campus community and recommend that the high school students in their lives explore UWG.

The objectives for this campaign, all to be accomplished by December 31, 2013, included the following:

- Increase awareness from 82.6% to 85.1%.

- Increase familiarity from 64.2% to 66.1%.

- Increase microsite visits and visits to the UWG home page by 2% to 3%.

- Increase social media following by 5% to 10%, dependent on the platform.

- Maintain a high level of students recommending UWG to other students.

- Maintain the number of applications in 2013 (which had slightly dipped in 2012).

- Collaborate with enrollment management/admissions to increase enrollment by 2.3%.

BURSTING WITH IDEAS AND PASSION?

HEAD WEST. Going West means having plenty of room for your mind to roam. Whether you're an artist in need of a canvas or an up-and-coming entrepreneur with a revolutionary business idea, you'll have plenty of opportunities to change the world as you know it at the University of West Georgia. With 106 mind-opening majors, more than 150 student organizations, and countless research and internship opportunities, you'll create your own path to success. Ready to explore West? **gowestgeorgia.com**

UNIVERSITY *of*
West Georgia.

Source: University of West Georgia, www.westga.edu/admissions/. Reproduced with permission.

COMMUNICATION

The UWG brand story was first shared internally to rally support, engagement, and excitement. The campus roll-out included each of the following:

- Multiple consensus-building presentations: The UWG brand rollout was presented to key constituencies to seek support and enthusiasm for the campaign. Presentation settings included UWG leadership, the brand committee, the presidential advisory council, three campus town hall meetings, the faculty senate, admissions and recruiters, business and finance partners, student organizations (including the UWG Student Government Association, the Public Relations Student Society of America, and the UWG Center for Student Involvement), athletics, and local and Atlanta-area alumni and key influencers.

- Campus engagement campaigns: Teaser chatter went viral on social media channels and the UWG website to target students, faculty, and staff with messaging to generate intrigue and excitement, such as "Watch for something BIG at UWG!" and "Get on the Brand Wagon!"

- Go West "Pack Pride" card: Students, faculty, staff, community members, and alumni presenting their branded Go West "Pack Pride" card or key fob received discounts from local area merchants.

The external campaign included advertising and publicity launched locally and in Atlanta:

- Paid placement/advertising: Spanning television and cable, outdoor, cinema, radio, digital, newspaper (local and west Georgia region), and targeted area business and chamber publications, the incorporation of paid media was foundational in the success and outcomes of the comprehensive communications campaign due to its mass reach appeal.

- Digital presence: The UWG website takeover featured high-interest stories, testimonials, and vibrant imagery that made a significant splash and provided the opportunity to optimize the site for efficient Internet searches. In addition, Google AdWords (the display of advertising copy and/or imagery linked to targeted keywords) provided a solid place for inquiry and interest. Digital display ads were placed on premium sites based on key target audience demographics (gender, age segmentation, geographic location, etc.). The campaign used video to capture attention and placed messages on targeted music-streaming service platforms. Multiple digital screens across campus featured branded content.

- Press mentions: The UWG Go West brand story was featured as a cover story in the national *Higher Education Marketing Report* publication. Local newspapers and magazines in the west Georgia region featured news of the Go West campaign. The UWG student newspaper, radio and television stations, and social media platforms featured the brand launch with periodic follow-up pieces.

- UWG Go West microsite (www.westga .edu/admissions): All aforementioned communications strategies pointed prospects to a dedicated microsite full of information for how to "apply west." The fully branded site showcased stories and videos featuring "best of west" students, faculty, and alumni. This included a "who's going west" section for students to share their individual experiences from all walks of academic and campus life, a Go West gear tab, and, most prominently, the "apply" button. Prospects requesting more information on UWG received Go West magnetic shields.

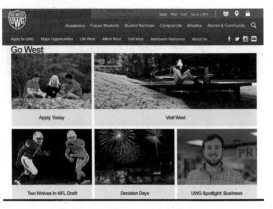

EVALUATION

A 2014 telephone survey of the 10-county area surrounding UWG revealed 80.9% of respondents had heard of UWG (slightly down from 82.6% in 2013) and were familiar with the institution (up from 64.2% in 2013). Go West microsite visits were up 93.4% (2015 peak of 8,830 vs. 2010 benchmark of 4,565). Go West microsite unique visits were up 120.3% (2015 peak of 8,301 vs. 2010 benchmark of 3,768). University home page total visits were up 0.3% (2015 peak of 595,716 vs. 2010 benchmark of 593,814). Evaluation of social media found that Facebook likes were up 283.4% (2015 peak of 21,681 vs. 2010 benchmark of 5,655). Twitter followers were up 1203.7% (2015 peak of 3,846 vs. 2010 benchmark of 295). LinkedIn company connections were up 1070.3% (2015 peak of 5,945 vs. 2010 benchmark of 508). LinkedIn university connections were up 40.4% (2015 peak of 33,354 vs. 2013 benchmark of 23,748). A 2014 web-based survey of faculty and staff revealed the main message of the campaign seen or heard by faculty and staff was overwhelmingly Go West. Of respondents, 90% reported having been exposed to brand messaging through the top four media—billboards, radio, television, and social media.

A 2014 student web-based survey mirrored this. Go West was overwhelmingly cited as the main message of the campaign. Additionally, three-quarters (76%) of respondents reported recommending UWG to other students. UWG's Admissions Office tracked significant increases in campus visits and attendance at scheduled campus preview days. Attendance was up 41.1% (2015 peak of 1,957 visitors vs. 2011 benchmark of 1,387 preview day visitors). The number of prospective students visiting campus increased 26.6% (2015 = 5,459 campus visitors vs. 2012 = 4,312 campus visitors). Submitted applications were up 23.8% (fall of 2015 = 7,878 vs. fall of 2010 benchmark = 6,361). Student enrollment was up more than 15% (fall of 2017 = 13,520 vs. fall of 2010 benchmark = 11,283).

From 2011 to 2015, the Go West campaign itself garnered three Telly Awards, four *Higher Education Marketing Report* Awards (including Best of Show), and 11 Council for the Advancement and Support of Education Region III Awards (including the Grand Award).

RACE PIT STOP

Discussion Questions

1. The UWG campaign used both qualitative (focus groups and interviews) and quantitative (surveys) research methods to help inform the campaign strategy. What are the benefits of using both types of research, and how did it help this campaign?

2. The authors indicate that name recognition, awareness, and familiarity surveys were conducted on an ongoing basis throughout the campaign. What is the benefit of doing this? Would all communications campaigns benefit from this? Why or why not?

3. Why was it important to share the new "brand story" with internal audiences first?

4. Based on the results reported in the evaluation section of the case, did the campaign achieve all the objectives laid out in the action planning section. Would this campaign be considered a success? Why or why not?

Trendlines

Higher education, as an industry, is facing an increasingly complex landscape. As *Inside Higher Ed* notes, decreasing student enrollments,

costs, an increasing focus on applied skills, and declining funding from states are some of the issues colleges are struggling with now.[1] In addition to these issues, traditional higher education institutions face increasing competition from for-profit colleges for students. While some institutions are searching for ways to attract students and gain a competitive edge, others have been forced to close. Smaller, liberal arts colleges are particularly at risk, since they have fewer resources than some of the larger universities. Examples of these closings can be seen across the country at schools such as Bethany University in California, which closed in 2011.

With the increasing pressure on higher education to be competitive, cost-efficient, and self-sustaining, schools are creatively finding ways to raise their visibility with various audiences. UWG's campaign focused on raising its profile with more regional audiences. Would the university have benefited from a nationwide strategy? Research some of the other public universities in your area. What can you determine about those schools' public relations strategies? How do they compare to the strategies and tactics UWG used?

REFERENCE

1. Rudgers, L. M., & Peterson, J. A. (2017, January 13). Coming in 2017. *Inside Higher Ed*. Retrieved from https://www.insidehighered.com/views/2017/01/13/upcoming-trends-2017-colleges-should-prepare-essay

GROWING THE POPE'S FLOCK

Fred Cook, Chief Executive Officer, Golin

SITUATION

In anticipation of Pope Francis's historic first visit to the United States in September 2015, the United States Conference of Catholic Bishops (USCCB) recognized the welcome opportunity to make a big social media splash surrounding the Pope and increase Hispanic engagement on USCCB social media channels. The USCCB, with the availability of cutting-edge 21st century social media tools and techniques, could now bring the Pope's message, developed over the first 20 centuries, to the people like never before and encourage Catholics and non-Catholics to perform acts of mercy in accordance with the Church's mission.

RESEARCH

In preparation for relevant content and messages, the team conducted a robust social listening audit in both English and Spanish to understand the issues and attitudes surrounding the Catholic Church and the Pope. Those topics—from climate change, the Middle East conflict, and poverty to marriage and family, child abuse, and immigration—informed communications strategies. A comprehensive communications playbook mapped out potential issues and opportunities, and identified actionable engagements and trending conversations that were preplanned for release during real-time moments throughout the visit. For example, the Church found that Spanish conversation differed from English in several key topics, such as immigration and the canonization of 18th century priest Junípero Serra. Understanding that those topics would drive significant Hispanic conversation, the Church prioritized engagement with influencers and the sharing of real-time content that aligned to the messages that the Pope would deliver to the Hispanic audience.

ACTION PLANNING

The USCCB's goal was to amplify the message of the visit, "love is our mission," and joyously move people to merciful action. Merciful action was defined as anything from praying to showing compassion for another human to sharing a message from the Church that resonated with individuals.

The USCCB wanted to appeal to a total marketing audience that included Catholics and non-Catholics. It appealed to the important millennial audiences (knowing how active they are on social media) through content that resonates with them including GIFs and video, and its total market approach to certain topics such as immigration helped ensure the USCCB reached the Hispanic audience. Additionally, when communicating with policy makers or Church leaders, at times the USCCB needed to be mindful of emphasizing Catholic beliefs or correcting misinterpretations of the Pope's actions or statements. Still, for all targets, love and mercy was the central message emphasized.

Campaign objectives were as follows:

- Protect and promote the messages of Pope Francis by driving impressions and engagements with the USCCB's messages.

- Engage with the faithful to share and encourage their acts of mercy.

- Spread messages of love and unity around the world.

- Achieve a more positive view of the Catholic Church.

COMMUNICATION

Golin developed a holistic media strategy that encompassed social content, influencer outreach (i.e., making connections with influential people), and proactive media mes-

Source: Courtesy of Golin. Reproduced with permission.

saging. In recognizing the significant media coverage and social conversation that the Pope's visit would spark, the team created a unique social presence for the USCCB that would distinctly amplify the Pope's messages. New Twitter and Instagram handles were created in both English and Spanish (@PopeInUS and @PapaEnUSA), and, in partnership with Twitter, a hashtag emoji of the Pope in front of an American flag was auto-populated for #PopeInUS and #PapaEnUSA. To successfully execute significant media outreach and social engagement, the team relied on The Bridge—Golin's approach for real-time insights, influencer engagement, and media outreach— comprising strategists, writers, editors, designers, and creative content developers. This team created 2,268 pieces of social media content in the form of creative images, messages, and GIFs, including 62 videos. For example, the USCCB shared a video at the end of each day highlighting the moments and shared quotes and GIFs from Pope Francis that aligned with the goal of his visit. In addition, the team responded to more than 1,500 influencers and Pope fans in both English and Spanish in inspiring ways that the Church had never done before. To do this, the USCCB identified people attending or watching events of the visit, and asked them individually via social media what they were praying for. People responded to the USCCB with prayers of peace, love, and health for Pope Francis, among many other things.

Throughout the six-day U.S. papal visit, there were 73 billion mentions of the Pope, which comes to about 10 million mentions per minute. The team analyzed these mentions, pinpointed the most influential voices advocating for the church, and then responded, creating relevant content to amplify their voices in real time (the average turnaround time between noticing these prime opportunities and then responding was seven minutes). For example, the USCCB hand-delivered a St. Genesius medal (the patron saint of actors and comedians) and note to Stephen Colbert, congratulating him on his new show. When notables such as Anderson Cooper tweeted about how amazing it was to be close to the Pope, the team shared a celebratory response and commented on what a joyous occasion it was. And when a potentially negative topic surfaced, the team shared real-time quotes from Pope Francis to help amplify the messages of love and mercy.

Source: Twitter/@PopeInUS.

EVALUATION

Overall, the USCCB efforts contributed 30 million earned media impressions in English and Spanish toward the Pope's visit, and 5.1 billion impressions of the campaign's hashtags, #PopeInUS and #PapaEnUSA. This was more than 8% of the total papal visit conversation, ushering in a new era of evangelism for the Pope and the Catholic Church in the United States.

The team created 2,268 pieces of content, including 62 videos, in real time. Over the course of the visit, the USCCB drove 1.65 million video views (more than 13,000 views per hour) and engaged with more than 1,300 individuals. Of those individuals, 120 were influencers, such as Bette Midler, Anderson Cooper, and Shakira. Following the visit, 28% of U.S. adults said they had a more positive view of the Catholic Church because of Pope Francis, according to the Pew Research Center,[1] and the USCCB gained influential followers such as Katie Couric and U.S. Speaker of the House John Boehner.

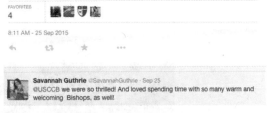

Source: Twitter/@SavannahGuthrie/@USCCB.

RACE PIT STOP

Discussion Questions

1. As part of this campaign in anticipation of Pope Francis's visit, research was conducted on both English- and Spanish-speaking audiences. Why do you think it was particularly important for the public relations team to research both of these audiences?

2. The target audiences for this campaign were very broad (e.g., millennials). Most campaigns try to target very specific audiences. Does it make sense for the public relations team to have such broad target audiences? Why or why not?

3. The public relations team countered any potentially negative topics with quotations from the Pope that reinforced the key messages of mercy and love. Was this a good strategy for handling negative comments? Were there different approaches that could have been used as well?

4. Review the objectives for the campaign. What changes would you recommend, if any?

Trendlines

Organized religion in the United States is at a crossroads, with modest decreases in the number of Americans identifying themselves as religious—from 92% to 89% over a seven-year period.[2] While the decrease is small, it is expected to rise in the coming years with a growing number of millennials avoiding affiliation with any organized faith. As the Pew Research Center notes, the "none" demographic, who are religiously unaffiliated, has increased by 6% over a seven-year period, and while members of this group are not necessarily atheists or agnostics, they do not wish to be part of any organized religion. This could be a concern for established religious institutions if this number continues to rise in the years ahead.

The decrease of religiously affiliated Americans could be of great concern for the Catholic Church, and as the most visible Catholic official, the Pope could play a big role in retaining members in the Church. In addition to the strategies and tactics discussed in this case study, what other ways could the Church use public relations to both retain members and recruit new ones?

REFERENCES

1. Positive impact of Pope Francis on views of the church, especially among Democrats and liberals. (2015, October 7). *Pew Research Center.* Retrieved from http://www.pewforum.org/2015/10/07/following-visit-two-thirds-in-u-s-view-pope-francis-favorably/

2. U.S. public becoming less religious. (2015, November 3). *Pew Research Center.* Retrieved from http://www.pewforum.org/2015/11/03/u-s-public-becoming-less-religious/

MISSISSIPPI, BELIEVE IT: ELEVEN YEARS AND MOVING FORWARD

Jesse McCraw, Brand Strategist, The Cirlot Agency

SITUATION

Mississippi is rooted in its rich culture and history, though much of its history is negative. The perception of the state echoes stereotypes of a region occupied by uneducated, obese, poor, and racist citizens. *Forbes*'s "Best States for Business" list has Mississippi at the bottom in economic climate and quality of life. *Education Week*'s Quality Counts report shows Mississippi at the bottom for academic achievement. The United Health Foundation places Mississippi as 50th in America's Health Rankings, its findings based on the state's high rates of infectious diseases, low adolescent immunization rates, low birth weights, high number of deaths associated with cardiovascular diseases, and high infant mortality rates. Though the state remains at the bottom of many national lists, The Cirlot Agency found an opportunity to use the stereotypes of Mississippi as a means of communicating the greatness that stems from the state. In March 2003, Rick Looser, president and chief operating officer of The Cirlot Agency, was seated next to a 12-year-old boy from Connecticut on a plane headed from Washington, DC, to Jackson, Mississippi. After hearing his southern accent, the boy asked where Looser was from. When Looser said that he lived in Mississippi, the 12-year-old asked: "Do you see the Ku Klux Klan on your streets every day, and do you hate all black people?" Looser was surprised that this was the image of Mississippi as seen through the eyes of a private school–educated child; but he also saw that the state's negative reputation could be a launching point to capture the attention of an audience and to highlight the accomplishments of the state. Starting in December 2005, The Cirlot Agency, headquartered in Jackson, debuted the Mississippi, Believe It! (MBI) campaign, a pro bono initiative that the agency took on for the state. MBI's intent was to tell Americans that the stereotype that stemmed from the Mississippi of 1960 is not who Mississippi is today. In 2015, during its 10th year, those associated with the MBI campaign saw a continued need to heighten awareness of these aspects of the state of Mississippi.

RESEARCH

Although many states have implemented promotional campaigns in the past, The Cirlot Agency had no knowledge of a public relations campaign like MBI. While researching other campaigns, the agency discovered most were for tourism or for taking up residency, such as the famous "Virginia

From Humble Beginning to Hero
The Soaring Spirit of Mississippi's Ensign Jesse Brown

Source: The Cirlot Agency (2016), www.mississippibelieveit. com/. Reproduced with permission.

It's Official.
Mississippi's Sarah Thomas Is the First Female NFL Ref.

Source: The Cirlot Agency (2016), www.mississippibelieveit. com/. Reproduced with permission.

Is for Lovers" campaign, which has been an ongoing, successful campaign since 1969. These efforts, however, are not like MBI in that the campaign does something that most public relations campaigns would never do—repeat the worst things people have said about you.

As its 11th year approached, the MBI campaign had established itself as a voice for greater public understanding about the state. The agency's effort was greatly centered on placing public service advertisements in newspapers throughout Mississippi. Agency members met with the editorial boards of Mississippi's daily newspapers, resulting in almost all agreeing to feature the ads in their publications for free. Over the years, MBI messages played against negative and offensive stereotypical statements to highlight the positive aspects of the state. Ads used humor to get individuals to have an "I didn't know that" moment about the state.

ACTION PLANNING

The goal was to expose as many people as possible to the message that the Mississippi of 1960 is not the Mississippi of today. The campaign targeted all those within and outside the state who call Mississippi home. This began as an internal effort, because unless the

people of Mississippi feel positive and passionate about their state, it is hard to convince anyone else to feel the same. The intent was to help make the people of Mississippi its best ambassadors. MBI also focused on all fourth-grade students in Mississippi with the message that they can be whatever they want to be in life. The posters act as an example of all those who came from Mississippi and what they have been able to achieve. For some of these students, sitting in classrooms located in the poorest state in the country, that message will resonate for a lifetime. Finally, the agency wanted the campaign to reach those outside of the state who have preconceived, stereotypical, and negative opinions regarding Mississippi, or simply know little to nothing about the state.

As the campaign entered its 11th year, Cirlot sought to deliver one set of all 22 posters to approximately 1,100 schools in Mississippi by April 2017. The central approach for the campaign was to continue using negative stereotypes to highlight the accomplishments of Mississippi through four new ads and through lesson plans for fourth-grade students. Two of the new ads focused on Mississippi being the first, as opposed to the last: honoring the first female NFL referee and the first African American aviator in the U.S. Navy.

COMMUNICATIONS

Within the state of Mississippi, press releases announcing the campaign were sent to select newspapers, magazines, and trade publications, along with the Associated Press and other wire services. Posters were sent to approximately 1,100 public and private K–12 schools and every college and university in the state.

In December 2016, Cirlot hosted a press conference celebrating the campaign's 11th anniversary with the release of four new ads, and announced that the campaign had been integrated into lesson plans, which were made available to all fourth-grade teachers in the state. The first two ads focused on Mississippi being the first, as opposed to the last: honoring the first female NFL referee, Sarah Thomas, and the first African American aviator in the U.S. Navy, Jesse Brown. The third ad continued to highlight Mississippians' accomplishments with Malaco Records, known as the "Last Soul Company." The final ad used the same theme and play on words to recognize one of its most famous artists, naturalist Walter Anderson (Mississippians are often referred to as "backwoods").

The Cirlot Agency added elements to the MBI website to complement the communications tactics, which included media kits, frequently asked questions, lesson plans, poster request forms, and all the ads in downloadable formats. The agency also aired the press conference through Facebook Live, as well as promoted the campaign through paid social media ads. Prior to the announcements, Rick Looser met with the publisher of Jackson, Mississippi's *Clarion-Ledger* to talk about the campaign. Subsequently, in its Sunday edition, the *Clarion-Ledger* ran a story on the campaign and dedicated a full page to the most recognized ad: "Yes, we can read. A few of us can even write."

With the set of posters, Cirlot included a specialty ad, which combines elements of several ads to highlight Mississippi as "The Birthplace of America's Music," featuring W. C. Handy, Jimmie Rodgers, and Elvis Presley.

EVALUATION

Prior to 2015, the campaign received coverage from several TV outlets in Mississippi, along with Mississippi Public

Source: The Cirlot Agency (2016), www.mississippibelieveit.com/. Reproduced with permission.

Source: The Cirlot Agency (2016), www.mississippibelieveit.com/. Reproduced with permission.

Broadcasting and university and college publications. The campaign also received a long line of coverage, including from the *New York Times, USA Today, U.S. News & World Report*, the *International Herald Tribune*, the Associated Press, the *Washington Post*, the *Dallas Morning News*, and the *Seattle Post-Intelligencer*. MBI was also featured on NBC's *Today* show as well as NPR's *All Things Considered* and *Morning Edition*, Fox News Radio, and Voice of America radio. Across these news stories, media coverage normally emphasized the stark contrast that the campaign portrays versus the stereotypical caricature of Mississippi and the people who live there. *Washington Post* journalist Neely Tucker, a Mississippi native, said, "I can tell you the best part of the ads is that they leave out the full wording. This is good writing. You say one thing and people know you mean something else." From 2005 to its 11th year, the campaign was viewed by an estimated 150 million people.

Finally, an ongoing relationship with Mississippi public schools helped Cirlot realize that there was an opportunity to further integrate MBI messages into lesson plans. People had begun reaching out to Cirlot to describe how the posters were being used in elementary schools, especially in fourth-grade classrooms, where Mississippi history is first taught. Teachers began requesting additional posters as materials to help teach their lessons. One Mississippi sixth-grade teacher said, "I had the most wonderful time reading these ads to my class. I want them to feel as proud of Mississippi as I do. I made a copy of each ad for them to share with their families. Thanks for the positive spin on our state. We always knew what we had. Thanks for sharing it with everyone else."

RACE PIT STOP

Discussion Questions

1. The public relations team in this case study did not articulate specific measurable objectives. In reviewing the case, particularly the evaluation section, what types of measurable objectives do you think could be applicable to the type of campaign that was executed?

2. The campaign focused first on communicating with residents within Mississippi. Do you think this was a good strategy? Why or why not?

3. A significant strategy for this campaign was engaging schools, teachers, and students in Mississippi. Why do you think the public relations team took this approach? Was this an effective strategy?

4. Why do you think the public relations team made the decision to openly acknowledge all the criticism about the state? Do you think this strategy was beneficial?

Trendlines

State and city convention and visitors bureaus often conduct highly visible public relations and ad campaigns to try to encourage tourism to the state or region. Virginia's "Virginia Is for Lovers" campaign and Las Vegas's "What Happens in Vegas Stays in Vegas" campaign are indicative of this. Virginia's campaign began in 1969 and continued to evolve over the years and helped bring in more than $24 billion in tourism revenue to the state in 2016,[1] while also adding an emphasis on attracting the lesbian, gay, bisexual, and transgender community to the state.[2] While tourism is a key driver for many campaigns, the MBI effort tried to change perceptions of an entire region. This is important to keep residents from leaving the area, to attract businesses and new residents, and to draw visitors.

While the Mississippi campaign attempts to change internal and external perceptions of the state, many other U.S. states and counties have very negative images in terms of health, education, poverty, personal safety, and other areas. Research your city, state, or county. What negative perceptions do people have of it? What creative campaign ideas and messages could help change those perceptions?

REFERENCES

1. Governor McAuliffe announces tourism revenue reached $24 billion in 2016. (2017, May 8). *Office of the Governor of Virginia*. Retrieved from https://governor.virginia.gov/newsroom/newsarticle?articleId=20229

2. Foley, D. (2016, September 25). Virginia now welcoming a broader array of "lovers." *WTOP*. Retrieved from http://wtop.com/virginia/2016/09/virginia-now-welcoming-broader-array-lovers/

A STRATEGIC VIEW: Public Relations and Tech Startups: A Case of OnlineVisas.com

Anna Klyueva, University of Houston–Clear Lake and Velie Law Firm

In the age of digital media, public relations has become increasingly important, especially with the boom of content marketing, which focuses on delivering value-driven subject matter to potential customers. The effectiveness of online content marketing strategies often depends on good material. This is where public relations can offer the most by bringing knowledge and insight to elevating brand perceptions, raising awareness, and positively engaging with publics through content. Public relations offers a variety of cost-effective strategies, and it can serve as a starting point for growing the audience and customer base for many tech startups.

Source: Velie Law Firm (2016), www.onlinevisas.com. Reproduced with permission.

In 2016, Velie Law Firm launched a startup—a global collaboration platform aimed at bringing together immigration attorneys, companies, and individuals from around the world. From the start, OnlineVisas.com's campaign focused on building relationships with publics and using inbound strategies to drive traffic to its new website (www.onlinevisas.com). In general, inbound strategies are about attracting the attention of prospective

Velie Law Firm
April 3, 2016 · ⊘

OnlineVisas has a 94% success rate! We would love the opportunity to assist you in your application process for a variety of visas. Want to know more? Check out our website! www.onlinevisas.com #OnlineVisas #VelieLawFirm #Visas #Visa #immigrationlaw #WeDeliverDreams #Success #Dreams #International #UnitedStates

All you need is a *Dream*

www.onlinevisas.com

👍 Like   💬 Comment   ↪ Share   🌐 ▾

Source: Facebook/@Velie Law Firm.

customers by providing useful content that generates new visitors, fosters a loyal audience for the site, and helps build client leads. The idea behind the inbound strategy for OnlineVisas.com rested on the notion that making friends on social media was more important than making contacts. After all, social media remains social if the content allows users to engage and to socialize. For an inbound strategy to be effective, search engine optimization strategies need to raise the client's online visibility. Moreover, onsite content should offer value and originality, and social content must emphasize genuine engagement, with scheduled posts and promotional content carefully constructed so that they do not counter authenticity.

The campaign aimed to generate website traffic and increase visit duration by 10%, as well as to establish Jon Velie, founder and CEO, as a thought leader and an expert, whose opinion the media might seek. To achieve these goals, the startup team developed a set of social media tactics focused on creating quality content and developing meaningful hashtags that allowed connecting to a larger conversation on immigration.

First, the campaign team made sure messaging and branding was consistent across platforms. An audit of accounts ensured the use of the uniform company description, logos, and website links. Building upon the company's vision, two principal messages were developed: "Delivering Dreams" and "Together, We Move the World." Other messages included slogans such as "94% Success Rate," "Your Visa Is a Click Away," "All You Need Is a Dream," and "Free Re-file in Case of Denial."

Second, messages were paired with appropriate website pages to drive traffic and then hold the visitor's interest, thereby decreasing bounce rate (i.e., the percentage of visitors to a website who leave after looking at only one page). Landing pages with a call to action allowed the website visitors to contact Velie Law and OnlineVisas.com representatives and request a free consultation and a strategy session.

Third, all posts were accompanied by meaningful hashtags that brought together publics interested in the topic, such as #P1visa, #B2visa, #H-1Bvisa, #HR, #OnlineVisas, #flatfeevisaapplication, and #immigration. One important consideration in piggybacking on generic hashtags was to follow the conversation and ensure it was relevant to the campaign's goals. For example,

Velie Law Firm
Published by Teallie Bee [?] · April 14 · ⊘

How is OnlineVisas #MovingTheWorld?
By helping clients obtain: #P1Visa #H1BVisa #B1Visa #B2Visa #E1Visa #E2Visa #H3Visa #IVisa #J1Visa #L1Visa #O1Visa #P3Visa
www.OnlineVisas.com #VelieLawFirm

Immigration Outsourcing
http://www.onlinevisas.com/outsourcing-immigration-services/ If your company or law firm needs to resolve an immigration case, here are some great reasons yo...
YOUTUBE.COM

259 people reached   Boost Post

👍 Like   💬 Comment   ↪ Share   🔻 ▾

⊙ 4

1 share

Source: Facebook/@Velie Law Firm.

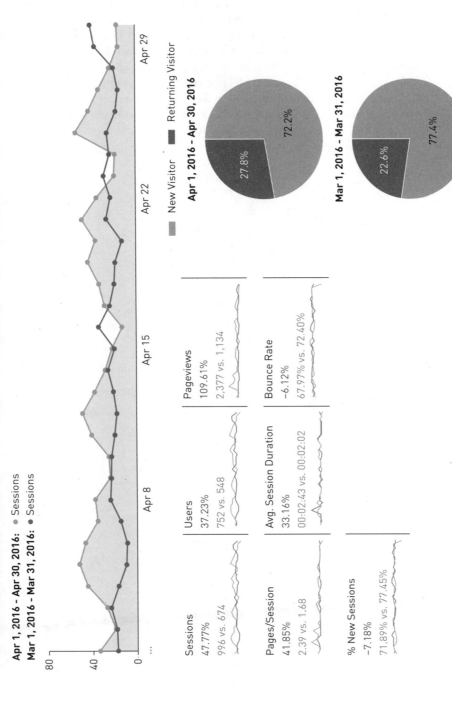

FIGURE 1.1 ■ Analytics of Views for OnlineVisas.com

Apr 1, 2016 - Apr 30, 2016: ● Sessions
Mar 1, 2016 - Mar 31, 2016: ● Sessions

Apr 8   Apr 15   Apr 22   Apr 29

■ New Visitor   ■ Returning Visitor

Apr 1, 2016 - Apr 30, 2016
27.8%   72.2%

Mar 1, 2016 - Mar 31, 2016
22.6%   77.4%

Sessions
47.77%
996 vs. 674

Users
37.23%
752 vs. 548

Pageviews
109.61%
2,377 vs. 1,134

Pages/Session
41.85%
2.39 vs. 1.68

Avg. Session Duration
33.16%
00:02:43 vs. 00:02:02

Bounce Rate
-6.12%
67.97% vs. 72.40%

% New Sessions
-7.18%
71.89% vs. 77.45%

Source: Facebook, Instagram, Google Analytics.

#immigration attracted conversations about sometimes controversial statements from then presidential candidate Donald Trump on the topic and brought in unnecessary negativity. The hashtag was later replaced with #immigrationlaw.

Social analytics data from Facebook, Instagram, and Google Analytics confirmed the campaign's successes. Overall traffic to the website increased by 37%, and the session duration rose by 33%. In addition, the campaign increased page views by nearly 100%, meaning that visitors had accessed rarely viewed content. Overall success of the campaign can be attributed to aligning the campaign's strategic thinking with sound knowledge of appropriate use (and measurement) of social media platforms. Both these strengths led to the creation of value-driven content and meaningful hashtags that targeted publics interested in the subject matter.

2

COMMUNITY RELATIONS

Community relations is an important, but often overlooked, aspect of public relations. With trust in organizations falling dramatically over the past decade, according to the Edelman Trust Barometer, engaging with the community can be extremely valuable in helping rebuild that trust. But it is not enough to just talk about being a good community citizen; an organization actually has to put boots on the ground to effect positive change in stakeholder attitudes and actions.

The case studies that follow in this section depict several avenues of community engagement. "Lights in the Night" illustrates the connections that arts and culture open for those involved with the experience. "Success, Value, Advocacy" demonstrates the benefit of bringing groups together for a common cause. And "The Cleveland Foundation Centennial Campaign" shows that even long-standing organizations formed with the specific purpose of making the community better need to engage stakeholders proactively lest they fade into obscurity.

LIGHTS IN THE NIGHT: LANTERNS MAKE COMMUNITY CONNECTIONS

Adrienne A. Wallace, Assistant Professor of Advertising and Public Relations at Grand Valley State University and Former Director at 8ThirtyFour Integrated Communications

SITUATION

The ArtPrize competition features contributions from around the world displayed in various venues in three square miles of downtown Grand Rapids, Michigan. A free and open event, ArtPrize brings in more than 2,500 entries and attracts more than 500,000 attendees whose votes help determine winners of cash prizes that amount to more than $500,000.

September 21, 2012
Grand Rapids, MI
www.lightsinthenight.org
ArtPrize Vote Code: 52910

Your hope.
Your community.
Your night.

Facebook: /LightsintheNightGR
Twitter: @LightsGR

Source: 8THIRTYFOUR Integrated Communications. Reproduced with permission.

First-time ArtPrize artists Dan Johnson and Mark Carpenter presented a dream to 8ThirtyFour Integrated Communications (8ThirtyFour) in May 2012: 20,000 Chinese sky lanterns, launched at one time by attendees, carrying wishes and hopes as a "community's entry." Called "Lights in the Night: Where Hope Takes Flight" (LITN), the approach for this venue inherently brought numerous risks. Obstacles such as fire, crowds, open water (the Grand River flows through downtown Grand Rapids), nearby highways and traffic on secondary roads, pedestrian traffic, and increased waste at the launch location (a park) loomed as significant concerns. But Johnson and Carpenter saw that these potential hurdles could be overcome to offer a safe event that could communicate a message of unity to the community and convey the importance of art.

RESEARCH

Research revealed that only two ArtPrize competitions since 2009 involved performance art, and therefore it was important to research the unique safety aspects of this event. The Grand Rapids fire chief expressed confidence that the product and the approach would not be a threat to the safety of people, places, or things. The team also researched what lanterns could be selected that would minimize litter and related environmental effects (fuel cells that do not drip, flame-resistant structure, etc.). Additionally, research established what lanterns were legal to launch in Michigan. Research from the ArtPrize website gave us the information that we needed to differentiate LITN from other artists' entries. An interview with the ArtPrize development manager helped provide a profile of the people who come to ArtPrize, including voter demographics, voting statistics, online participation, and behavior/trends from previous years, such as perceptions of performance art pieces and their relative success in the contest.

Further research found that one of the most important factors for success in ArtPrize is location. Mapping out the locations of the finalists in previous years pointed to a locale for the best visibility. The exact venue was chosen after a traffic study of pedestrians and the availability of open green space. After significant secondary research into voter trends, historical perspectives, and historical weather conditions (including consulting a local TV meteorologist), the team was able to settle on five important dates—two dates for "preview launches," the launch date, and two backup dates for the launch.

As primary research, 8ThirtyFour hosted two small "pre-launch" focus groups, which involved members of the media and their close friends and family. From this research, we observed the effectiveness of lantern launching on two different types of weather days (one cool and breezy, one cool and still), noted the intensity of emotional connection within a group dynamic, and determined further safety contingencies for before, during, and after the event.

ACTION PLANNING

Within a budget of about $15,000, the client's ultimate goal was not to win the competition, but rather to safely and successfully provide the public with a once-in-a-lifetime experience. From the beginning, a public relations campaign with event execution was more valuable to the client than accumulating votes or winning a cash prize.

The message for multiple stakeholders—including teens/tweens, young families, and young adults—was simple: create a "magical moment." Tapping into the popularity of the Disney movie *Tangled* (and its memorable use of lanterns), the campaign sought to unite the community in an opportunity to ascribe individual meaning to people's participation in LITN as it was the "community's entry." We emphasized that the event was a time for community members to offer up their dreams in a night of inspiration that honors the whole community.

The campaign had two key measurable objectives, both to be achieved by the September 2012 launch:

- Attract at least 5,000 participants to launch more than 5,000 lanterns.

- Attain top 25 or better standing in the ArtPrize competition.

COMMUNICATION

8ThirtyFour grew a Facebook page organically through tagging, following, and jumping on relevant media conversations. Using Twitter more as a listening tool than as a transmission tool provided the team with valuable intelligence to use in developing Facebook-specific conversations, and steered us clear of any pre-event controversy. Using social media in this way kept the event's reputation secure and allowed us to rapidly debunk anything that was untrue on social media or inaccurately reported on local news websites.

As .this was our fastest-growing tool and the most cost-effective tactic, we were able to articulate our key messaging in the "notes" section of Facebook, through status updates, answering questions, and delivering sound content throughout. We thought that an e-newsletter and blog might be primary ways of reaching audiences, but found that there was more engagement and shares through Facebook than on other platforms. We adjusted our content calendars (e.g., dumped our blogging duties and began more abbreviated content) and posted more regularly on Facebook. Here we were able to share videos,

Source: 8THIRTYFOUR Integrated Communications. Reproduced with permission.

stories, and instructions as things changed with weather and launch locations. Members of the community began to use language and keywords inspired by our media talking points, and they engaged with the artists' stories of why they offered this lantern launch.

At the launch site, we offered launch instructions (mostly for public safety) on large banners at the distribution locations and music courtesy of another performance artist (pianos on the bridges downtown playing classic Americana tunes). We decided to take a huge risk and intentionally left the voting number off of the launch instruction posters as well. While this worked in our favor to create classic conversations on the ground and on social media, it could have massively backfired.

The second thing responsible for this "feeling" on the ground was the movie *Tangled* released by Disney and Pixar earlier in the year. We did not have to go far, or work very hard, to make associations to this film. The movie was basically full of tribal or "cult" knowledge, and both its messaging (about hope) and its ambiance (the light of the lantern) took care of much of the emotional underpinnings.

The campaign pursued a "ground up" media relations tactic. The higher-profile journalists in the West Michigan market were covering the more popular ArtPrize entries, and they were saturated with pitches from across the United States and around the globe. Competition for media outlet attention was fierce. 8ThirtyFour focused instead on journalists who were

Lanterns released at the Lights in the Night event were environmentally friendly—they were made with no metals, allowing them to be compostable.

Source: Derek DeVries. Reproduced with permission.

covering the less popular ArtPrize entries, or who covered a beat that was relevant to the motivation behind LITN and the local community. For example, the campaign held a mock launch at 4:30 in the morning for a local Fox News affiliate and helped *Good Morning America* interview two camera-shy artists.

Following the event, and for the next week, 8ThirtyFour used (with permission) user-generated content for stories, photos, videos, tweets, Facebook status updates, and Instagram posts, with some of it finding its way into traditional news media. Some of the most powerful content came from unexpected places such as registered nurses at the children's hospital and hospice nurses. To help prevent litter from the event, anyone who found a lantern after the launch was encouraged to follow the instructions on the lantern tag for how to return it. Those who returned the lanterns received coupons for a free appetizer and were also eligible for raffle prizes (including the Grand Prize—a seven-night stay for two in Redstone, Colorado). Volunteers with the campaign were dispatched to collect lanterns that residents were not interested in redeeming through the bounty program. In addition, when reports of lantern-related trash in the nearby Grand River began to spring up, staff or volunteers fished out those lanterns and, through social media, showed that they did not match the LITN lanterns.

EVALUATION

The original campaign objectives were surpassed:

- Attract at least 5,000 people to the event to launch lanterns. Result: ArtPrize estimates 50,000–70,000 people were present at the event.

- Launch 5,000+ lanterns depending on the amount of public participation present. Result: 15,000+ lanterns launched.

- Attain top 25 or better standing in the ArtPrize competition. Result: Finished in the top 5 (with a cash prize of $5,000).

Of note, in addition to 8ThirtyFour's original objectives:

- LITN was the first performance entry to break into the top 25 in the history of ArtPrize after securing the most votes in a 24-hour period for any piece in the popular vote, and set a record as the first performance piece to place in the top 10.

- The LITN digital campaign netted more than 4,000 likes on Facebook and 500 Twitter followers with a possible reach of more than 150,000 with each post.

- LITN took roughly 25% of all ArtPrize votes cast.

- LITN resulted in more than 250,000 crowdsourced photographs of the event published online, and the event got more than 9,000 mentions in digital news media both domestically and internationally including blogs, vlogs, and traditional media.

- LITN achieved international coverage in the UK's *Daily Mail* and on Norwegian television. Regional affiliate MLive conveyed the mood perfectly, with Editor Julie Hoogland writing:

It was a singular spectacle: Thousands of glowing round Chinese lanterns launching into a black sky. The magical gleams multiplied as they reflected off the Grand River waters beneath and the windows of the city skyline above. . . .

For 20 magical minutes, we were Sparkle City, USA.

Friday had a special feel in Grand Rapids. ArtPrize crowds crescendoed all day, building to the lantern launch.

Rome? Hong Kong? Sydney? Sao Paulo? How I long to travel the world someday. Set sail. See the wonders. But on Friday, I remember thinking it clearly: There is nowhere I would rather be than right here. Right now. Grand Rapids.[1]

One of the most important lessons from this campaign is to anticipate what could go wrong and have a plan. For example, because of copyright restrictions about background music, some of the most spectacular and most viewed videos about the lanterns were taken down from YouTube. A video posted to YouTube by Jason Grzybowski, a freelance visual designer from Grand Rapids, netted over 180,000 views within 24 hours of the event, but was taken down due to such copyright claims. In contrast, "official" videos from local media outlets WOODTV 8 and WZZM 13 each had under 3,000 views, showing that we are all content creators and that user-generated content and personal connections were far more valuable in creating word-of-mouth public relations than content generated via traditional media channels, digital or otherwise. Had 8ThirtyFour not followed alerts and performed searches for new user-generated media every few hours, we would have likely missed some of the most beautiful (and, yes, illegal), meaningful, and heart-tugging media involved with this event. Before they disappeared, we were able to get a quick screenshot for evaluation purposes to establish that online crowdsourced videos featured anywhere from 55 to 180,000 views. It is worth noting that the budget did not allow for, nor did 8ThirtyFour pay for, a photographer or a videographer.

RACE PIT STOP

Discussion Questions

1. The Lights in the Night case study indicates that a public relations campaign with event execution was more valuable to the client than accumulating votes or winning a cash prize. At least one of the objectives, however, keyed on attaining a top 25 standing. How would you rewrite that particular objective to more closely match the campaign goal?

2. 8ThirtyFour made the decision to avoid messaging at the launch site. Do you think this was a good decision? Why or why not? And what environmental considerations was 8ThirtyFour thinking about in making this decision?

3. 8ThirtyFour also intentionally left the voting number off the launch instructions. The firm claimed this worked in the client's favor by creating "classic conversations on the ground and on social media." What do you think 8ThirtyFour used to measure these conversations? Do you think this decision actually worked for the firm? Why or why not?

Trendlines

A study by the Urban Institute found that, for most people who participate in arts and culture, the experience involves community connections that represent "paths of engagement."[2] It found that a deeper understanding of those everyday connections can open new opportunities for arts and cultural organizations to build participation. How could 8ThirtyFour build upon the success of Lights in the Night to provide new opportunities in arts and culture in Grand Rapids? Could the momentum achieved by the success of Lights in the Night be used to grow additional paths of engagement not necessarily tied to arts and culture?

REFERENCES

1. Hoogland, J. (2012, September 29). Prettiest sky in the country? Last night, it belonged to Grand Rapids. *MLive*. Retrieved from http://www.mlive.com/opinion/grand-rapids/index.ssf/2012/09/prettiest_sky_in_the_country_l.html

2. Walker, C. (2002). Arts and culture: Community connections. *Urban Institute*. Retrieved from https://www.urban.org/sites/default/files/publication/67426/310512.pdf

Media Contact

Kim Bode

8ThirtyFour Design and Marketing

(616) 299-2677

kim@834design.com

FOR IMMEDIATE RELEASE

100% Community-Driven, Interactive, and Executed Entry Makes ArtPrize Top 10

Fifteen thousand lanterns lifted into the night sky as part of the ArtPrize entry, Lights in the Night, on September 28, 2012.

Grand Rapids, Michigan: Lights in the Night: Where Hope Takes Flight was voted into the ArtPrize top 10 on Sunday, September 30. The epic ArtPrize entry was staged on Friday, September 28, and could not be ignored as over 15,000 glowing orbs lifted into the air from downtown locations garnering attention from around the world.

As described by local artists Dan Johnson and Mark Carpenter, the lantern launch was symbolic of the hopes and dreams of thousands of Grand Rapidians and visitors/volunteers alike. When eco-friendly Chinese sky lanterns ascended into the sky at 8:00 p.m., thousands looked and formed a new instant community in what was arguably the most awe-inspiring and breathtaking ArtPrize experience in history.

"The response was unbelievable; lines were wrapped around the park and down the street with people waiting to get a lantern. People showed up hours early to find a spot and wait for the signal," said Johnson. "We had to shut down Bridge Street Bridge and parts of Pearl Street to make room for all those in attendance—it was magical."

Lights in the Night Grand Rapids was the first ever 100% community-driven, interactive, and publically executed event in ArtPrize history. Over 15,000 lanterns were launched into the Grand Rapids sky, with the community itself becoming the ArtPrize entry.

Source: 8THIRTYFOUR Integrated Communications. Reproduced with permission.

"When the community came together to launch the lanterns, it mimicked life in the most profound way, with all of us uniting to lift the hopes and dreams of our community . . . that to me is art," said Carpenter.

Facebook fans agree. One fan posted, "There is something to this that touches to the very heart of what it means to be an American. It took everyone working together to make your vision happen. Thanks for taking what you could see and making all of us a part of the art."

Another fan commented, "Art is created to invoke feelings . . . whether performance, visual, or otherwise. This piece was art and was simply stunning!"

The lanterns are **100% biodegradable** and have a burn time of approximately 5–7 minutes with a radius of less than 2 miles, and then float gently to the ground. The community is encouraged to return lanterns to The B.O.B. (Big Old Building) where they will be honored with a special gift from the Gilmore Collection and entry into a Grand Prize drawing for a dream getaway, thus completing the lantern's journey.

SUCCESS, VALUE, ADVOCACY: BUILDING AWARENESS FOR STUDENT VETERANS OF AMERICA ON COLLEGE CAMPUSES

*Christie M. Kleinmann, Associate Professor, Belmont University**

Source: Student Veterans of America. Reproduced with permission.

SITUATION

Student Veterans of America (SVA) is a 501(c)(3) non-profit dedicated to ensuring student veteran success on the college campus and beyond. SVA provides a variety of resources to help student veterans excel in the classroom and succeed in the workforce, and though this nonprofit's work is imperative to student veteran success, it is not a well-known entity. Belmont University's student public relations agency Red, White and Bruin (RWB) sought to increase awareness of this nonprofit and positively affect SVA's work with student veterans on college campuses in the Greater Nashville community.

RESEARCH

Secondary research showed that SVA was not well known throughout Nashville. There were only five chapters affiliated with Nashville universities, and there were no mentions of the nonprofit in local news networks' archives. Although this nonprofit had little presence in the Nashville community, the colleges and universities in the region displayed a strong commitment to student veteran education through their participation in the Tennessee Veteran Reconnect grant, which was designed to provide financial assistance to veterans returning to school. This information provided an opportunity for RWB because it showed that student veteran education already had some resonance in the community. As a result, the campaign sought to explain SVA's mission to support student veteran education as well as heighten the awareness of this organization in the Greater Nashville area.

An environmental scan supported RWB's previous research and identified a statewide commitment to educational benefits for student veterans. Tennessee governor Bill Haslam expressed the desire that Tennessee would be the premiere state for student veteran success nationwide. This desire was supported by two important initiatives. One was

---

*Special thanks to the members of the Red, White and Bruin agency: Haley Charlton, Julia Couch, Lindsey Barchent, Haley Hall, and Jessica Martin.

the Yellow Ribbon Program, which originated from the Post-9/11 Veterans Educational Assistance Act of 2008 and offered financial assistance for post-9/11 veterans wishing to return to school. The initiative enjoyed widespread support among community colleges and universities in the Greater Nashville area. The other sign of commitment was the Tennessee Higher Education Commission award of $1 million to veterans' education, with nearly half of that sum dispersed among five institutions in Middle Tennessee.

Primary research clarified the campaign opportunity and helped identify the key campaign stakeholders. RWB created two surveys—one for civilian students and one for student veterans—that used quantitative, Likert, and semantic differential scales to ascertain the level of awareness and acceptance of SVA. Survey results found that 61% of civilian students and 47% of student veterans were unaware of SVA. In addition, only 27% of civilian students were aware of a student veteran group on their campus, while only 21% of student veterans felt SVA was an important part of the student veteran experience. These percentages showed that RWB had the opportunity to grow awareness exponentially among both groups.

ACTION PLANNING

Primary and secondary research suggested that the campaign's major stakeholders, civilian students and student veterans, were segregated from, and knew little of, one another. The campaign's goal was to raise awareness of SVA and its role in student veteran success as well as highlight the value of student veterans on college campuses in the Greater Nashville area. To help create and maintain mutual understanding, RWB's campaign focused on how SVA could help student veterans learn about SVA resources available to them and how civilian students could support their veteran peers. RWB focused on students at Belmont, Lipscomb, Vanderbilt, and Tennessee State universities. Success, value, and advocacy were the key messages for the campaign. "Success" meant providing students with the support necessary to reach their full potential. "Value" signified recognizing the worthiness of others—especially as individuals add value and contribute to a shared community for student veterans. "Advocacy" pointed to the campaign's active support for student veteran success. In addition, the SVA messages reiterated the acronym for the Student Veterans of America, further raising awareness for the nonprofit in a subtler manner.

The campaign began on February 15, 2016, with four objectives:

- To increase awareness of the SVA among student veterans in the Greater Nashville area by 20% by March 15, 2016

- To increase awareness of the SVA among civilian students in the Greater Nashville area by 20% by March 15, 2016

- To increase student veteran understanding of the student veteran community by 10% by March 15, 2016

- To transfer awareness and conversations about the student veteran experience to a digital space by gaining 500 interactions across social platforms by March 15, 2016

COMMUNICATION

SVA's mission and values were shared via red, white, and blue support ribbons attached to information cards throughout the 30-day campaign. In addition to the support ribbons, RWB successfully launched a student veteran Week of Honor, February 21–27, across the state of Tennessee. The week began with the reading of a proclamation signed by Governor Haslam during a news conference at the Tennessee State Capitol. A student veteran Week of Honor video was then released on social media, using #StudentVetsWeekTN, as well as a video encouraging students to wear the campaign's red, white, and blue ribbon to support the SVA and, in turn, stu-

Source: Student Veterans of America, www.studentveterans.org. Reproduced with permission.

dent veterans. RWB posted pictures of civilian students wearing the SVA support ribbons and included quotes from each individual about what the Week of Honor meant to them. The campaign then launched a social media event in early March titled Benefits Week, which used Twitter and Facebook to offer trivia and facts about G.I. Bill benefits.

The campaign also offered multiple opportunities for civilian students and student veterans to engage in conversation. One such opportunity was with the academic keynote address of retired Lieutenant General Keith Huber. The event morphed into a dialogue between civilian students and student veterans, allowing the two groups to gain a better understanding of the other through a Q&A opportunity at the end of the address. The event concluded with a private roundtable bringing together Lieutenant General Huber and student veterans from various universities for a more intimate conversation.

RWB utilized many one-way communication tactics, including traditional print tactics as well as digital resources. For instance, red, white, and blue ribbons/information cards were provided at every event, and students were encouraged to wear the ribbons during the campaign. RWB also disseminated fact sheets about the organization, which included different examples of SVA involvement for civilians and student veterans. The campaign's social media links were also included in campaign materials in an effort to engage stakeholders in online conversations.

Finally, RWB distributed digital newsletters for student veterans at the beginning and the end of the campaign. These newsletters created virtual bookends that served as information hubs for student veterans. The newsletters contained information about the campaign, interviews with Nashville student veterans, quick facts about veteran education benefits, and links on how to become involved with SVA chapters in the Greater Nashville region.

Source: Twitter/@HopeFloats019/@RedWhiteBruin. Reproduced with permission.

EVALUATION

Post-campaign survey results were used to determine if the objectives were met. Specifically, the campaign accomplished many things:

- Increased the level of awareness of the SVA among student veterans by 33%

- Increased the level of awareness of the SVA among civilian students by 51%

- Increased student veteran understanding of the student veteran community by more than 23%

- Created conversations about the student veteran experience in a digital space by gaining 13,036 total interactions from Twitter, Facebook, and YouTube

Other results included the following:

- The news conference for Student Veterans Week garnered media coverage on Nashville's Fox 17 evening news; *The Leaf Chronicle* in Clarksville, Tennessee; Belmont University News; and *Tower Notes*, a community newsletter published by Belmont University.

- The social media component for Student Veterans Week reached 2,138 and provided 184 interactions.

- Student Veterans Week videos reached more than 1,100 users and garnered 266 interactions. In addition, students wore the support ribbons and shared their pictures on social media, reaching more than 5,500 users and gaining more than 1,100 interactions.

Beyond these evaluation measurements, several lessons were also learned from this campaign:

1. **Keep the central purpose central**—Great ideas and honest enthusiasm can easily alter the campaign's focus. If a new idea does not fit the purpose, it should not be part of the campaign.

2. **Understand your audience**—Practitioners should seek key figures within their campaign's stakeholder groups to help them understand the often complex nature of their audience.

3. **Measure, measure, measure**—Strategic measurement is key to showing campaign success. To do so, practitioners need clear definitions of what they want to measure, and then measure those things often.

4. **Recognize emerging opportunities**—Additional organizations in the Greater Nashville area wanted to participate in honoring student veterans during the Week of Honor. This desire was recognized too late. Practitioners should continue to scan for challenges and opportunities throughout the campaign process in order to make timely campaign adjustments.

5. **Leave a legacy**—For RWB, this campaign's success was about leaving a legacy where student veterans would feel valued and find community, and where civilian students would recognize the value of student veterans and be provided with tangible means to honor student veterans.

RACE PIT STOP

Discussion Questions

1. The campaign's goal was to raise awareness of the Student Veterans of America and its role in student veteran success as well as highlight the value of student veterans on college campuses in the Greater Nashville area. Why was it necessary to raise student awareness of SVA *among civilian students* to achieve this goal?

2. One of the campaign strategies was to engage student veterans and civilian students in dialogue, yet the one event designed to do so slowly "morphed" into that dialogue. What could the planners have done to ensure that dialogue occurred from the beginning?

3. A campaign tactic was to distribute digital newsletters for student veterans at the beginning and end of the campaign. Was this an effective strategy? Why or why not?

Trendlines

In the spring of 2017, two University of Florida scholars—Ann Christiano and Annie Neimand—wrote in the *Stanford Social Innovation Review* that "too many organizations concentrated on raising awareness . . . without knowing how to translate that awareness into action by getting people to change their behavior or act on their beliefs."[1] They pointed out four elements crucial to a successful public interest campaign: (1) a clear layout of objectives, tactics, and evaluation methods; (2) narrow targeting of audiences; (3) campaign messages with clear calls to action; and (4) having the right messengers to carry forth those messages. With these steps in mind, could this campaign have been translated from awareness into action? Why or why not? What elements would need to be changed to make the transition toward emphasizing audience action?

REFERENCES

1. Christiano, A., & Neimand, A. (2017, Spring). Stop raising awareness already. *Stanford Social Innovation Review*. Retrieved from https://ssir.org/articles/entry/stop_raising_awareness_already

THE CLEVELAND FOUNDATION CENTENNIAL CAMPAIGN

Michael Murphy, Chief Marketing Officer, Cleveland Foundation

Emily Foote-Huth, Marketing and Communications Coordinator, Cleveland Foundation

SITUATION

Established in 1914 as the world's first community foundation, the Cleveland Foundation's centennial was a milestone not only for the organization, but also for the place-based philanthropy movement it pioneered. Cleveland Foundation founder Frederick Harris Goff envisioned an alternative to the private foundations established by ultra-wealthy individuals. Community foundations pool contributions from a group of donors to create a permanent endowment, managed by independent citizen trustees and dedicated to serving the needs of a designated geographic area. This model now includes nearly 1,848 community foundations around the world, spanning every continent except Antarctica. Seizing this landmark opportunity to leverage the centennial spotlight, the Cleveland Foundation developed a campaign to celebrate its 100-year history and the birth of the community foundation field, while elevating the foundation's reputation locally and nationally as it entered its second century.

Source: Cleveland Foundation. Reproduced with permission.

RESEARCH

Focus groups and interviews with board members, foundation leaders, and other key stakeholders revealed that, despite the foundation's long-standing presence and widespread impact in the community, many were unfamiliar with its catalytic role supporting key community assets and institutions. Measures of external engagement with, and awareness of, the Cleveland Foundation brand also indicated that there was room for growth in these areas. For example, an external survey of Cuyahoga County, Ohio, residents conducted in 2011 revealed that the Cleveland Foundation was not among the top five nonprofit or charitable organizations that county residents identified as making the biggest difference in Cuyahoga County, despite the foundation being among the largest funders of nonprofits and charitable causes in the county (and country). Before launching the centennial campaign, the foundation's Facebook page influence was ranked 13 among 17 local and philanthropic sector pages with similar audiences and content. The foundation identified its centennial campaign as an opportunity to reintroduce the Cleveland Foundation brand to new audiences and reinforce its value proposition to existing stakeholders.

ACTION PLANNING

The overarching goals of the Cleveland Foundation's centennial campaign were to increase awareness of the foundation's history of impact and current leadership in the community among members of the general public in Greater Cleveland. The foundation also sought to underscore its reputation as a philanthropic leader among such national peers as the Ford Foundation, Rockefeller Foundation, Kresge Foundation, Charles Stewart Mott Foundation, and Knight Foundation. To accomplish these goals, the foundation planned to increase its visibility and engagement with Greater Cleveland residents in strategic settings that showcased the foundation's long history of support and impact in the community. The foundation also planned to engage with its national philanthropic peers in strategic settings to deliver the message that the foundation has been—and continues to be—a pioneer in the field of community philanthropy. The following objectives were set, to be achieved between January and December 2014:

- Increase earned media impressions by 50% year-over-year between 2013 and 2014.

- Increase public engagement with the foundation's social media and web properties by 20% year-over-year between 2013 and 2014.

COMMUNICATION

Tactic: Digital Communications

On January 1, the foundation launched an internet microsite, with help from the Cleveland graphic design firm Nesnadny + Schwartz, commemorating the joint centennial of the Cleveland Foundation and the community foundation movement. Graphically powerful and easy to navigate, this legacy site (www.clevelandfoundation100.org) provided rich content that was repurposed for other communication channels, including a social media campaign and the foundation's centennial annual report.

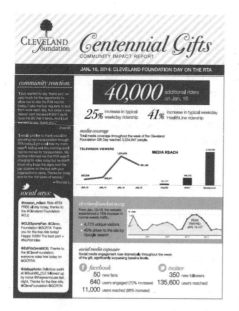

Source: Cleveland Foundation. Reproduced with permission.

Tactic: Community Relations

To thank Greater Cleveland for a century of support and celebrate the foundation's ties with many of the community's premier assets, the foundation's cross-disciplinary centennial team developed the concept of giving a gift to the community each month during the foundation's 100th year. The monthly gifts provided free access to some of the community's premier assets and attractions, from a day of free public transportation on the Greater Cleveland Regional Transit Authority to tickets for a Cleveland Orchestra concert at the Blossom Music Center. By providing free access to these community assets, the foundation could introduce itself to new audiences while taking the opportunity to educate attendees about its role in building and enhancing these grantee organizations over the years. The foundation secured a free partnership with Cleveland Fox affiliate WJW-TV 8 to reveal the gifts each month on the city's top-rated morning news show. Cleveland Foundation leadership became familiar faces for Fox 8 viewers as on-air guests each month to announce the gifts.

Tactic: Special Events

To highlight its centennial nationally, the foundation convened a conversation on May 12 in Washington, DC, attended by 22 philanthropic leaders from across the country, representing community foundations as well as private philanthropic institutions, the federal government, professional organizations, and higher education. Attendees engaged in an on-the-record dialogue with *Chronicle of Philanthropy* editor Stacy Palmer about the next century of place-based philanthropy. The next night, the foundation convened a public town hall in Washington, DC, inviting the community to NPR's national headquarters to participate in a similar conversation and preview an upcoming documentary from Cleveland's National Public Radio/Public Broadcasting Service affiliate on the Cleveland Foundation's first century. The conversation was streamed live to Cleveland, where a similar gathering for VIP Cleveland Foundation donors was held.

Tactic: Centennial Meeting Presented by KeyBank

On June 11, 2014, the Cleveland Foundation hosted a once-in-a-century celebration at Cleveland's Playhouse Square theater district. The Cleveland Foundation Centennial Meeting presented by KeyBank featured a historic address from the Cleveland Foundation president and a keynote speech by retired general and former secretary of state Colin Powell. A record 1,200 individuals attended this Centennial Meeting.

Source: Cleveland Foundation. Reproduced with permission.

Tactic: FRED Talks

Honoring the legacy of Cleveland Foundation founder Frederick Harris Goff, the foundation launched a series of quarterly "idea incubator" events called FRED Talks. These gatherings invited the community to listen to, engage in, and contribute to conversations with local and national thought leaders. The ideas generated from FRED Talks informed the foundation's grant-making strategies, harkening back to Goff's early practice of conducting surveys on community issues. The launch event in the FRED Talks series, "E3: Education, Economic Development, Empowerment," focused on opportunities for communities to connect young students with real-world work experiences that better prepare them for tomorrow's workforce.

Tactic: Council on Foundations' Fall Conference for Community Foundations

The Cleveland Foundation was a presenting sponsor of the 2014 Council on Foundations' Fall Conference for Community Foundations, the largest annual gathering of associates from community foundations around the world. Staff from the Cleveland Foundation, a

Guests at the Cleveland Foundation's Centennial Meeting and monthly gift days were invited to share a message and sign their name on a giant birthday card.

Source: Cleveland Foundation. Reproduced with permission.

number of whom served on the conference's advisory committee, worked closely with the Council on Foundations to plan programming that would showcase Cleveland as the birthplace of the community foundation field. Cleveland Foundation leadership presented eight sessions and a meeting of all participants, and hosted 120 conference attendees on four site tours that highlighted community projects, neighborhoods, and assets around Cleveland.

EVALUATION

A marketing and communications team tracked a variety of metrics to evaluate the performance of the centennial campaign. Between January and December 2014, nearly 61 million total impressions were generated through media outreach and across print, broadcast, and online platforms. This represented a nearly 200% year-over-year increase in media impressions from approximately 21 million impressions in 2013, far exceeding the goal of a 50% increase. Media impressions generated through monthly gift promotion alone totaled 22 million, and the Council on Foundations conference by itself received media coverage across online, print, and broadcast channels totaling 2.82 million impressions. The partnership with Fox 8 to announce the gifts each month amounted to nearly one hour of free airtime.

The foundation's centennial year activities also translated into strong growth in digital engagement across the foundation's online properties. Throughout the year, the Cleveland Foundation's social media properties grew their audience and influence significantly. The foundation's Twitter followers grew by 51.9%, from 10,894 on January 1 to 16,551 on December 17. Its Facebook followers grew by 103.6%, from 3,457 on January 1 to 7,038 on December 17. By the end of 2014, the foundation's influence rank on Facebook had moved from 13 to 8 out of 17 ranked local and sector pages with comparable audiences and content.

Contributing to this growth in social media engagement was the foundation's use of social media at its centennial year events. The foundation's tweets of its special events earned 61,723 impressions and 499 engagements. Social media was especially effective over the course of the Council on Foundations conference.

The Cleveland Foundation's posts on its social media properties drew more than 28,000 impressions on Facebook and 15,000 impressions on Twitter. The Cleveland Foundation's centennial history microsite attracted 13,111 unique visits, and held the attention of readers for an average duration of two minutes and 29 seconds. Content from the history site was repurposed for a social media campaign, which generated 446,933 impressions and 7,777 engagements throughout the year. The foundation's homepage, ClevelandFoundation.org, experienced year-over-year growth in traffic of more than 31.4%, from 206,306 sessions between January 1 and December 31, 2013, to 271,163 sessions between January 1 and December 31, 2014.

While the centennial history microsite remains a valuable reference tool for information about the foundation's history, its value likely would have been enhanced had the microsite been more fully integrated into the foundation's main website. As a separate domain, the microsite has a limited shelf life and potentially cannibalizes traffic from the foundation's primary website.

The foundation's centennial marketing and communications strategy also could have benefited from the use of stakeholder perception tracking and reporting. Although the centennial campaign heightened the foundation's profile among target stakeholders, it would be valuable to more closely measure and track the effect of the centennial activities on stakeholders' perceptions of the foundation.

RACE PIT STOP

Discussion Questions

1. The campaign had two goals: (1) increase awareness among the general public, and (2) underscore the Cleveland Foundation's reputation among its national peers. Do you think the campaign would have been more effective if it had more narrowly targeted its stakeholders? Why or why not?

2. One of the objectives focused on "increasing earned media impressions." Is this an effective measure of awareness? Why or why not?

3. Another objective sought to strengthen digital engagement with the foundation's social media and web properties. Is this an effective measure of action? Why or why not?

4. The case study included several tactics. What strategies would these tactics fall under?

Trendlines

Individual donations to nonprofits and charitable organizations went up about 4% in 2016, with giving to foundations up by 3.1%.[1] Millennials (born between 1982 and 2000) are a potentially key stakeholder group for such giving—84% of them made a charitable donation in 2015.[2] With such an important group, practitioners need to keep in mind six key factors about millennials: (1) they are consistently connected through digital platforms, (2) they have a strong preference for sharing information with others, (3) they care more about results than about the the institutions they give to, (4) they find stories particularly relevant (i.e., they want to know how their personal stories relate to the nonprofit's cause), (5) they keep track of causes through social media, and (6) they want to know how donations are being used.[3] Consider a nonprofit that you care about. If that organization is not sure that millennials are a key audience, how would you help it make such a determination? Once you have identified some important millennial groups, what advice would you give this nonprofit on how to best approach them? It is apparent that millennials consume information through digital platforms; however, what else would you recommend to complement online approaches?

REFERENCES

1. Giving USA 2017: Total charitable donations rise to new high of $390.85 billion. (2017, June 12). *Giving USA*. Retrieved from https://givingusa.org/giving-usa-2017-total-charitable-donations-rise-to-new-high-of-390-05-billion/

2. Hawthorne, J. (2017, May 2). Six ways millennials are changing charitable giving. *Business Connect*. Retrieved from https://businessconnectworld.com/2017/05/02/6-ways-millennials-are-changing-charitable-giving/

3. Ibid.

INTEGRATED COMMUNICATION

Integrated communication focuses on how public relations strategies and tactics work within, and complement, a wider mix of marketing, advertising, and public information messages. In this regard, public relations attempts to make these various components work together seamlessly so that an organization can present a complete, reliable, and believable message that aligns with stakeholders' interests and desires.

The cases in this chapter show this kind of integration at work. The CLOROX® Ick Awards campaign used a combination of humor and social media to amplify the continuing importance of a well-established product. The Optical Society reached out to its stakeholders through multiple platforms to celebrate its centennial year. Finally, the Greater Fort Lauderdale Convention and Visitors Bureau tied its efforts into both ongoing news events and the availability of a high-profile celebrity ambassador to reassert its prominence in the tourism arena.

THE CLOROX® ICK AWARDS

Leslie Schrader, Partner and Director, Ketchum

Whitney Press, Managing Account Supervisor, Ketchum

Fran Bernhards, Senior Content Manager, Ketchum

SITUATION

Spontaneity often creates life's most memorable moments and some of life's biggest messes, especially if young children are involved. That unpredictable combination created a perfect opportunity for the Clorox® Company. Clorox® has been making quality cleaning products for more than 100 years and is considered by many to be a household staple—largely

by older generations. Today's younger parents have a dual-income, on-the-go lifestyle. To them, CLOROX® means grandmothers and bleach. Time-starved, they do not want to spend their precious free time cleaning like their grandmother's, or even their mom's, generation. By 2013, the company already had in place, with Ketchum's help, the "CLOROX® Ick-tionary" (www.icktionary.com), an online, wiki-style dictionary made for parents. The interactive forum allowed parents to gain a fun and positive perspective about the ick in their lives, with terms such as the following:

- *Petrifries* (pet-ruh-frahyz): Week-old French fries found stuck in the toddler's high chair

- *Sasplotch* (sass-ploch): Mysterious giant footprint through the house

- *Spillates* (spil-lah-teez): Stretching exercises that tone muscles and improve flexibility when you're wiping up spills under tables and on countertops

Clorox wanted to build on this approach and convert this younger generation into brand enthusiasts, highlighting the important role CLOROX® products play not only in cleaning up life's messes, but also in freeing up time for the important things in life, like spending quality time with family.

RESEARCH

Today's parents are normally between the ages of 25 and 40—some are millennials, and others are younger Gen Xers. Millennials, in particular, are often starting new life stages with expanding responsibilities. Whether these parents are caring for a new baby or raising multiple children, they have hectic schedules and are multitasking mavens. They sometimes just need to get through the day without *another* potty accident. Balancing work and family is hard for moms and dads, and life today is increasingly a high-pressure balancing act. Many moms and dads struggle to strike this balance and find themselves not spending enough time with their children.[1] Likewise, the "traditional" realm of modern moms and dads changed drastically in the past half century, and roles are converging, inspiring a greater reliance on teamwork.[2] Dads, a traditionally untapped audience for bleach and other CLOROX® cleaning products, are taking a larger role in parenting. Among fathers with a wife in the workforce, 31% were a regular source of care for their children under age 15 in 2011, up from 26% in 2002.[3] Research into modern parents' social media habits revealed the following insights:

- 70% of modern moms visit social media sites weekly, with one-third of moms visiting several times daily. Many moms (one in three) rely heavily on "expert" recommendations from family and friends.[4]

- 48% of consumers think social media posts created by others in their networks are a good way to discover new products, brands, trends, or retailers.[5]

- 88% of consumers trust online reviews as much as personal recommendations.[6]

- Today's parents enjoy sharing and hearing from their peers in real time about child-rearing experiences and messy mishaps they encounter daily. Research indicates that conversations about kids' messes—pee, poop, and puke—occurred on blogs, forums, social networks, video-/photo-sharing sites, and Twitter. While parents love sharing "messy moments" stories online, they generally do not discuss cleaning solutions, especially in relation to brands.[7]

Modern moms and dads are increasingly time-starved and do not want to spend free time cleaning.[8] Many do not know Clorox makes a full line of products that can help them spend less time cleaning and more time living.

ACTION PLANNING

Through research, we knew where to find modern parents: on social media, looking to share and commiserate with their peers. We noticed they did not hold back, sharing their ickier family moments. Why? Because once you have cleaned up the messes and looked back on them, you realize they *were* pretty funny. The campaign strategy emphasized the point: "Get Icky . . . Be Funny . . . Clean Up." We needed to show this audience that Clorox understood. The goal was to get them to think of Clorox as a peer, along with friends, family, and social media influencers they interact with online, often several times a day. The key overarching message emphasized that CLOROX came to the rescue, tackling the ickiest messes. The strategic message components included the following:

- Diaper-changing disasters, milk and cereal splattered across the kitchen floor, ketchup landing right on your white shirt—mess and ick are an inevitable part of everyday life, especially if you are a parent, but they are also part of what makes life interesting and humorous.

- These are the stories you can't wait to share with friends and family, especially over social media. Sometimes it's best to just laugh through the mess, knowing it can all be cleaned up later.

- The next time you're faced with a mess, CLOROX has your back with a number of products to help you take them on in every room of the house. CLOROX helps you spend more time enjoying life with your family—and less time cleaning.

The campaign objectives included the following:

- Engage at least 500 unique Twitter followers and generate 50 million Twitter impressions during the event.

- Make cleaning a social media trending topic during the four hours of the Twitter party.

- Shift parents' perception of "mess" from a negative one to a more positive fact of everyday modern parenting life, and directly associate the CLOROX brand and family of cleaning products as a powerful solution and dependable ally in helping moms and dads clean up the worst messes.

- Increase CLOROX brand conversation on social channels by at least 25% during the campaign execution.

- Brand CLOROX in social media conversations and traditional media coverage, and produce relevant, shareable, new content for CLOROX's social media properties.

- Secure 25 stories in traditional media about the event and generate 10 million traditional media impressions with at least 80% CLOROX message penetration.

- Generate 500 million views of the YouTube videos produced and posted during the event within 60 days.

COMMUNICATION

In early 2014, the CLOROX® Ick Awards took real-time marketing to the next level, letting parents co-create content with us on the fly. We recruited Rachel Dratch, a mom and former *Saturday Night Live* star, along with actors from the Second City comedy troupe, to improvise a live awards show on Twitter. We invited parents to call the shots in real time: Moms and dads participating in the live Twitter party became the creative force behind the CLOROX® Ick Awards, sharing funny stories from parenthood in real time using the hashtag #Ickies. Chicago's best improvisers then reenacted these messes for award categories like "Showdown Mess" and "Most Epic Mess"—creating multiple ick-prov videos, which were quickly uploaded to CLOROX's YouTube channel so parents could vote on their favorite cleaning disasters. The result became a chronicle of messy mishaps told through personalized video content any parent can laugh at, and very likely relate to.

Rachel Dratch conducts a mock red carpet interview with a Second City actor.

Source: AP Images for Clorox.

For the awards show, Dratch and Second City actors improvised a recorded red carpet scene and awards acceptance speech scene for each award category. In dramatic fashion, Dratch announced the winning nominee's Twitter handle and tweet. During the acceptance speeches, a Second City actor representing the winner thanked the CLOROX cleaning or laundry product that helped clean up that particular mess. This process was repeated for seven different award categories (#MysteriousMess, #SuperParentMess, #EpicMess, #CraziestKidMess, #BestDateMess, #HorrificMess, and #ShowdownMess). We produced 35 videos in real time during the awards show Twitter party. But the fun didn't stop there—Second City and Dratch continued improvising with some of the night's best tweets in a segment called "Mess'N Around Awards Show After Party"—to create eight additional videos that ran live on the CLOROX laugh hub.

EVALUATION

Clorox surpassed all of its goals for the CLOROX® Ick Awards, including use of the campaign hashtag #Ickies, and campaign exposure as measured through both social and traditional media impressions. Some measures of how Clorox turned cleaning into an engaging social media topic included the following:

- Engaged 1,434 unique Twitter followers in the CLOROX® Ick Awards conversation during the event (287% of goal)

- Generated more than 163 million Twitter impressions (326% of goal) and 16,500 uses of #Ickies, along with other category hashtags like #MysteriousMess and #SuperParentMess, becoming a worldwide trending topic on Twitter

- Of all keywords, *ick* earned the highest penetration in social media (15,394 mentions), followed by *mess* (3,150 mentions), *clean* (459 mentions), and *laugh* (245 mentions)

Some measures of how the campaign offered relevant, shareable content included the following:

- Secured 90 stories (360% of goal) for a total of 19.6 million media impressions (196% percent of goal); key placements included the WGN Morning Show (Chicago), ET Online, and *Star* Magazine Online.

- 96.9% included CLOROX's "laugh through the mess" messaging (121% of goal).

- 95.3% included CLOROX product messaging (119% of goal).

- Increased CLOROX brand conversation volume online by 63% during the campaign's execution (252% of goal).

- Generated more than 32% of conversation online, compared to CLOROX competitors (18% of goal).

- Co-created a total of 43 CLOROX® Ick Awards videos in one evening—inspired by parents' messy mishaps—and drove more than 1.4 million YouTube views (280% of goal). Average video view duration was around one and a half minutes, suggesting absorption of the video's material and messaging.

- The CLOROX® Ick Awards received numerous award distinctions including a Global SABRE Award, a Gold SABRE Award, two In2 SABRE Awards, and two Silver Anvil Awards from the Public Relations Society of America.

Our evaluation also pointed to some learning lessons:

- Have more hands on deck to help with the multitude of logistics in pulling off a four-hour improv awards show.

- Be in one large room, so everyone can see everything in real time. Our social media war room was in a separate area from the studio where the ick-prov was filmed, due to the space we used. If there were a way to have a window into the studio or a monitor to observe the ick-prov in real time, it would help everyone anticipate what videos were coming next so that one could pace the online conversation accordingly.

- Make a widget on CLOROX.com to house the event. The conversation took place on Twitter, where participants followed along using the hashtag. A widget on CLOROX.com, however, would have allowed for pulling in the conversation automatically, broadening exposure of this event.

RACE PIT STOP

Discussion Questions

1. There are quite a few social media objectives in this campaign. What other measurable objectives might you have added? Explain your reasoning.

2. The case mentioned the importance of dads in today's child-rearing activities. How did the Ick Awards campaign work to engage this target audience? What other campaign strategies and/or tactics would you suggest Clorox have used to accomplish this?

3. Do you believe the campaign would have been as effective in other countries/cultures? What kinds of considerations might one need to explore before investing in the campaign elsewhere?

Trendlines

This campaign is notable for its effective use of humor, something that is not customary in public relations campaigns. In this case, however, humor was an essential component that could work because humor was connected to an issue or problem that was of benefit to key audiences.[7] One public relations professional maintains humor can be very effective because it "increase[s] comprehension and [will] help you win over your audience."[8] Consider a favorite product or service of yours—how could comedic messages and approaches be used to help promote its usefulness? Alternatively, where have you seen ineffective use of humor used in public relations campaigns? Why did those attempts to be funny fall flat?

REFERENCES

1. Parker, K., & Wang, W. (2013, March 14). Modern parenthood: Roles of moms and dads converge as they balance work and family. *Pew Research Center*. Retrieved from http://www.pewsocialtrends.org/2013/03/14/modern-parenthood-roles-of-moms-and-dads-converge-as-they-balance-work-and-family/

2. Ibid.

3. Laughlin, L. (2013, April). Who's minding the kids? Child care arrangements: Spring 2011. *U.S. Census Bureau*. Retrieved from https://www.census.gov/prod/2013pubs/p70-135.pdf

4. North American technographics consumer deep dive survey. (2012, August/September). *Forrester Technographics*. Retrieved from Forrester.com

5. Engaging consumers where it matters most: How to win fans and influence people in today's "social customer lifecycle." (2013). *Wildfire by Google*. Retrieved from http://www .ufsa.ufl.edu/uploads/mcda/Engaging_Consumers_Where_It_Matters_Most.pdf

6. Anderson, M. (2014, July 7). 88% of consumers trust online reviews as much as personal recommendations. *Search Engine Land*. Retrieved from http://searchengineland .com/88-consumers-trust-online-reviews-much-personal-recommendations-195803

7. Klotz-Guest, K. (2005, June 21). Humor in PR: Can you hear me now? *MarketingProfs*. Retrieved from http://www.marketingprofs.com/5/klotz-guest2.asp

8. Scudder, K. (2013, January 31). Funny business: Does humor belong in PR writing? *Public Relations Tactics*. Retrieved from http://apps.prsa.org/intelligence/tactics/articles/ view/10073/1073/funny_business_does_humor_belong_in_pr_writing#.WfNJajBryUk

THE OPTICAL SOCIETY'S CENTENNIAL YEAR CELEBRATION: REFLECTING A CENTURY OF INNOVATION

Rebecca B. Andersen, Director, Public Relations, The Optical Society

Tracy Schario, Former Chief External Relations Officer, The Optical Society

SITUATION

The Optical Society (OSA) serves as a global catalyst for the science of light. Founded in 1916 in Rochester, New York—an internationally renowned center for optics education and industry—OSA is the "leading professional organization for scientists, engineers, students, and entrepreneurs who fuel discoveries, shape real-life applications and accelerate achievements in the science of light."[1] One hundred years after its founding, OSA has grown from a small group of luminaries to a diverse worldwide membership of more than 20,000 dedicated to advancing knowledge and applications of optics and photonics (the science of light detection, generation, and manipulation). The society impacts 275,000 customers annually—they subscribe to one or more of OSA's 17 scientific journals and/or attend the approximately 50 meetings, conferences, and trade shows managed by OSA. The society also supports more than 350 student chapters globally and engages with over 250 corporate members. Still, when an organization turns 100, it is an opportunity to raise visibility and promote the role the organization plays in the industry and in supporting advances in society.

RESEARCH

OSA engaged in comparative research in 2011 to look at what other science-based societies had done to capture 100 years in the making. That year it interviewed members of the centennial planning committee for an oral history project on the global impact of optical science. This led to the creation of 366 facts about optical science, video testimonials from members, and the capturing of scientific advances that were later printed in a *Century of Optics* textbook.

Focus groups with various members, including students, a board of directors, and governance committees, as well as a survey of staff, found that capturing the essence of OSA's 100 years would be challenging. From the media relations perspective, primary research in 2015 found that OSA was receiving an average of 350 mentions per month in both industry and general scientific news media outlets. These were mostly news release pickups related to research-related news from the research journals published by OSA.

ACTION PLANNING

The four goals of the centennial campaign were as follows:

1. Capture the legacy: Acknowledge the role OSA has played in the evolution of the field of optics and photonics by highlighting the standards of expertise over the past 100 years.

2. Connect members: Highlight the active role OSA has taken in enhancing the scientific community by connecting its members.

3. Light the future: Call attention to the momentum that OSA leadership has always brought to the field of optics and how these leaders continue to inspire the next generation of scientists.

4. Spark inspiration: Celebrate every little idea and how those ideas become transformative through the ingenuity of applied thinking.

Target audiences for OSA's Centennial campaign included the following:

- Internal: members, the board, volunteers, and staff; 350+ student chapters globally; 250+ corporate members (OSA Industry Development Associates); and donors to the OSA Foundation

- External: customers and prospects; scientific societies; U.S. policy makers and staff; and corporate partners

- Influencers: top-tier media and trade publications; high-profile personalities in science

Messages for these audiences included the following:

- OSA is the leading global professional association in optics and photonics, supporting research and collaboration in the science of light that enhance nearly every aspect of our lives.

- OSA is an innovator and convener offering world-renowned publications, meetings, and membership programs and providing quality information and inspiring interactions that power achievements in the science of light.

- OSA celebrates its centennial in 2016, marking a century of sparking inspiration and smart innovation driven by more than 270,000 scientists, students, engineers, and business leaders in 177 countries.

- Throughout its centennial, OSA will honor the legacy of optical pioneers who have made countless modern technologies possible while also lighting the future by inspiring the next generation of optics and photonics leaders.

Capture the Legacy	Connect with Members	Light the Future	Spark Inspiration
Capture and preserve the last 100 years of OSA history; recognize and thank the pioneers and supporters.	Increase involvement and community recognition of our members around the world.	Inspire the next generation of OSA leadership.	Raise public awareness of the value of optics and photonics in everyday life.

Reflecting a Century of Innovation

Source: The Optical Society. Reproduced with permission.

The measureable objectives included the following:

1. *Media relations:* Execute a media outreach strategy that creates a steady stream of stories and builds awareness of the centennial.

   - Expected Outcome(s):

     Secure at least 20 media placements generated from interviews or bylined content including op-eds and media partnerships.

     Secure at least three media partnerships.

2. *Social media:* Enhance OSA's social media presence on Twitter, Facebook, and LinkedIn by publishing content daily on at least two channels.

   - Expected Outcome(s):

     Track #OSA100 with a goal of exceeding more than 136,000 impressions monthly during the centennial year, the current reach of OSA's Twitter presence.

     Increase our social media subscribers by 20% during the centennial year.

3. *Event support:* Promote the *Light the Future* speakers' series at OSA's events, and pitch related stories to targeted media.

   - Expected Outcome(s):

     Secure two to three media attendees at each *Light the Future* session through October 2016.

4. *Public relations writing*: Create an OSA Centennial Media Kit (e.g., news releases, fact sheets, and bylined articles); develop CAKE (Centennial Anniversary Kit Experience) materials for all of the society's chapters and affiliated organizations; and create key messages to include in all activities and materials.

   - Expected Outcome(s):

     Draft at least 20 to 25 news releases, fact sheets, web content, and/or bylined articles.

     Have at least 30 downloads of CAKE by student chapters.

COMMUNICATION

With a $120,000 budget, we began the centennial public relations program with a soft launch in 2015—a 100-day countdown to the official start on January 1, 2016. Then, the campaign began with the tagline "Reflecting a Century of Innovation." The key tactical elements included the following:

Media relations. We conducted media training in December 2015 with key leaders in OSA, including reviewing briefing materials and offering an in-person interview preparation course. We provided media outreach materials to OSA chapters. We distributed media kits and conducted media tours to create relationships with key media targets and secure briefings. We worked to identify milestones and events that can be used for news release development as well as media pitching. OSA partnered with industry publication *Laser Focus World* to publish a monthly Q&A with OSA members. Another industry media publication, *Photonics Media*, created a dedicated OSA 100 video channel and published our ads in its print magazine.

Social media. We amplified OSA's social media presence on Twitter, Facebook, Reddit, and LinkedIn by creating ongoing centennial content (e.g., updates/events, blog posts, milestones, member videos), all under the banner of an "I am #OSA100 proud" promotion. More specifically, we conducted social media contests, including a trivia contest and "video the future" contest. We created a social media CAKE tool kit with sample content for student chapters, industry partners, and sister societies to help promote contests, centennial events, and #OSA100. Videos on OSA's YouTube page featured members saying what the organization means to them. Throughout the year, we distributed 366 OSA and optics/photonics history facts, with corresponding graphics and the #OSA100 hashtag.

The Optical Society @OpticalSociety · 2h
#OSA100 @MilesPadgett takes part in a @Reddit AMA session on 28 Sept. Get your questions ready now ow.ly/Qnol304skyP

Reddit "Ask Me Anything" with Professor Miles Padgett on September 28

Source: Twitter/@OpticalSociety. Reproduced with permission.

Website. The centennial website featured the 100 icons from the exhibit, OSA centennial publications including the *Century of Optics* book, the CAKE tool kit with presentation templates, event guidelines and social media suggestions, member videos, and a timeline.

Special events. Public relations played an important part in our onsite events throughout the year. We worked to promote a *Light the Future* speakers' series—featuring Ira Flatow of Public Radio International's *Science Friday*, technology pioneer Mary Lou

Jepsen, Nobel Laureate Steven Chu, and futurists Ray Kurzweil and Michio Kaku, among others—at eight international meetings in 2016. Each event was open to the public and videotaped. We hosted celebrations at OSA meetings throughout the year, including the 100th birthday bash at the annual meeting.

EVALUATION

Developing an integrated public relations campaign to honor 100 years of scientific discovery was all-encompassing. With the support of our members, who willingly shared their stories, and an organized communications effort, we were able to measurably increase the visibility of OSA and promote the advancements of science around the world.

The most significant returns on investment were increasing membership by 5% to more than 20,000 worldwide and securing the society's first $1 million gift to the OSA Foundation. The key tactical results, which exceeded expectations, included the following:

Source: The Optical Society. Reproduced with permission.

1. The "OSA 100" exhibit of iconic inventions and inventors was showcased globally at 30 trade shows, attracting more than 27,000 visitors. At eight conferences, it was accompanied by a *Light the Future* visionary keynote speech and reception, which reached another 4,700 participants. This 10' × 20' exhibit was loaned to the Rochester (New York) Museum and Science Center through April 2017, and a portable version of the exhibit was displayed at 16 universities in nine countries.

2. The *Light the Future* program met the stated goal of two to three media in attendance at every event. The media were a variety of industry, general science, and physics press.

3. OSA wrote and distributed 18 news releases, resulting in 1,734 stories, 26 interviews, and 25 bylines/blogs with a total of nearly 4 million impressions.

4. Twitter followers increased by 29%, Facebook by 14%, and YouTube by 35%.

5. We shared 148 videos of members—by far the most popular OSA 100 content on Facebook—and distributed the CAKE tool kit to student chapters through nearly 400 downloads.

6. The website had more than 71,000 visitors with nearly 3,000 publication downloads.

7. The centennial attracted 17 corporate sponsors providing more than $200,000 in contributions and in-kind media services.

RACE PIT STOP

Discussion Questions

1. How far in advance did OSA begin planning for its centennial year celebration, and what kind of research did the organization do first? Do you believe its planning timetable was reasonable? Why or why not?

2. What strategies and/or tactics could OSA have used the following year and the year after to help maintain the momentum of its yearlong celebration?

3. Examine the objectives, then look at the evaluation section. What objectives do you think are most useful to OSA? What objectives would you change or add?

4. OSA's centennial celebration plan consisted of media relations, social media, and special events. Think about the tasks involved in each of these areas and create an individual plan for one of the centennial campaign elements (i.e., a media relations plan, a social media plan, or a special event plan) based on what you know about these activities from the case. When doing so, think about the timing of these tasks and include a mock calendar that specifies them.

Trendlines

In 2010, the American Society of Association Executives (ASAE), an association dedicated to excellent association management, estimated there were 92,000 trade and professional associations in the United States. Although associations have long served as industry advocates for political and regulatory purposes and worked to strengthen professions and professional bonds, association membership is reported to be declining across the board. The proliferation of social media networks, easy access to professionally oriented content online, and the growing costs of association membership have been cited as reasons why. As a result, a number of associations are rebranding themselves with new names, such as the Consumer Electronics Association did when it became the Consumer Technology Association (CTA) in 2015.[2]

Think about what you value in the clubs and organizations to which you belong. Now imagine you work for a professional association, such as the Public Relations Society of America (PRSA), the International Association of Business Communicators (IABC), or the Arthur W. Page Society. What niche value, or unique selling proposition (USP), can your organization offer current and prospective members to sustain and grow the group? Are there elements or aspects of your own experience that you could draw upon to help spur increased membership?

REFERENCES

1. The Optical Society presents Nick Holonyak Jr. Award for 2018. (2018, April 3). *Optical Society.* Retrieved from https://www.osa.org/en-us/about_osa/newsroom/news_releases/2018/the_optical_society_presents_nick_holonyak_jr_awa/

2. Yohn, D. L. (2016, January 5). To stay relevant, professional associations must rebrand. *Harvard Business Review.* Retrieved from https://hbr.org/2016/01/to-stay-relevant-professional-associations-must-rebrand

"LOVE IS LOVE" WEDDING IN FORT LAUDERDALE

Virginia Sheridan, Managing Partner, Finn Partners

SITUATION

In mid-2014, it became evident that Florida would repeal the state's same-sex marriage ban. Finn Partners encouraged its longtime client, the Greater Fort Lauderdale Convention and Visitors Bureau (GFLCVB), always a tourism category leader, to come out early in support of the repeal—becoming the first government bureau to do so. The GFLCVB released an announcement of its unconditional support for the overturning of bans on same-sex marriage. In the announcement, Nicki E. Grossman, then president of the GFLCVB, said:

Source: Greater Fort Lauderdale Convention & Visitors Bureau. Reproduced with permission.

> We fought and won this debate more than 20 years ago when we expanded the Broward County Human Rights Act to include sexual orientation as a protected classification in 1995. We restated this stance when we unanimously amended the Act in 2008 to include gender identity or expression. Today, we reconfirm our commitment to the human rights of gay couples, gay families and transgender residents and travelers following recent laws that discriminate against the LGBTQ (lesbian, gay, bi-sexual, transgender and questioning) community in some U.S. states.[1]

Under the leadership of its director of LGBTQ marketing, Richard Gray, and with marketing dollars to support LGBTQ tourism, the GFLCVB had long promoted Fort Lauderdale to LGBTQ travelers and businesses since the first ad campaign in 1996 called "Rolling Out the Rainbow Carpet." With the impending repeal of the same-sex marriage ban in Florida, the next step was the creation of a "big idea"—which turned into the "Love is Love" wedding—to celebrate marriage equality and extend a congratulatory message to the LGBTQ community as same-sex marriage became legal.

RESEARCH

Greater Fort Lauderdale enjoys an enviable destination image of being warm, welcoming, and inclusive. It has the highest concentration of same-sex couple households in the United States, and has become the destination of choice for LGBTQ travelers with its hundreds of LGBTQ-owned and -operated businesses. Featuring the world's first AIDS museum and the Pride Center at Equality Park—a nonprofit whose mission is to offer a safe, welcoming, and inclusive space for the LGBTQ community—Greater Fort Lauderdale is also home to the Stonewall National Museum, one of the only permanent spaces in the United States devoted to exhibitions related to LGBTQ history and culture. In 2014, more than 1.3 million LGBTQ travelers visited Greater Fort Lauderdale and spent approximately $1.4 billion. While there is little research on actual worldwide LGBTQ travel-related economic impact, some organizations estimate it could be $66 billion per year in the United States and $165 billion globally.

In deciding on the Love is Love wedding celebration, Greater Fort Lauderdale looked to other cities that had previously approved same-sex marriage, as well as research generated by organizations such as the 2012 *Global Report on LGBT Tourism* by the World Tourism Organization. Research indicated that the very act of allowing same-sex marriage, in addition to demonstrating positive attitudes toward the LGBTQ community, was economically beneficial for both the travel and wedding markets. For instance, in 2012, one year after the passage of New York State's Marriage Equality Act, NYC & Company (a marketing firm) and the city of New York released the first statistically reliable study (*The Economic Impact of Same-Sex Marriage in New York City: 2011–2012*) to quantify the economic impact of same-sex marriages. It found that in the first year that same-sex marriages were legal in New York, at least 8,200 same-sex marriage licenses were issued in New York City and more than 200,000 .guests attended these wedding celebrations, totaling about $259 million in local economic impact.[2]

Based on these data, as well as a strong conviction that the Love is Love wedding approach would be a proper celebration of a long-fought issue (and a thank-you for continued support and loyalty by the LGBTQ community), the GFLCVB gave approval to move ahead with the event and to accelerate planning and execution to be the first in Florida to offer this event.

ACTION PLANNING

The goal of the Love is Love wedding was to further GFLCVB's positioning as the undisputed destination of choice for LGBTQ travelers. The strategy was to show Greater Fort Lauderdale's connection to these audiences by providing couples from all walks of life with the chance to marry, en masse, in sunny romance for all the world to see. Overarching Love is Love celebration objectives included the following:

- Stage a celebration that demonstrates the destination's commitment to the LGBTQ community.

- Communicate Greater Florida's support and celebration of equality in marriage—and be the first destination to do this as a specific campaign.

- Create participation and inclusiveness through destination partners and the community.

- Generate significant awareness through traditional and social media avenues, as well as website traffic.

- Demonstrate the GFLCVB's thought leadership and progressive marketing capabilities.

- Increase the number of LGBTQ visitors.

- Position Greater Fort Lauderdale as the best travel destination for LGBTQ travelers.

- Highlight the innovative aspects of Greater Fort Lauderdale as a destination that promotes itself as a friendly destination within the LGBTQ community.

Source: Greater Fort Lauderdale Convention & Visitors Bureau. Reproduced with permission.

GFLCVB, Finn Partners, and the GFLCVB's advertising agency (Starmark), with a $50,000 budget, conceived and rolled out a comprehensive plan to execute a notable Love is Love event in Greater Fort Lauderdale. What evolved was a group sunrise wedding (and vow renewal) for 100 LGBTQ and straight couples from around the globe. The strategy was to execute a festive, caring, and noncommercial celebration that would cast a favorable light on Greater Fort Lauderdale as a leader in LGBTQ rights. The Love is Love destination wedding would commemorate the landmark announcement for same-sex marriage equality in Florida and the GFLCVB's commitment to the LGBTQ community and, by marrying 100 couples, offer a nod of recognition to Broward County's centennial celebration, which also took place in 2015. The invitation to both straight *and* LGBTQ couples to participate signified the destination's inclusiveness and open-mindedness, especially Broward County's open arms and open hearts hospitality.

COMMUNICATION

When the ban on same-sex marriage was lifted and marriage equality became state law on January 6, 2015, the GFLCVB vowed to execute the wedding by February 5, 2015. From florals and photography, to wedding licenses and champagne, to wedding cake and officiants, every detail had to be seen to, and in a hurry.

The first step was to invite and welcome 100 couples, both LGBTQ and straight (plus friends and family), to show the world that love is possible in Greater Fort Lauderdale. An activation plan solicited couples to participate, with an invitation that included travel, accommodations, a destination beach wedding, and a reception. A microsite (www.sunny.org/LoveIsLove) was created with an entry form for couples to submit their photos and love story to be chosen for one of the 100 spots.

LGBTQ and straight couples registered, representing 18 U.S. states, the United Kingdom, Italy, and South America, reflecting the universal acceptance that the Love is Love wedding represented. Of the participants, 30% were renewing their vows. Once the GFLCVB selected the couples, Finn Partners secured their interest in media interviews to tell their personal stories and the significance of the Love is Love wedding to them. After a vetting process, the agency arranged hometown media interviews for the couples, including Ohio's *Plain Dealer* and Maryland's *Frederick News-Post*. Target media for this phase of the promotion included mainstream outlets as well as such LGBTQ publications as *Curve*, *GayCities*, *Instinct*, *Passport*, and *Here Media*.

Source: Greater Fort Lauderdale Convention & Visitors Bureau. Reproduced with permission.

The campaign formed partnerships with travel companies to enhance the event—including JetBlue, Cruise Planners, and the W Fort Lauderdale hotel—to provide a complimentary two-night stay, round-trip airfare, and an opportunity for one lucky couple to win a seven-night Celebrity Cruises honeymoon. More than 50 local hospitality partners provided items for a "Hello Sunny" welcome bag for each participating couple. The Broward County government supported the initiative by offering extended hours on the eve of the wedding to issue marriage licenses to out-of-town participants, with the GFLCVB providing transportation to the courthouse.

To add extra excitement and media appeal, Finn Partners secured celebrity performer Lance Bass as the event's Love is Love ambassador. Bass, a former member of *NSYNC and a *Dancing With the Stars* alum, is an active LGBTQ advocate. He joined the wedding procession with his new husband Michael Turchin. Finn Partners leveraged the timing of Lance's appearance in Greater Fort Lauderdale to coincide with his history-making televised wedding on the E! network special *Lance Loves Michael: The Lance Bass Wedding*—the first American television broadcast of a celebrity marriage between two men—which aired the same night as the Love is Love wedding. A national press release and outreach to celebrity and entertainment media were activated to garner coverage and media interviews for Bass. The press release was supported by social media posts on the GFLCVB's Twitter and Facebook channels.

LGBTQ and straight couples say "they do" at the W Fort Lauderdale in a historic group wedding ceremony hosted by the Greater Fort Lauderdale Convention and Visitors Bureau. Lance Bass and husband Michael Turchin (lower front, center) led the "Love is Love" procession on the same day as the premiere of *Lance Loves Michael*, the first televised wedding between two men.

Source: Greater Fort Lauderdale Convention & Visitors Bureau. Reproduced with permission.

Symbolic of new beginnings, the wedding ceremony was timed with sunrise. A wedding set was created at the W Fort Lauderdale; couples were invited to a predawn breakfast, and hair and makeup touches were provided by the hotel's Bliss Spa (led by Ted Gibson of TLC's *What Not to Wear* fame). Throughout the morning, the agency arranged more than 40 interviews with print and broadcast media with the wedding couples, guests, Lance Bass, and GFLCVB representatives. Immediately post-event, the agency distributed Associated Press–quality wedding photos across the wire, and a press release was distributed internationally with images and video links to broadcast-quality footage. The footage was also posted on the client's dedicated YouTube channel. All six local affiliates of the major news networks covered the live event, which was picked up nationwide by affiliates coast-to-coast.

EVALUATION

Earned media included 201 unique broadcast placements with a total potential reach of 58,322,236 impressions. TV highlights were aired on MSNBC, CNN, and NBC, CBS, ABC, and Fox affiliates coast-to-coast. Print coverage totaled a potential reach of 2,930,894 impressions, while online coverage totaled 1,312 articles and 667,892,234 unique viewers. Major print and online coverage included the *New York Times*, the *Huffington Post*, *Us Weekly*, the *Toronto Sun*, *Yahoo! Travel*, the *Miami Herald*, the *Baltimore Sun*, *Brides*, and *Travel Weekly*.

Social media/online success included the following:

- The #LoveIsLove and #HelloSunny hashtags featured 1,137 posts (January 1–February 8, 2015) and a potential reach of 13,637,433 and 13,638,570, respectively.

- Lance Bass was a tweet machine, with an average of 700 likes per post and 400,000 potential reach.

- The Love is Love landing page on the Sunny.org website received 29,159 page views (January–February 2015).

- The Sunny.org/Wedding page doubled in visits from December 2014 (7,741 visits) to January 2015 (14,753).

The integrated campaign also included 15- and 30-second video spots and print and digital ads that ran in the *Huffington Post* and the *New York Times*, as well as LGBTQ publications *Curve*, *GayCities*, *Instinct*, *Passport*, and *Here Media*. Results included the following:

- Advertising impressions totaled 10,235,063.

- Facebook video ads were the best-performing ads in the GFLCVB's social media history, with 103,756 complete video views.

The Love is Love event garnered several prestigious awards, making it one of Fort Lauderdale's most awarded single campaigns, including *PR Week*'s Promotional Event of the Year, *Bulldog Reporter*'s Silver Award for a PR Campaign, and the Hospitality Sales and Marketing Association International Adrian Gold Award for Feature Placement in a Marketing Program and Special Event.

Source: Greater Fort Lauderdale Convention & Visitors Bureau. Reproduced with permission.

RACE PIT STOP

Discussion Questions

1. With less than a month to organize, promote, and carry out the Love is Love event, little time was available beforehand for research. What other types of research may have been done quickly prior to the campaign's launch? If more time had been available, what kinds of primary research would you suggest be conducted? Why?

2. Revisit the campaign's objectives. Knowing what you do about this case, revise them to be measurable and time-specific. What other objectives would be germane to this case?

3. Given the objectives of this campaign, do you believe the contest to engage participants was a good strategy? Why or why not? What would be possible risks in using this strategy? How would you go about minimizing or preparing for the risks you have identified?

4. What other strategies or tactics could build upon the success of the Love is Love wedding to further engage its participants and their families and friends?

Trendlines

Political and social climates change over time, with societies becoming more or less accepting and conservative or liberal, depending on current cultural concerns. What are the risks associated with an organization/company being a thought leader and trailblazer for social change? What about the benefits? What considerations do you believe a company or organization should employ before embarking on a campaign as a social change leader?

In 2017, the World Tourism Organization released an updated *Global Report on LGBT Tourism*. The report lists recommendations for tourism-related entities who want to attract LGBTQ consumers. Both the first report in 2012 and the latest one discuss trends in LGBTQ tourism.[3] Read this section of each report and discuss the differences in the trends reported in 2012 and those reported in 2017. What additional insights might you apply to a future GFLCVB tourism campaign?

REFERENCES

1. Greater Fort Lauderdale Convention and Visitors Bureau. (2016, April 19). Gender identity a human right in Broward County/Greater Fort Lauderdale. *PR Newswire*. Retrieved from https://www.prnewswire.com/news-releases/gender-identity-a-human-right-in-broward-county--greater-fort-lauderdale-300253806.html

2. Ellis, B. (2012, July 24). Gay marriage boosts NYC's economy by $259 million in first year. *CNN Money*. Retrieved from http://money.cnn.com/2012/07/24/pf/gay-marriage-economic-impact/index.htm

3. Global report on LGBT tourism. (2012). *World Tourism Organization*. Retrieved from http://www.e-unwto.org/doi/pdf/10.18111/9789284414581; Second global report on LGBT tourism. (2017). *World Tourism Organization*. Retrieved from http://cf.cdn.unwto.org/sites/all/files/pdf/lgtb_report_compressed_0.pdf

FOR IMMEDIATE RELEASE

LOVE IS LOVE IN GREATER FORT LAUDERDALE!

SUNRISE BEACH WEDDING CELEBRATES MARRIAGE EQUALITY IN THE GAY CAPITAL OF FLORIDA

Greater Fort Lauderdale Convention and Visitors Bureau to Host 100 Couples With Free Air, Hotel, and Historic Group Wedding Ceremony

GREATER FORT LAUDERDALE, Florida (January 6, 2015)—To celebrate the landmark announcement for same-sex marriage equality in Florida, the Greater Fort Lauderdale Convention and Visitors Bureau (GFLCVB) has launched a "Love is Love" initiative to marry both LGBTQ and straight couples from across the nation in a historic collective wedding ceremony.

The sunrise beach wedding will take place on Fort Lauderdale beach in front of the W Fort Lauderdale hotel on Thursday, February 5. Registration to win a "Love is Love" wedding trip is available at www.sunny.org/LoveIsLove starting today.

Reverend Dr. Durrell Watkins, senior minister of the Sunshine Cathedral, will preside. The GFLCVB, JetBlue, W Fort Lauderdale, and area partners have joined together to provide a wedding to remember.

Following the sunrise beach wedding, the newlyweds will be invited to the W Fort Lauderdale for a post-ceremony champagne toast and reception to commemorate the unique occasion. In addition, a lucky couple will receive an ultimate cruise wedding getaway to begin their new life together. W Fort Lauderdale also is offering a "Love is Love" wedding package for an extended stay in Greater Fort Lauderdale.

"I'm extremely proud of the willingness and openness of our hospitality community to effect change for the better. And as we commemorate the 100-year anniversary of the founding of Broward County in 2015, we're excited to extend our never-wavering support of the LGBTQ community, and provide couples gay and straight from across the country a chance to be a part of this significant day in history," said Nicki E. Grossman, president of the GFLCVB.

In a ruling handed down in December, the U.S. 11th Circuit Court of Appeals in Atlanta turned down a request by Florida's secretaries of health and management services and the clerk of the court in the Panhandle's Washington County to extend a stay in the state's same-sex marriage ban case. A federal judge based in Tallahassee had ruled in August that the state's same-sex marriage ban is unconstitutional, but stayed his decision until January 5 to give the state time to appeal.

"Greater Fort Lauderdale has long been a pioneering advocate of the LGBTQ community in Florida, and our 'Love is Love' campaign is another example of how we hope to continue to positively impact our resident community and visitors by offering this special day to rejoice as now we all can say 'I Do' legally," said Richard Gray, managing director of the LGBTQ market for the GFLCVB.

Home to the highest concentration of same-sex couple households in the country, and as one of the top LGBTQ vacation destinations in the world, Greater Fort Lauderdale is one of the most diverse LGBTQ capitals and continues to be a destination of choice for LGBTQ travelers with hundreds of LGBTQ-owned and -operated businesses.

For more information on the "Love is Love" wedding celebration, visit www.sunny.org/LoveIsLove.

Editor's Note: Please click here for a broadcast-quality video about the Greater Fort Lauderdale Convention and Visitors Bureau's "Love is Love" wedding celebration. Please click here for high-resolution images.

Nicki E. Grossman and Richard Gray are available for interviews on this subject.

###

(Continued)

(Continued)

About Greater Fort Lauderdale

From the seagrass to the sawgrass, Greater Fort Lauderdale boasts more than 34,000 lodging accommodations at a variety of hotels, luxury spa resorts, and Superior Small Lodgings reflecting a "beach chic" vibe. Visitors enjoy 23 miles of Blue Wave certified beaches, discover 300+ miles of inland waterways that run from the Intracoastal Waterway to the Everglades, dine at thousands of restaurants and eateries, get immersed in a thriving arts and culture scene, and indulge in top shopping. For more info, contact the Greater Fort Lauderdale Convention and Visitors Bureau at (800) 22-SUNNY or visit www.sunny.org.

The Greater Fort Lauderdale Convention and Visitors Bureau can also be followed on Twitter at www.twitter.com/visitlauderdale and Instagram at www.instagram.com/visitlauderdale. Become a fan on Facebook at www.facebook.com/visitlauderdale or join us on Foursquare at www.foursquare.com/visitlauderdale. To have Greater Fort Lauderdale in the palm of your hand, download the free iPhone applications, *Fort Lauderdale* and *Defrost Your Swimsuit* at www.sunny.org/apps.

Media Contact

Virginia Sheridan

Finn Partners

(212) 715-1600

virginia.sheridan@finnpartners.com

Source: Greater Fort Lauderdale Convention & Visitors Bureau. Reproduced with permission.

FINANCIAL COMMUNICATION

Financial communication, traditionally managed by the investor relations function within companies, is an important link between the organization and those who invest in the organization. It is a rapidly changing aspect of public relations as the lack of trust in major institutions is at an all-time high, and stakeholders and regulators are demanding greater corporate accountability and transparency.

This chapter features case studies involving one state's tax amnesty efforts, a venture capitalist firm's campaign to build brand equity to attract new investment dollars, and the financial turnaround of a technology investment company based on communication. All three cases should provoke thinking about how people approach facts and information, especially as confidence in major institutions has eroded over the past several years. The VantagePoint case study provides details on a potentially new functional area of public relations as more venture capitalists bring on public relations experts. Finally, both the VantagePoint and Alcatel-Lucent cases point to how, even with an extensive outreach to investors, an organization might not ultimately achieve longer-term financial goals.

TAX AMNESTY 2015: ACT NOW. GET RIGHT. MOVE FORWARD

Amanda Jo Stanley, Former Director of Public Relations, Indiana Department of Revenue

SITUATION

The Indiana Department of Revenue (DOR) was created by an act of the Indiana General Assembly on February 18, 1947. The DOR is responsible for providing services

to Indiana citizens regarding state tax matters. Additionally, the department administers state tax laws, develops regulations, and makes decisions about tax policy.

House Enrolled Act (HEA) 1001 was signed by Indiana governor Mike Pence in May 2015. The legislation required the DOR to establish a tax amnesty program and stated the program would last eight business weeks. The legislation provided that any liability due and payable for a period ending before January 1, 2013, would be eligible for amnesty. Tax Amnesty 2015 was held from September 15, 2015, through November 16, 2015; taxpayers could file an original or amended return to report a tax liability. If a taxpayer paid all taxes due, the department would release any existing liens and not seek civil or criminal prosecution. If a taxpayer was eligible for Tax Amnesty 2015 and did not pay the tax due or did not comply with the payment plan agreement established with the department, the original penalty would be doubled after Tax Amnesty 2015. Anticipated funds collected from the program were targeted primarily for the state's regional cities development fund, the operation of the state's rail line, and the state's general fund.

RESEARCH

Indiana offered its first amnesty program in 2005, collecting more than $244 million from $1.3 billion in outstanding liabilities, exceeding its originally anticipated $65 million. The Tax Amnesty 2015 campaign relied heavily on available data from that earlier campaign, analyzing media coverage, taxpayer letters, website statistics, and program reports. From that campaign, the department learned two crucial lessons:

- The vast majority of amnesty collections occurred in the last two weeks of the program.

- A direct marketing public relations campaign is the most cost-effective promotional method.

Identifying and analyzing current taxpayer data was a crucial step in the research process. For example, the department identified approximately 260,000 eligible taxpayers with more than $500 million in outstanding tax liabilities. The number of eligible taxpayers by tax type was identified. Geographic application of the total number of eligible taxpayers by county helped identify key counties for advertising and presentation purposes. A specific target list by tax type and amounts of outstanding tax liability was developed to prioritize efforts on high-value opportunities, and corresponding target media lists for earned and paid media were developed. For example, business taxpayers accounted for the majority of eligible liabilities. To reach these taxpayers, media efforts focused on business and manufacturing media outlets. The department determined that taxpayers in 15 Indiana counties accounted for more than 67% of the total eligible tax liabilities.

ACTION PLANNING

With a budget of $13.4 million, the campaign's goal was, over four months, to persuade eligible taxpayers to participate in Tax Amnesty 2015 by paying their past-due taxes. The execution phase of the campaign ran from July 20, 2015, through November 16, 2015.

The campaign focused on reaching all eligible taxpayers, along with tax professionals, general and trade media reporters, and legislators and government leaders in Indiana. The overarching strategy included positive messages in all communications. Key messages for eligible taxpayers included the fact the taxpayer was eligible to participate, how and when to participate, and the benefits of doing so (e.g., "penalty, interest, and collection fees are waived if the tax is paid in full"). Key messages for tax professionals, media, legislators, and government leaders focused on using these audience segments (tax professionals, trade media reporters, etc.) to reach eligible taxpayers with the same positive messages.

Objectives included the following:

- Inform 95% of eligible taxpayers about Tax Amnesty 2015 by November 16, 2015.

- Provide more than 12,000 Indiana tax professionals with basic Tax Amnesty 2015 information by November 16, 2015.

- Place at least 200 total stories in Indiana general media and in trade media about Tax Amnesty 2015 prior to November 16, 2015.

- Provide 75% of all Indiana elected officials and staffs with Tax Amnesty 2015 information by August 17, 2015.

- Collect $110 million in outstanding tax liabilities by December 31, 2016.

COMMUNICATION

To reach taxpayers through local, trusted sources, the department partnered with community and business organizations and Indiana legislators to host more than 60 Tax Amnesty 2015 informational seminars. The department partnered with local libraries, chambers of commerce, tax preparation offices, and certified public accountants to host these seminars. More than 500 taxpayers attended the in-person seminars. A

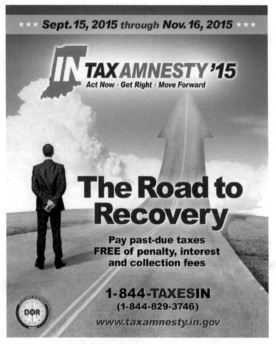

Source: The Indiana Department of Revenue. Reproduced with permission.

asher

Media:	Radio – Air Dates:
Client:	**Indiana Department of Revenue**
Date:	08/26/15
Job#:	dor-24422
Title:	**Tax Amnesty**
Time:	:60
Revision:	3

SFX (:02):	*(Spinning wheel from Life game; click, click of a piece "moving".)*
VO (:03):	In board games taxes are simple:
PLAYER 1 (:03):	Aww, noooo…pay taxes…$20,000. **(Group laughter)**
SFX :	*(Music up and under through next spin.)*
VO (:05):	But that's just a game.
VO (:10):	In real life — if you fail to meet your tax obligation — the penalties, interest, and fees can really add up. But, the Indiana Department of Revenue is offering a great opportunity for both individuals and businesses.
VO (:14):	It's called Tax Amnesty Twenty-Fifteen. A short, two-month window to pay back taxes between September fifteenth and November sixteenth. Free of penalties, interest and fees. You can learn all about Tax Amnesty Twenty-Fifteen at TAX AMNESTY DOT I-N dot GOV
SFX (:02):	*(Spinning wheel; click, click, click of "moving" a piece.)*
PLAYER 2 (:03):	More taxes. Not again. **(Group laughter)**
VO (:08):	We should all pay our fair share…in board games and real life. If you haven't been, it's time. Get it done by November sixteenth.
TAG (:10):	**Tax Amnesty Twenty-Fifteen…Act Now…Get Right…Move Forward. Learn more at TAX AMNESTY DOT I-N dot GOV or by calling ONE EIGHT FOUR FOUR TAXES-I-N**

Source: The Indiana Department of Revenue. Reproduced with permission.

webinar version also was made available on the Tax Amnesty 2015 website. To promote the outreach presentations, the campaign provided turnkey materials and posters and handouts to partnering organizations. The campaign created a Tax Amnesty 2015 website, which allowed taxpayers to easily find important program-related information, including forms, the program payment portal, fact sheets, and department contact information. On the website's homepage, a Tax Amnesty 2015 informational video featuring the department commissioner introduced the program. The department drove traffic to the program website through links and graphics on the department's external website and internal intranet site. The campaign used social media (Facebook and Twitter) to provide general Tax Amnesty 2015 information (including payment plan options) and to provide an outlet for taxpayers to contact the department with questions. The campaign also found social media ideal for promoting the in-person seminars, and to cross-promote publications, news releases, and blogs.

The campaign developed and placed radio and digital advertisements. News releases announced the program, promoted presentations with partnering organizations, and updated taxpayers on the program's status and success. Tax Amnesty 2015 was covered in all major media markets in the state through radio, print, and television. Business, law, and finance trade publications provided important coverage of the program.

EVALUATION

More than 81,000 taxpayers participated in Tax Amnesty 2015 by paying in full or establishing a payment plan. As of December 31, 2015, the program had collected $168.75 million, exceeding the $110 million collection goal. Final program collections would total approximately $188 million. The success of Tax Amnesty 2015 led to new legislation in 2016 to fund additional economic development programs. Other achievements included the following:

- 100% of eligible taxpayers were notified of their Tax Amnesty 2015 eligibility prior to the start of the program.

- More than 270 Tax Amnesty 2015 stories were placed in Indiana general media during the Tax Amnesty 2015 campaign period. Media in all 92 Indiana counties covered the Tax Amnesty 2015 program.

- More than 13,000 Indiana tax professionals were provided with Tax Amnesty 2015 information during the Tax Amnesty 2015 campaign period.

- 100% of all Indiana legislators were provided with Tax Amnesty 2015 information by August 17, 2015.

Should the state decide to conduct a third tax amnesty program in future years, the results of the Tax Amnesty 2015 campaign will provide valuable insight and guidance. As technology advances and how taxpayers interact with government changes, the department must adapt and meet taxpayers where they are. During Tax Amnesty 2015, the DOR learned most taxpayers preferred to participate online rather than in person.

RACE PIT STOP

Discussion Questions

1. The Tax Amnesty 2015 campaign relied heavily on available data from the 2005 tax amnesty program. What other data could have been researched?

2. Most of the objectives in this campaign identify measurables that relate to information distribution. What other kind of objectives do you think would have been useful for this campaign?

3. What other strategies could the campaign planners have used?

Trendlines

The Pew Research Center recently published a report on how people approach facts and information.[1] Quoting from the executive summary:

[People] fall along a spectrum ranging from fairly high engagement with information to wariness of it. Roughly four-in-ten adults (38%) are in groups that have relatively strong interest and trust in information sources and learning. About half (49%) fall into groups that are relatively disengaged and not very enthusiastic about information. . . . Another 13% occupy a middle space: They are not particularly trusting of information sources, but they show higher interest in learning than those in the more information-wary groups.

What are the implications of the results of the Pew Research Center study for this case? Distrust of the government, especially tax entities, would figure to reduce engagement with tax amnesty information. What can be gleaned from this study that would inform potential changes as involves government entities communicating with the public on personal finance concerns?

REFERENCES

1. Horrigan, J. B. (2017, September 11). How people approach facts and information. *Pew Research Center*. Retrieved from http://www.pewinternet.org/2017/09/11/how-people-approach-facts-and-information/

BUILDING BRAND EQUITY TO ATTRACT INVESTMENT DOLLARS IN CLEAN TECHNOLOGY

Arlene Guzmán Todd, Independent Public Relations Strategist

Kate S. Kurtin, Assistant Professor, California State University, Los Angeles

Source: VantagePoint Capital Partners (2018).

SITUATION

VantagePoint Capital Partners (VP) is a Silicon Valley venture capital investment firm founded in 1996 with a mission to identify and invest in companies looking to revolutionize industries and change the world. In 2007, the crumbling global infrastructure and increased dependence on fossil fuels created a unique opportunity to shift the firm's investment focus in information technology (IT), digital media, health care, and financial technology toward focusing primarily on companies making breakthroughs in energy innovation and efficiency, known as clean technology (cleantech). VP worked to position itself as a leader in cleantech and actively sought investment dollars and U.S. Department of Energy grants and loan guarantees on behalf of their portfolio of startup companies. The firm quickly learned the tremendous capital demands required to build viable cleantech companies, and in 2010, it announced a commitment to raise a $1.25 billion cleantech fund. In order to accomplish the goal, VP implemented a comprehensive public relations strategy, the first of its kind for the firm.

RESEARCH

Primary research for the public relations campaign came in the form of acquiring knowledge from holding investor pitch meetings and media interviews (through which we could track firsthand some media coverage trends on cleantech/green issues), monitoring the emergence of cleantech-focused conferences, and gleaning insights through conversations with industry, government leaders, and entrepreneurs. Findings confirmed the transformative economic opportunities surrounding the cleantech industry and the opportunity for VP to position itself as an emerging leader driving cleantech innovation. The confidential nature of investor relations required VP to focus on a qualitative competitive analysis on the activities of two leading Silicon Valley venture firms: Khosla Ventures and Kleiner Perkins Caufield & Byers. Like VP, these firms had joined the race to establish large cleantech investment funds. These firms began to leverage public relations as they competed for media coverage and investment dollars. The cleantech industry was new and without established best practices, which provided the competing firms the opportunity to originate and evaluate public relations activities that were unique to each firm's corporate DNA. Activities by each of these firms had a ripple effect that contributed to increasing the cleantech sector's appeal to investors.

Secondary research came in the form of a study of cleantech media coverage that measured industry mentions and tone.[1] Findings from these activities provided independent data revealing approaches that promoted the cleantech economic opportunity while also highlighting cleantech's broader industry, societal, environmental, and policy impacts. Our campaign would use these findings to create relevant and compelling content to drive feature media coverage.

ACTION PLANNING

The overall goal for this public relations campaign in 2010–2011 was to establish VP as the leading voice in modernizing the world's infrastructure. VP's messaging was designed to appeal to key audiences, including entrepreneurs developing cleantech products and solutions, existing and potential investors, and elected government officials who could enact policies that would support the emerging cleantech industry. Messaging included the following:

- VP is the voice for the next generation of transformative cleantech capital investing.
- VP plays an integral role in modernizing the world's infrastructure with investments in major cleantech sectors.
- VP has a strategic investment model designed to help create mainstream, scalable, global cleantech companies that have a major impact on the world's infrastructure.
- VP's knowledge of the cleantech market provides unparalleled reach and insight.

VP focused on accomplishing three main objectives that would be carried out and measured during the first six months of the fundraising campaign:

- Position VP as the leader of the cleantech industry by securing feature coverage in at least one high-profile, national-level business media outlet.
- Increase traditional and social media coverage of VP's role in cleantech.
- Obtain $1.25 billion to support cleantech opportunities.

COMMUNICATION

Media relations activities included developing and distributing press releases around substantial firm announcements concerning its network of advisers and portfolio companies. VP updated its corporate boilerplate messaging to reflect its cleantech leadership. The updated boilerplate read, "VantagePoint Capital Partners is a global leader in financing and supporting transformative companies focused on energy innovation, Internet and digital media." The campaign also provided access to high-level executives (including the CEO) to general business media, cleantech and financial sector media, and other high-profile publications such as *Bloomberg*, *Time* magazine, the *Wall Street Journal*, and *Fortune*. For online media, the campaign developed website materials that included editorials, investor communication, and social media profiles on Facebook and Twitter, all used to promote the firm's thought leadership and to push firm media and press coverage.

The campaign reached out to investors in numerous ways, including the following:

- Creation of investor materials that highlighted firm capabilities and team expertise, provided an overview of investment opportunities, and projected return on investment to potential investors.

- Development of a speaker's bureau focused on keynote and panel opportunities that featured VP executives. This bureau participated at high-profile conferences and events, including *Fortune*'s Brainstorm Green, the World Economic Forum, the *Wall Street Journal* ECO:nomics conference, the Clinton Global Initiative events, and the Milken Institute's Global Conference.

- Conceptualization and execution of the "ResourcePoint CleanTech Summit," a private, invitation-only multiday conference for 100+ thought, industry, and government leaders in the cleantech sector.

- Getting VP portfolio companies to add references to VP and its website on their official corporate materials.

- Using social media to track viral conversations about the brand, allowing VP to react quickly to online dialogues affecting the firm's reputation.

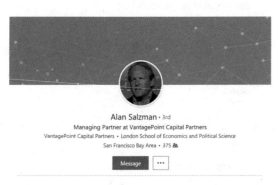

Alan Salzman · 3rd
Managing Partner at VantagePoint Capital Partners
VantagePoint Capital Partners · London School of Economics and Political Science
San Francisco Bay Area · 375 🖾

Message   ⋯

Alan Salzman, co-founder and CEO of VantagePoint, took on an active speaking role for the campaign, appearing before media and speaking at major forums such at the Milken Institute's Global Conference and *Fortune*'s Brainstorm Green.

Source: LinkedIn/@Alan Salzman.

The campaign also featured a government relations program that focused on discussing cleantech with local and national government officials and introducing VP's position as a thought leader in the space. To do this successfully, VP deployed the following tactics:

- Researched state and federal regulations affecting the cleantech industry and identified the individual proponents of cleantech-friendly policies

- Researched elected officials at the local, state, and national levels who had expressed commitment to cleantech and alternative energy and developed an outreach campaign to educate them on the firm's mission and investment focus

- Contributed political donations to candidates who campaigned on a cleantech-friendly platform

EVALUATION

The VP campaign focused on accomplishing three main objectives. In addition to achieving these three items, general evidence of campaign success is included below.

Objective 1: Position VP as the leader of cleantech in the venture capital industry.

The firm's CEO, Alan Salzman, was highly sought after by the press for conversations related to the cleantech space. Salzman was featured in press placements in leading outlets including *Forbes, Fortune, Bloomberg,* the *Wall Street Journal,* CNN, and Fox Business and also secured speaking opportunities in leading conferences including the World Economic Forum Annual Meeting, the Milken Institute's Global Conference, and *Fortune's* Brainstorm Green. In addition, Salzman was appointed finance chair of the World Business Summit on Climate Change, became a member of the BP Alternative Energy Advisory Board, and was placed on the Climate Group's international council.

Objective 2: Increase and enhance coverage in traditional and social media.

The firm was mentioned in leading media outlets including the *New York Times,* the *Wall Street Journal, Time,* and *Forbes* on multiple occasions. In addition, VP established a presence on Facebook and Twitter. During implementation, we learned that social media was effective in reaching entrepreneurs but was not an appropriate media channel to reach key investors, who tended to have nominal online presence due to their roles as fiduciaries.

Objective 3: Obtain $1.25 billion to support cleantech opportunities.

VP had made an aggressive bet on cleantech. Early portfolio company success, highlighted by the IPOs (initial public offerings) from Tesla, provided evidence of the firm's ability to invest in companies who were making significant impacts in the world and were yielding positive financial returns. For example, before Tesla's IPO, VP owned 7.13 million shares (9.11%) of Tesla, worth an estimated $121.2 million at the projected $17 initial public offering price. In 2013, however, the cleantech bubble burst, and investment in cleantech collapsed by almost half—down 46% to $2.2 billion. The downward spiral of the larger cleantech industry, and the corresponding lack of investor interest, forced VP to stop raising the planned $1.25 billion fund.

RACE PIT STOP

Discussion Questions

1. What additional research could the VantagePoint team have considered? What information could have come from these other research methods that could have added to the team's understanding of the challenge?

2. The tactical framework for this campaign seems to have been highly focused on media relations and outreach through social media. What other tactics might VP have considered?

3. Examine the objectives. How would you have constructed all of them in ways that point to measurable outcomes?

4. The evaluation covered all of the objectives, which were primarily focused on media relations. How would you have developed numerous indicators to measure the success or failure of the investor and government affairs portions of the plan?

Trendlines

Recently, we have seen a rise in the addition of top public relations and communications talent to venture capital (VC) firms. In many cases, these public relations experts are used primarily to help entrepreneurs and startup companies shape their public relations strategy. Other VC firms are bringing on public relations experts to boost their own images and promote them to the press. Smart entrepreneurs are thinking about public relations and branding at an earlier stage. This has led to an understanding of the value of being transparent and authentic with consumers (including investors) and a bigger role for public relations in building brands in the financial arena. What are the implications of this trend for the profession of public relations?

REFERENCES

1. National Renewable Energy Laboratory. (2013, December 3–4). *Clean energy finance: Challenges and opportunities of early-stage energy investing.* Retrieved from http://www .nrel.gov/docs/fy14osti/60882-1.pdf; Ernst & Young. (2012). *Cleantech matters.* Retrieved from http://www.ey.com/Publication/vwLUAssets/Global_cleantech_insights_and_ trends_report_2012/$FILE/cleantech_matters.pdf

THE ALCATEL-LUCENT SHIFT PLAN: A FINANCIAL TURNAROUND BOLSTERED BY COMMUNICATIONS

Marisa Baldo, Former Vice President of Investor Relations, Alcatel-Lucent

Wendy Zajack, Faculty Director in School of Continuing Studies, Georgetown University

SITUATION

Alcatel·Lucent

When Alcatel and Lucent Technologies merged in April 2006, the $34 billion consolidation created one of the world's biggest global communications equipment providers. Just two years later, the merger was already considered an enormous failure. Culture differences, inability to agree on strategy because of a complex management structure, a consolidated customer base, and price pressure by aggressive competitors had taken their toll. After almost a decade of floundering, the future of the company was in serious doubt when a hard-charging French telecom executive, Michel Combes, was announced as the company's new CEO on April 1, 2013.

Combes, formerly CEO of Vodafone Europe, had extensive experience in telecommunications turnarounds. The high-energy French executive had a reputation for getting the job done; however, the complexity and scale of Alcatel-Lucent would put all of his abilities to the test. When Combes walked in the boardroom doors of the Paris Alcatel-Lucent headquarters, located in an elegant building a stone's throw from the Eiffel Tower, the company was close to bankruptcy. Alcatel-Lucent was in a crisis situation with its financial investors, customers, and employees. One of the last financial steps taken by the previous executive team was to secure an emergency $2 billion loan from Credit Suisse and the Goldman Sachs Group. This was obtained by using Alcatel-Lucent's prized possession—key intellectual property from its Silicon Valley–based internet routing business, as well as a rich patent portfolio—as collateral. This gave the company a temporary financial respite, but put it in a situation that was not sustainable for the long term.

By the beginning of 2013, Alcatel-Lucent shares had become "penny" stocks. While many financial restructuring plans had been attempted at the company, Combes had a very short time to come up with what many considered a last-ditch attempt to save it. Where other leaders had time to strategize, Combes needed to leap into quick, decisive action and turn an extremely large global ship in the right direction.

RESEARCH

The research conducted by the team at Alcatel-Lucent consisted of a mix of initiating internal audits and perception surveys with investors (the key audience), and CEO Combes and his team holding hundreds of meetings with stakeholders, including employees, customers, and investors. In his first few months, he met with Alcatel-Lucent's top 25 global customers, including the top three U.S. customers, AT&T, Verizon, and Sprint, and, in France, the telecom firm Orange. He met directly with employees to gain unfiltered insights. While most customers considered Alcatel-Lucent to be a leader in innovations, they were unhappy with the company's ability to deliver its technology on time. And nearly all of them were extremely worried about the financial instability of the company. In a market where network technology is purchased in a 10-year buy, install, and upgrade cycle, this lack of confidence could be crushing.

Under the leadership of the finance department, the company consulted with a handful of major banks to assess the feasibility of the type of financing plan necessary to solve the balance sheet issues. The heart of this plan was to put together a simple, yet feasible, path toward profitability that included bolstering the products that were the company's growth engines, deeply cutting the staff, and reallocating both research and development (R&D) spending and the funding of nonprofitable products. This honest feedback played a role in building the right narrative for the plan's announcement. Several external firms were also called in to provide industry analysis and specific counsel on various elements, including PricewaterhouseCoopers. The firm conducted an audit on cash generation, helping to create a viable financial plan to return Alcatel-Lucent to a free cash-flow situation—quite simply, a situation where it was making enough cash to pay for its expenses (R&D, employees, and offices) and have some money left over.

A top management consultant also came on board to make a strategic and competitive assessment that led to the right market positioning. In a highly competitive telecommunications equipment market, where specialization had become the norm, Alcatel-Lucent had to show that it was able to leverage its depth and breadth of knowledge to its customers' benefit. Lastly, a global communications consulting firm worked with the leadership communications team to prepare messaging around the research findings.

Key findings from the research revealed concerns about the company's lack of focus, fragmented R&D, lack of accountability, uncompetitive cost structure, and unsustainable financial structure. Research also found where the company was strong, including its winning products, relationships with customers, and solid innovation capabilities. The key was communicating these findings to key audiences in a way that assured customers, employees, and investors alike that Alcatel-Lucent was a financially stable company that would be around in the future, that it was competitive, and that it offered innovations that would help its customers build the network of the future. This was not a onetime communications exercise, but a bold, strategic, and extremely transparent message that would need to be heard and believed by these key audiences. It came to be known as the Shift Plan.

ACTION PLANNING

On June 19, 2013, when Combes had been in the job just over two months, he publicly announced a new branded transformation plan—called the Shift Plan—that set a clear company course for the next three years. The key elements that distinguished this from past restructuring plans were its clarity and transparency. Broadly, the goals for the Shift Plan were to better position the company for the future by fostering employee accountability and, externally, improving the organization's financial reputation as a sound investment.

Equally important as the identification of issues was a clear set of business and financial targets and goals. These targets and goals were communicated repeatedly to all stakeholders—both internal and external. The plan focused particularly on product development objectives and controlling costs, with the end result of a return to positive free cash flow and increased investor confidence. The primary objectives included the following:

- Product development and focus

    o Core networking: Increase to over $8.75 billion U.S. dollars (USD) in revenues (implying mid-single-digit annual growth) and a 12.5% operating margin (from 2.4% in 2012).

- Cost containment and debt reduction aimed at returning to free cash generation

    o Achieve cost efficiency of more than $1.2 billion (USD) fixed cost reduction.

    o Turn around cash and debt profile through three streams of $2.5 billion (USD) each.

One of the key elements of the Shift Plan was creating communications that identified the company's main issues clearly and comprehensively. This included a number of dimensions: industrial, commercial, operational, and financial. The team then created an equity story that included both ambitious and realistic financial targets to be reached over a three-year horizon. These mileposts were the cornerstone of engagement with the audience, and progress was communicated regularly on the appropriate key performance indicators over the plan's lifetime.

Once the equity story was defined, the second key mission of the financial communications team was to evangelize this message within the financial community. One key aspect was to focus on communication with financial analysts—especially the sell-side analysts who were writing reports on the company and issuing buy/sell ratings that carried a lot of weight among the broader investment community. In parallel, the team focused on shareholders and on key institutional investors who manage large funds, such as mutual or pension funds. To both of these audiences, the first step was to clearly and openly communicate the plan to achieve financial health and how the company would reach a positive cash flow. The second phase was to continue to communicate on a regular basis that the company was on the road to recovery and determined to make progress on each of the defined dimensions.

The team also looked after its debt holders. This audience was made up of institutional investors who bought corporate debt by purchasing convertible bonds or high-yield bonds. This group was an essential part of Alcatel-Lucent's plan to refinance its own debt; these investors wanted to see positive progress before investing more to help Alcatel-Lucent finance its debt. They needed to clearly understand how the company planned to achieve its financial restructuring.

Employees were another key audience: The company sought to rally them around the Shift Plan. Providing extremely clear financial goals for employees and their business areas allowed them to make the sometimes very difficult decisions around terminating products and the staff and organizations necessary to support them. Having a deep understanding of the bigger picture made it possible for them to help drive the plan into their regions and business areas as well as exhibit increased accountability.

COMMUNICATION

The team created a specific shareholder program defined with a particular focus on regions that were underrepresented in the current shareholding structure—notably France and Continental Europe (Germany and Switzerland, in particular). The program also focused on attracting investors who had long-term investment approaches and moving away from its reliance on the current investor base that had a more short-term strategy. Short-term investors, who like to buy and sell often, like hedge funds, tend to bring more volatility to stock prices and are less likely to build long-term relationships with companies.

The Shift Plan relied on constant communications with all types of investors through targeted road shows, selective presence at brokers' conferences, and ad hoc one-to-one or group meetings. The team provided access to the top leadership as well as regular updates via calls around quarterly earnings releases, but also during key industry trade shows like Mobile World Congress and by hosting its own Investor Day where top management and executive committee members provided an in-depth review of the group strategy and prospects. At each communication event (including the publication of quarterly results and major product announcements), the investor relations team proactively called the analysts covering the stock (about 25 individuals) to ensure key points were understood and reflected in expectations. The team worked to provide timely responses to any inquiries as well as provide an adequate level of information, including allowing analysts to talk with experts within the business to answer specific technology or industry questions.

Alcatel-Lucent's investor relations team continually communicated Shift Plan messages, including calling individual stock analysts.

Source: Photo by startupstockphotos.com, https://www.pexels.com/photo/notes-macbook-study-conference-7102/, licensed under CC0, https://creativecommons.org/choose/zero/.

Bond holders were particularly important. Alcatel-Lucent was able to raise cash by selling its debt by issuing bonds aimed to attract these types of investors. Communication to this community was critical, so it was managed by a cross-functional team that included the investor team and the corporate treasury teams (both a part of the corporate finance organization), and Alcatel-Lucent participated in debt conferences two times a year to assure and attract these types of investors.

Significant external focus was placed on customer communications. Sales teams and senior leadership scheduled regular communication with key customers on financial metrics. The company scheduled monthly calls with top customers to provide an update on the evolution of the company's financial standing. Internally, Combes also valued the importance of frequent communication with employees. This included employee-focused briefings at each earnings announcement to keep the momentum going, rebuild confidence, and continue motivating a tired and beaten workforce. Alcatel-Lucent also created small group sessions organized by the investor relations team to explain the movements in the share price and to provide information about the perspective of respected organizations from the outside. Employees were kept apprised of every milestone that was reached and were clear on how their individual organizations and functions contributed to the success of the Shift Plan. The pace of change was difficult, painful, and exhausting; however, the goals were clear and constant.

EVALUATION

The Shift Plan's success depended on Alcatel-Lucent bringing in more revenue from its growth business areas, but also cutting costs and restructuring its debt. This happened. From a financial communication perspective alone, the key results were astounding. The main goal of the Shift Plan—a return to positive free cash flow in 2015—was largely exceeded when the company announced a free cash flow of $825 million for 2015 as a whole compared to a cash burn of $840 million. This strong commitment to communicating where it was during each step of the journey led to improved customer commitments, support from the financial markets in terms of investment, and improved employee engagement, support, and pride.

Other major achievements included the following:

- Successful repositioning as a leader in IP (internet protocol), cloud, and ultra-broadband technologies, evidenced by the growing share of next-generation technologies that went from around half of revenues in 2012 to 77% in 2015, growing at a double-digit pace on average over the period. At the same time, the share of R&D spending into next-generation technologies expanded from 67% in 2012 to 87% of total R&D in 2015.

- The fixed cost savings goal of $1.2 billion (USD) was surpassed, achieving $1.3 billion (USD) in savings.

- At the end of 2015, the group had a net cash position of $1.8 billion (USD), compared to a net debt position of just under $1 billion (USD) at the end of quarter 2 in 2013.

Other results included the following:

- Increased share of long-term investors. This was underscored with an investment made by Capital Group, which took more than 10% of the company's shares and stayed aboard throughout the Shift Plan.

- Increased interest from French investors, which moved from 11% of holdings in 2013 to 17% in 2015.

- Positive turnaround in broker ratings. In January 2013, among the 19 brokers rating the stock, there were 9 "sell," 8 "hold," and only 1 "buy." In early April 2015, among the 20 brokers covering the stock, there were 14 "buy," 5 "hold," and only 1 "sell."

While the Shift Plan was largely successful in terms of industrial repositioning, restoring cost competitiveness, and refinancing, the networking industry experienced a consolidating customer base. Alcatel-Lucent was unable to find growth in new markets as

FIGURE 4.1 ■ Share Price Chart

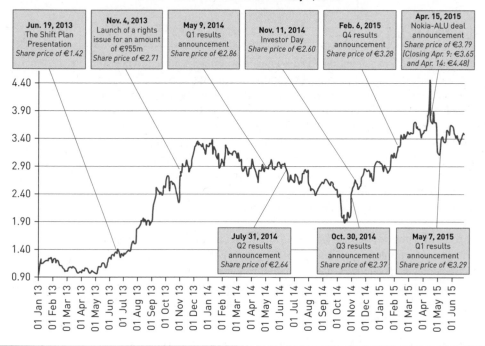

Stock Price Evolution Since January 1, 2013

Jun. 19, 2013	Nov. 4, 2013	May 9, 2014	Nov. 11, 2014	Feb. 6, 2015	Apr. 15, 2015
The Shift Plan Presentation *Share price of €1.42*	Launch of a rights issue for an amount of €955m *Share price of €2.71*	Q1 results announcement *Share price of €2.86*	Investor Day *Share price of €2.60*	Q4 results announcement *Share price of €3.28*	Nokia-ALU deal announcement *Share price of €3.79 (Closing Apr. 9: €3.65 and Apr. 14: €4.48)*

July 31, 2014	Oct. 30, 2014	May 7, 2015
Q2 results announcement *Share price of €2.64*	Q3 results announcement *Share price of €2.37*	Q1 results announcement *Share price of €3.29*

Source: Based on information from FactSet and Thomson Reuters.

well as the financial strength to make the right technological and financial investments to survive for the long term. On April 15, 2015, Alcatel-Lucent combined with Nokia (see Figure 4.1) in a transaction valuing the group at $19.5 billion (USD) intended to create an innovative and financially strong leader in next-generation IP technologies.

RACE PIT STOP

Discussion

1. Think about and discuss how a B2B (business-to-business) technology company that relies on long-term contracts (e.g., the purchase of financial instruments for investment) is different from B2B companies that provide more immediate, short-term products and services. How might communications with these distinct types of customers differ? How do they differ from traditional B2C (business-to-consumer) companies?

2. What role did interpersonal communications play in investor relations, employee relations, and media relations? How important do you believe this strategy was in achieving positive company results?

3. Search online for an annual report of a publicly traded company and read the CEO

letter to shareholders. Can you discern any key messages? Why would the CEOs of public companies, as opposed to private ones, be so important in helping to secure investor trust and safeguard corporate reputation?

Trendlines

Financial/investor relations firms and corporate teams use many of the same skills public relations practitioners employ. However, according to the National Investor Relations Institute (NIRI), people who desire to work in this space also need specialized finance and marketing knowledge. Find the NIRI code of ethics online and compare it to the code of ethics of the Public Relations Society of America (PRSA) members. How are these codes similar, and how are they different, if at all?

Today, a crisis can ruin a company or organization in a matter of hours, let alone days. What special challenges do publicly held companies face during times of crisis? If you were to develop a generic crisis communications plan for a publicly held company in the midst of a financial struggle, what key target audiences would you have to include, no matter the industry?

5

ISSUE ADVOCACY

Public relations is increasingly taking a larger role in advocating for causes and policy changes. The collection of case studies in this chapter provides insights into the various strategies and tactics that have successfully advocated for change.

The Compassion & Choices and Brittany Maynard case demonstrates the long lead time sometimes necessary to move the needle on important and controversial issues. It also shows the importance of understanding the positions of diverse stakeholders and highlights the critical role of research in identifying the most effective and relevant narrative on an issue. The James W. Foley Legacy Foundation case study points to the importance of social media in identifying and effectively communicating with the correct stakeholders. It also shows how to use big data to target an organization's advocacy efforts. Finally, the Oceana case reveals the challenges of global advocacy.

COMPASSION & CHOICES AND BRITTANY MAYNARD HELP CREATE NEW MEDICAL AID-IN-DYING LEGISLATION IN CALIFORNIA

Heather J. Hether, Lecturer, University of California, Davis

Sean Crowley, Media Relations Director, Compassion & Choices

Toni Broaddus, Former California Campaign Director, Compassion & Choices

Compassion & Choices (C&C) is the nation's largest and oldest nonprofit advocacy organization whose mission is to improve care and expand end-of-life options by working nationwide in state legislatures, Congress, and federal and state courts, and with medical

---

*The authors are thankful for the support and thoughtful feedback from Dan Diaz, Brittany Maynard's husband, in writing this manuscript.

groups and local communities. The organization's goals include empowering people with information and tools related to end-of-life care options; advancing policies that enable people to make fully informed decisions about their health care; and passing and implementing laws that give mentally capable, terminally ill adults the option of medical aid in dying. For more than 30 years, C&C, headquartered in Denver, Colorado, has been advancing its mission through a comprehensive strategy that includes legislative advocacy, grassroots organizing, media outreach, and litigation. The organization's work has significantly impacted the development and implementation of legislation and patient and physician support programs related to advance care planning and end-of-life support, pain management, and medical aid in dying.

SITUATION

Providing terminally ill adults with the means to peacefully shorten an unbearable dying process has been a contested issue in California for several decades. There is no federal constitutional right to medical aid in dying, but some states specifically authorize this practice. In January 2015, medical aid in dying was authorized in four states: Oregon, Washington, Montana, and Vermont. While medical aid in dying has been a public issue for about 30 years, the language and nuances of the issue have evolved. The current term, *medical aid in dying*, refers to a practice in which a physician writes a prescription for a lethal dose of medication for a terminally ill adult patient who may decide to self-administer it. In early 2014, C&C launched a five-year plan to use compelling, real-life stories and spokespersons to organize support and change state law via a ballot initiative or lawsuit, and/or through the legislature in California, a large, populous state often proven to be a national leader on social issues. In just a few months, this effort became a full-blown legislative campaign to make medical aid in dying an authorized option for terminally ill Californians.

RESEARCH

For more than 20 years, research has shown that "strong majorities" of Americans support medical aid in dying.[1] For example, a 2013 survey conducted by the Pew Research Center found that 66% of adults believed there "are circumstances where a patient should be allowed to die."[2] Similarly, a May 2014 Gallup poll found that almost 7 in 10 Americans (69%) believe that a doctor should be able to "end [a] patient's life by some painless means" if the person has a disease that cannot be cured and the patient and his or her family request it.[3]

C&C has engaged in research to better understand how stakeholders perceive medical aid in dying and to identify the most effective communication strategies. During this campaign, the organization hired a research team including a pollster, a media consultant, and a psychologist. The team conducted 16 focus groups, multiple in-depth interviews and dyad (two-person) interviews, two statewide telephone surveys, and an online survey to understand which demographics supported medical aid in dying and to determine the messages that would resonate with people conflicted about the issue. The research found that nearly 7 in 10 California voters (69%) supported the End of Life Option Act, including 70% of Latinos and 60% of Catholics. Initially, the intent of the research was to understand how California voters with diverse cultural backgrounds talk about death and dying. C&C was particularly interested in learning how Spanish-speaking Californians felt about the issue, but the organization also explored the thinking of African Americans and Asian/Pacific Islanders. The organization also used its public narrative to talk about medical aid in dying as an end-of-life option because people in the focus groups thought everyone should have all possible options at the end of life, even if medical aid in dying was not an option that they would choose for themselves.

ACTION PLANNING

In 2014, C&C launched a five-year plan to organize support and change California state law via a ballot initiative or lawsuit, and/or through legislative action to make medical aid in dying an authorized option for terminally ill Californians. The budget to prepare and conduct the legislative campaign for the first two years (2014–2015) was $2 million. C&C objectives were (1) in the first year, achieve the passing of six to eight local resolutions in California that would be in favor of medical aid in dying and (2) achieve, no later than 2018, the passage of a statewide law authorizing medical aid in dying.

C&C launched the California Campaign in the spring of 2014. Just a few months earlier, in early January, unbeknownst to C&C, a 29-year-old California woman named Brittany Maynard was diagnosed with a large, aggressive brain tumor and given a prognosis of three to five years to live. However, after surgery removed part of the tumor and it grew back quickly, doctors revised their prognosis in the spring of 2014 and advised Maynard she had only six months or less to live.

After thoroughly researching her condition in hopes of identifying treatment options that would extend her life, Maynard came to the conclusion that there were no medical options available that would treat her tumor without causing her debilitating pain, the possibility of losing the ability to communicate, possible blindness, and a reduced quality of life. During the course of her research, Maynard came across information on Oregon's Death with Dignity Act that authorizes medical aid in dying as an option to end unbearable suffering for terminally ill adults with six months or less to live. Subsequently, in March 2014, Maynard decided to pursue this option. She and her family relocated from California to Oregon to access it because there was no such law in California. They contacted C&C in August 2014 to discuss a plan to educate lawmakers and the public about this end-of-life care option. On November 1, 2014, Maynard took the prescription medication authorized by the Oregon law to gently end her life.

On October 6, less than a month before she died, Maynard went public with her story to advocate for a medical aid-in-dying law in California in partnership with C&C, which publicized three videos she had recorded about her decision. Maynard became an active partner in the advocacy effort to provide all Californians with access to medical aid in dying. Maynard recognized that most terminally ill individuals with a short time to live likely do not have the energy, resources, or time to establish residency in a state where medical aid in dying is authorized and find a new medical team there, as she had done in Oregon. C&C and Maynard developed an outreach strategy that leveraged her media appeal as a young, well-spoken advocate who presented a different image on an issue that was often regarded as concerning only the elderly.

Realizing the power of personal stories, C&C partnered with others who had experience with the issue and could advocate for its importance. The storytelling program reached out to more than the terminally ill; it also reached out to their families, those impacted by a previous death, and those in the medical and legal communities devoting their work to end-of-life care issues. The program prepared participants to speak publicly, as well as to the media and legislators. For example, research found that voters worried about the family members of people who wanted access to medical aid in dying, so storytellers were encouraged to talk about their families. Research also underscored the importance of people acknowledging the importance of faith in their end-of-life decisions, which was a topic that C&C had previously avoided or played down.

COMMUNICATION

In January 2015, the End of Life Option Act was introduced in the California Senate, and the C&C strategy was accelerated. C&C used the legislative campaign to organize a statewide network of supporters to provide the foundation for a ballot measure campaign in 2016. As it turned out, Maynard's story gave impetus to the legislative strategy. C&C waged the campaign to reach two primary stakeholders: (1) legislators and policymakers, and (2) California voters—both English speaking and Spanish speaking.

Compassion & Choices California's former campaign director Toni Broaddus speaking at a rally featuring religious leaders, dying Californians, and their families outside the state capitol office of Governor Jerry Brown urging him to sign the End of Life Option Act on September 24, 2015. Governor Brown signed the bill into law 11 days later on October 5, 2015.

Source: Compassion & Choices. Reproduced with permission.

Key Public: California Legislators

C&C managed 25 volunteer action teams and four lobbying firms to educate lawmakers about the need for medical aid in dying. In targeted districts, C&C set up meetings for legislators with a constituent trained to tell a personal story, a doctor who could explain how the law would work, and a clergy member who could address spiritual or theistic concerns. In local districts, volunteers rallied outside the offices of their state representatives. Educational outreach to policy makers included 300 community events across the state and more than 1,300 legislative visits to all of California's 120 legislators. C&C targeted every committee member across both political parties for increased visits and activities, as needed. Legislator outreach was designed to capture the votes C&C needed to support the legislation, so it did not follow a particular demographic or geographic strategy. C&C earned the support it needed to pass the bill, one legislator at a time. The persuasion campaign was customized for individual legislators, in terms of who was assigned to meet with them, specific talking points to address specific concerns, and follow-up visits and calls from constituents on an ongoing basis. At the community level, C&C volunteers continued to pass local resolutions in support of the proposed state law.

Key Public: California Voters

One of the most visible elements of this campaign was the media advocacy strategy to reach voters, opinion leaders, policy makers, and opposition groups in California. The media strategy relied

Compassion & Choices launched a website on October 6, 2014, in partnership with Brittany Maynard to support their advocacy work to pass medical aid-in-dying legislation nationwide.

Source: Compassion & Choices. Reproduced with permission.

upon the personal stories of terminally ill individuals, their families, and others who had been directly impacted by this issue and who were committed to taking part in the campaign.

Maynard's telegenic personality supported a strong media relations campaign that developed around her personal story. Working with C&C, Maynard advocated for medical aid in dying through both online and offline media. On October 7, 2014, Maynard wrote an online op-ed for CNN.com titled "My Right to Death With Dignity at 29." Maynard described the history of her illness and how the lack of a medical aid-in-dying law in California forced her to move to Oregon with her family to access its death-with-dignity law. Maynard also created a six-minute-long video that appeared on people.com and youtube.com, which featured her; her husband, Dan Diaz; and her mother, Debbie Ziegler. In the video, Maynard described her health condition and her thoughts about her illness and death. She also explained why she and her family were advocates for medical aid-in-dying laws. C&C also launched a website, TheBrittanyFund.org, telling her story and showcasing her video. As thousands of national news organizations shared Maynard's story, Twitter hashtags #BrittanyMaynard and #DeathWithDignity trended nationally.

Offline, C&C launched an aggressive media relations campaign about Maynard. Her story was covered by newspapers and magazines, radio shows, television news, and talk shows. Stories ran in *People* (cover story) and the *New York Times*; on *60 Minutes*, *CBS This Morning*, NBC's *Today* show, and PBS *NewsHour*; and in thousands of other media outlets worldwide. Maynard made a testimony video for C&C to share with California legislators. C&C released the video in concert with the first committee hearing; the timing was designed to generate renewed public attention and keep the momentum going as the legislators began to vote.

Dan Diaz, Brittany Maynard's widower, listening to testimony his wife recorded before she died urging lawmakers to pass medical aid-in-dying legislation during a news conference at the California state capitol on March 25, 2015. Afterward, the California Senate Health Committee approved the End of Life Option Act.

Source: Compassion & Choices. Reproduced with permission.

Key Public: Spanish-Speaking California Voters

C&C reached out to members of the Latino community through a Spanish-language earned media campaign. In television, C&C successfully pitched stories for multiple interviews with national Spanish language television networks Telemundo and Univision. In addition, Emmy-award winning journalist Jorge Ramos, often called the "Latino Walter Cronkite," publicly endorsed the bill after an interview with Maynard's husband.

In print, C&C successfully pitched op-eds written by Catholic Latino advocates to large-circulation national and California media outlets. C&C told the stories of Latino ministers who counseled terminally ill adults in their final days. C&C's outreach to Latino media also involved giving presentations to the editorial boards of major newspapers, which led to the endorsement of the End of Life Option Act by multiple Spanish-language newspapers, including *La Opinión*, *Hoy*, and *Latino California*.

C&C also engaged in media relations that promoted the endorsement of the End of Life Option Act by leaders in the Latino community, including Latino labor leader and civil rights activist Dolores Huerta (who also personally lobbied Latino legislators); actor, director, and activist Edward James Olmos; and actor Mauricio Ochmann from the popular Telemundo telenovela *El Señor de los Cielos*.

EVALUATION

By all measures, C&C's advocacy campaign, in partnership with Maynard, was a success. The California legislature passed the End of Life Option Act authorizing medical aid in dying as an option for terminally ill adults, and Governor Brown signed it into law on October 5, 2015—one day before the first anniversary of the launch of C&C's partnership with Maynard, and less than 10 months after the bill's introduction in January 2015. Among the campaign's other achievements are the following:

Policy making: Inspired by Maynard's story, more than 200 lawmakers from across the political spectrum introduced or cosponsored bills to authorize medical aid in dying in 25 other states and the District of Columbia—more than a threefold increase over 2014, when bills were introduced in only seven states.

Media coverage: The California legislative campaign generated more than 840 media placements, including 500+ news stories, 170+ letters to the editor, 120+ op-eds, and 30+ endorsements of the bill nationally by at least 18 newspapers across the political spectrum, ranging from the *New York Times* to the *San Diego Union-Tribune*.

Less than four days after the story of Maynard's death was published on People.com, it had garnered more than 16.1 million unique visitors and reached nearly 54 million views on Facebook, by far the most of any *People* article.[4] Finally, the business news media outlet *Quartz* concluded, "Compassion & Choices . . . put into motion a brilliantly savvy national campaign to leverage her [Maynard's] unique appeal as a spokesperson for their movement."[5]

Internet traffic: Within a month of its launch, TheBrittanyFund.org drew more than 5 million viewers from 235 countries, and website traffic peaked at nearly 250,000 viewers per hour, resulting in the site crashing for hours and requiring C&C to dramatically increase its capacity. Only three weeks after Maynard and C&C launched their partnership, a YouGov poll conducted October 26–28, 2014, showed 38% of Americans knew about Maynard and her advocacy for medical aid in dying, the equivalent of more than 100 million Americans.[6] Cision media analytics showed that online searches related to California and aid in dying had 10.7 billion unique visitors from October 2014 to October 2015, and this coverage more than doubled the following year (2015–2016) to more than 23.5 billion unique visitors online.

The Hispanic Public Relations Association (HPRA) awarded C&C its 2016 ¡Bravo! Awards for "Non-Profit Campaign of the Year" and "Public Education Campaign of the Year" for its Latino media outreach campaign that helped pass California's historic End of Life Option Act.

Support from the medical community: By October 2015, 148 doctors and 115 health care professionals in California joined the Doctors for Dignity initiative, as well as 18 national and state health care organizations that endorsed the End of Life Option Act. In addition, the California Medical Association dropped its 28-year opposition to medical aid in dying.[7]

Community support: Endorsements of medical aid in dying were received from more than 100 organizations and almost 100,000 individual supporters statewide.

Signature drive: Signatures of 22,000+ supporters were gathered at nearly 240 local community events.

RACE PIT STOP

Discussion Questions

1. The objectives in this case appear to be modest when compared to the actual results. In retrospect, should the objectives have been more ambitious, or is there value in keeping objectives limited for this kind of campaign?

2. Does the state in which you live have a law similar to the ones advocated by Compassion & Choices? If not, are there any special challenges communicators might face in your state that are different from the ones the group faced in California?

3. If you were to plan a campaign to pass this type of legislation in your state (or in a state nearby that does not have such a law), what kinds of research would you propose first be conducted? Why? Who would be your primary target audiences?

Trendlines

This case reignited the debate over medical aid in dying, a divisive topic on a personal and political level. However, an increasing number of states are taking up the cause; six states and the District of Columbia have authorized medical aid in dying, and 27 states are in various stages of considering such legislation. Bottom line, there will be many changes in laws and practice soon. What role should the public relations profession take as the trend for legalizing medical aid in dying continues? Why have the opponents of medical aid in dying been less successful in their efforts to prevent legalizing the practice?

REFERENCES

1. McCarthy, J. (2014, June 18). Seven in 10 Americans back euthanasia. *Gallup*. Retrieved from http://www.gallup.com/poll/171704/seven-americans-back-euthanasia.aspx?utm_source= alert&utm_medium=email&utm_campaign=syndication&utm_content=morelink&utm_ term=Politics

2. Views on end of life medical treatment. (2013, November 21). *Pew Research Center*. Retrieved from http://www.pewforum.org/2013/11/21/views-on-end-of-life-medical-treatments/

3. McCarthy (2014).

4. Sebastian, M. (2014, November 6). Brittany Maynard story leads to record digital traffic for *People*. *AdAge*. Retrieved from http://adage.com/article/media/brittany-maynard-story-sets-digital-traffic-record-people/295738/

5. Yang, J. (2014, November 5). 752 people have exercised their right to die in Oregon— why you've only heard about Brittany Maynard. *Quartz*. Retrieved from http://qz.com/ 291687/752-people-have-exercised-their-right-to-die-in-oregon-why-youve-only-heard-about-brittany-maynard/

6. YouGov. (2014, October 28–30). Assisted suicide poll. Retrieved from https://d25d2506s-fb94s.cloudfront.net/cumulus_uploads/document/dl6fbt2baj/tabs_OPI_assisted_suicide_ 20141030.pdf

7. White, J. B. (2015, May 20). California Medical Association drops opposition to assisted suicide. *Sacramento Bee*. Retrieved from http://www.sacbee.com/news/politics-government/ capitol-alert/article21433962.html

SPREADING AWARENESS OF JAMES W. FOLEY'S LEGACY

*Gemma R. Puglisi, Assistant Professor, American University**

SITUATION

In August 2014, James "Jim" W. Foley, a freelance journalist for *GlobalPost*, an international digital news site, was killed by the Islamic militant group known as ISIS, and they videotaped his death for millions to see. The tragedy forced action to help further protect journalists, prevent hostage-taking, and educate young journalists and news

*Several students were essential to developing this case study, including Meshari Abokhodair, Zachariah Barehmi, Olivia Bell, Katherine Boryeskne, Kimberly Cate, Nina D'Agostino, Marissa Da Silva, Jasmine Day, Yenis Guevara, Heidi Hokanson, Alyssa Hyacinthe, Kathryn Kirchner, Aimee Manjarres, Quinn McGourty-Holland, Ezra Menelik, Kerry Milazzo, Sarah Peterson, Zachary Powell, Alexander Seyb, Jamie Silverman, Riley Tarver, and Franny Valour.

organizations about the dangers in news reporting. Shortly after their son's death, Diane and John Foley created the James W. Foley Legacy Foundation to raise awareness about these issues. Through a mutual friend, a connection was made between Diane Foley and the students in American University's spring 2015 Public Relations Portfolio class; the students dedicated the semester to helping the nonprofit achieve its goals. The foundation wanted to raise awareness about Jim both as a freelance journalist and as a hostage who was in captivity for two years before he was killed.

People knew that an American journalist had been killed, but most did not know the young freelancer's name. Therefore, there was an opportunity to spotlight his death as a way to reach news organizations, the government, and the White House, and to increase their knowledge about the dangers journalists face in their work, including the threat of being held hostage. However, there was a challenge related to this messaging: The United States has a policy of not negotiating with terrorists. If family members or organizations were to do so, they could be prosecuted for breaking the law.

In the case of the Foleys, various branches of government assured the family that they were working on finding their son and doing what they could to free him. The family was asked not to contact the press to avoid any complications the coverage might bring. After their son's death, the Foleys, along with other families of journalists killed, made it their mission to alert the White House and the government agencies that the loss of their loved ones could have been avoided had there been more transparency and communication among the U.S. entities involved.

RESEARCH

Both primary and secondary research was done to better understand journalists' risks and legal protections, and to assess journalism students' knowledge of journalism's risks, particularly as they relate to freelance journalists. Primary research included consulting with a professor who was an expert in international news and with one of Jim Foley's former professors. In addition, students reached out to various news organizations that work to protect journalists, including the Committee to Protect Journalists, Reporters Instructed in Saving Colleagues, Columbia's Dart Center, the Rory Peck Trust, the Canadian Journalism Forum on Violence and Trauma, and the Ochberg Society for Trauma Journalism.

A 25-item Qualtrics survey was developed with students at Northwestern University's Medill School of Journalism and administered through colleges/universities with journalism programs. More than 15 universities were contacted across the United States. The method was via social media; teachers, deans, and student organizations were encouraged to ask students to participate in the survey to help assess what they knew about freelance journalism and its risks. The survey was live from March 30, 2015, to April 16, 2015, with 267 participants. Results revealed the following:

- 70% of respondents found news involving foreign correspondents to be extremely or very important.

- 69% of respondents thought that violence against journalists in conflict zones abroad had increased in the past two years.

- 44% of respondents thought that between 41% and 60% of news was sourced by freelancers.

- 41% of respondents thought large news organizations provided little protection to freelancers abroad.

- On a scale of 1 to 10, with 1 being *no danger* and 10 being *extremely high danger,* most respondents believed that freelance journalists face danger levels of 7 to 10; and on a scale of 1 to 10, with 1 being *not at all informed* and 10 *being perfectly informed,* 22% of respondents said their knowledge level concerning U.S. hostage policy was a 1. More than half of the respondents scored below 5. (See Figure 5.1.)

For secondary research, a report was developed from research findings comparing/contrasting U.S. hostage policies with those of other countries—especially those with better track records of successfully gaining hostages' release—to provide logical appeals and options to U.S. administrators. Students looked at various sources including a PBS report on the Iran hostage crisis, documents from the United Nations News Centre,[1] a brief from the *Cardozo Law Review* about captives and their exodus,[2] and a report by the Center for Security Studies on ransoms and terrorist funding.[3]

ACTION PLANNING

The overall goal of the campaign was to increase awareness about the dangers journalists face and to seek changes to U.S. hostage protocols to help increase the odds of release. Identified Foley Foundation stakeholders included young journalists, freelance

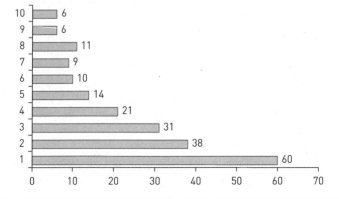

FIGURE 5.1 ■ Survey Respondents' Awareness of U.S. Hostage Policy

On a scale of 1 to 10, with 10 being extremely informed and 1 being not at all informed, how informed are you of the United States hostage policy?

Source: Courtesy of Gemma Puglisi.

journalists, news organizations, college students interested in pursuing journalism careers, families who had loved ones as hostages, and advocates who could put pressure on the administration and government to make hostage protocol changes.

Overall, the plan was to articulate and bring the message home that

- the current hostage policy is not working,

- both young audiences and the general public do not understand the risks that freelance journalists take to cover regions that are in conflict,

- freelance journalists who risk their lives need to be protected by news organizations as well as their countries.

The overall approach was to use various student teams to convey these messages. For the events team, this meant working with current journalists and having events at American University, as well as working with two nationally known news organizations—the Newseum and the National Press Club—as a means to open the discussion internationally and get the public's attention.

For the research report team, the idea was to help the public understand (1) what the U.S. policy was and (2) how that policy differed from other countries' policies. Furthermore, this team set out to identify what students knew about the policy and what freelancers do. Many journalism students want to be reporters, and many may not understand the risks associated with covering stories in war-torn areas. Thus our action plan was to use the research and develop questions and get the results from the survey distributed.

For the social media team, the goal was to have a social media campaign for one day in April 2015 targeting the White House, and getting young people involved in tweeting to the president to change the policy for families and hostages. The White House, under the Obama administration, used social media actively, so the students knew that their tweets would be seen.

COMMUNICATION

The campaign included the following tactics:

- An "online day of action" was held April 8, 2015, targeting the Obama administration in advance of a U.S. hostage policy review the president had ordered. Students were asked to tweet at the White House on the issue, using the hashtag #ProtectUSHostages. Other hashtags included #RememberingJimDC. Sample tweets included the following:

  o @WhiteHouse—as the threat of #ISIL and kidnapping abroad

Source: Aimee Manjarres. Courtesy of Gemma Puglisi.

continues to grow, the US must reevaluate our hostage policies. #ProtectUSHostages

- ○ What is the worth of an American citizen abroad? @BarackObama, reevaluate US hostage policy. #ProtectUSHostages

- ○ I want to know my government will protect me in a crisis abroad. #ProtectUSHostages @BarackObama @WhiteHouse

- Because the Foley Foundation was fairly new and in the beginning stages—and did not have a strong social media presence at the time—the students used the Facebook page they created to promote the day of action with, for example, this message:

  - ○ Happening TODAY! Please take a few minutes to tweet in support of the White House reevaluating our hostage policy, a process that's in its final stages. Families of hostages deserve transparency and accountability. #ProtectUSHostages

- Several special events were held in Washington, DC, to help increase awareness of and engagement around journalism dangers and hostage policy issues. The class helped the Foley Foundation with events at the Newseum and the National Press Club and worked with these entities to reach journalists. A panel discussion was held at American University to educate journalism and communication students about the challenges freelance journalists face. Students promoted this event using several tactics, including posters placed on the campus shuttle and an event Facebook page.

- The survey findings were used as a media hook and were published in the college edition of *USA Today*, which helped reach college students across the country.[4]

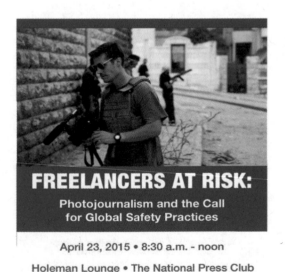

Source: Manu Brabo. Courtesy of Gemma Puglisi. Reproduced with permission.

EVALUATION

Because awareness was a key objective of the campaign, and pre- and post-surveys would be difficult in such a short time frame, overall impressions helped the class understand their potential audience reach. The campaign totals are provided below:

- The Newseum outreach resulted in 657,461 impressions, which includes social and legacy media as well as the number of attendees.

- The American University panel promotions resulted in 26,086 impressions.

- The online day of action had 24,932 impressions.

- The Facebook page had a potential reach of 17,348 users.

- The legacy media impressions for all events totaled 35,000.

- Twitter impressions were calculated to be 7,584.

- Combined impressions across events totaled 743,479.

Diane Foley attended the class's final presentation and was so impressed by and grateful for their work, she sent each student a note card that featured a photograph taken by Jim while in Syria before his capture. The class also received recognition from the university by having an article placed on the university's website about their work.

Overall, because of Diane Foley's incredible courage and voice as well as the voices of other families, President Obama publicly discussed our country's hostage policies on June 24, 2015,[5] at the White House, when he invited the families of those who lost loved ones. He said that, although our country's formal policy remains the same, families may now take steps without fear of being prosecuted by their own government.

RACE PIT STOP

Discussion Questions

1. Examine the action planning part of this case, then review the evaluation of the campaign. What measureable objectives could have been put in place at the campaign's outset?

2. What were the campaign's key messages?

3. What do you believe were the most effective tactics used in the campaign? Why? What other tactics would have been feasible for this campaign?

4. Visit the James W. Foley Legacy Foundation website and its social media channels. Looking ahead, what additional communication strategies and tactics might the foundation employ to further fulfill its mission?

Trendlines

Two of the biggest trends in advocacy public relations are the use of social media for government relations and thought leadership, and the use of data-driven advocacy. Creating engaging social media content allows public relations professionals to aid their organizations in reaching influential audiences, such as policy makers, reporters, grassroots supporters, and other online stakeholders. Social media can also be used to elevate an organization's policy expertise around an issue, establishing the organization as a thought leader in that space. Using data to target an organization's advocacy efforts can greatly improve key performance metrics. Coupling these two factors increases the likelihood of an advocacy win. Big data also allows organizations to find potential advocates, increase advocacy action rates, target specific lawmakers, and help move advocates further along the engagement continuum.

How could this campaign have taken better advantage of these two trends to be even more successful? What additional primary and secondary research could the portfolio class have done to further identify potential advocates? Finally, what social media strategies could the portfolio class have implemented to further elevate the Foley Foundation as a thought leader in this discussion?

REFERENCES

1. Security council adopts Resolution 2133. (2014, January 27). *UN News Centre*. Retrieved from https://www.un.org/press/en/2014/sc11262.doc.htm

2. Weill, R. (2014). Exodus: Structuring redemption of captives. *Cardozo Law Review, 36*(1).

3. Nunlist, C. (2013, October). Kidnapping for ransom as a source for terrorist funding. *CSS Analyses in Security Policy, 141*, 1–4.

4. Foster, P. (2015, May 2). With Foley in mind, students survey peers about freelance journalists. *USA Today*. Retrieved from http://college.usatoday.com/2015/05/02/with-foley-in-mind-students-survey-peers-about-freelance-journalists/

5. Davis, J. J. (2015, June 23). Obama ordering changes in U.S. hostage policies. *New York Times*. Retrieved from https://www.nytimes.com/2015/06/24/world/obama-ordering-changes-in-us-hostage-policies.html?_r=0

CUT THE BAIT: STOP OVERFISHING SUBSIDIES

Courtney J. Sakai, Former Managing Director, International Trade and Food Security, Oceana

SITUATION

Oceana is the world's largest international advocacy organization exclusively focused on ocean conservation. Oceana was created to protect the oceans and marine life on a global scale by winning national and international policy victories. Oceana was founded in 2001 by a group of leading philanthropists after they learned that less than one-half of all environmental funding was directed to marine conservation and that there was no dedicated international oceans organization. Oceana regularly produces scientific reports that drive policy change and that, along with other efforts, generate thousands of media hits per month. Oceana collaborates with thousands of community and business leaders and organizations and has several million supporters who engage in Oceana's campaigns through direct, social media, and online advocacy.

The world depends on the oceans for food and livelihood. Fish provide animal protein for nearly one-fifth of the world's population, and at least 15% of the animal protein in the diets of 4 billion people.[1] However, nearly 800 million people still do not have enough to eat.[2] The United Nations predicts that the world will need to produce 70% more food by 2050 to meet the hunger needs of a growing population.[3]

In addition to food, fishing activities economically support coastal communities and hundreds of millions of people. Of the world's fishers, more than 95% engage in small-scale and artisanal activity and catch nearly the same amount of fish for human consumption as the highly capitalized industrial sector.[4] Fishing and fishing-related activities are also a source of livelihood and empowerment for women, who comprise half of all those employed in the fisheries sector.[5] Therefore, it is of grave concern that nearly all of the world's fish populations are being rapidly depleted by overfishing and destructive fishing practices. According to the United Nations Food and Agriculture Organization, 90% of marine fisheries are either overexploited, fully exploited, significantly depleted, or recovering from overexploitation. The global catch of wild fish reached its peak in the mid-1990s and has been declining ever since.[6]

Source: Oceana. Reproduced with permission.

Oceana found that, despite the lack of international consensus that the world's oceans are in trouble and that there is inadequate management in every part of the world, many governments continued to provide subsidies to their fishing sectors. Research revealed that, although some types of subsidies supported beneficial programs such as management and research, the vast majority of subsidies promoted or facilitated increased and intensified fishing, such as programs for boat construction and modernization, fuel, equipment, and other operational costs. These "overfishing subsidies" allow fleets to fish longer and farther away than otherwise would be economically possible. The scope, magnitude, and effects of these programs were so significant that addressing harmful fisheries was the greatest single action that could be taken to protect the world's oceans.

Oceana identified the World Trade Organization (WTO) and the multilateral trading system as the best, and possibly only, opportunity to address the problem of fisheries subsidies on a global scale. It realized that while environmental groups often play "defense" in international trade agreements, there was an opportunity to play offense and work to reduce harmful fisheries subsidies.

RESEARCH

Oceana researched existing literature on the WTO, trade and the environment, and fisheries subsidies. It also reviewed past media stories on these subjects. It held listening sessions with people who had experience in international trade and/or the WTO, including representatives of business associations, think tanks, law firms, and academic institutions, and interviewed several key decision makers. Key findings included the following:

- There was a general recognition about the importance of fisheries and the problem of subsidies, but there was low knowledge about the issue of overfishing and its relationship to WTO negotiations.

- There was low visibility (fewer than 15 news stories) and scant political support for the issue.

- Few outside organizations were engaged in the WTO fisheries subsidies negotiations, and none had attempted a comprehensive campaign or any significant communications activity around the issue.

- Inside the WTO, the fisheries subsidies negotiations had a low profile and low levels of attention.

- Impact in the fisheries subsidies negotiations could be achieved by targeting a smaller group of countries (approximately 15) with influential roles in trade blocs, geographic alliances, or other political groupings.

- There was no good information on fisheries subsidies at the country level.

ACTION PLANNING

The campaign was designed to increase visibility of the overfishing issue and create external pressure on the key audiences to act. A major strategy was to use science-based messages to demonstrate the WTO's opportunity to address overfishing and the urgency for action. Oceana was engaged with the WTO and the fisheries subsidies negotiations for more than a decade, particularly in a policy capacity. Oceana's public relations campaign primarily took place over five years, from 2007 through 2011. The campaign was conducted during the most active and critical periods of the WTO negotiations.

The campaign had two basic taglines: "Cut the Bait: Stop Overfishing Subsidies" and "Subsidies are fishing the world's oceans to death. It's time to Cut the Bait." Oceana decided that the campaign must raise the stakes for failure to act on fisheries subsidies as well as provide positive recognition for doing so. Specifically, the campaign messages would clearly convey the unique responsibility and opportunity the WTO and its members had to address one of the world's most important environmental challenges—global overfishing. An expanded message based on these taglines appears as follows:

> The WTO has a once-in-a-lifetime chance to demonstrate that it can not only balance trade and the environment, but make one of the greatest contributions to protecting the world's oceans. The WTO needs to seize the opportunity presented by the fisheries subsidies negotiations to address global overfishing because, as the world's leading scientists have declared, if we wait it will be too late.

The campaign's major goal was to establish international recognition and political commitment to addressing the problem of fisheries subsidies. Accordingly, it established the following:

- Objective 1: By the end of 2011, achieve expanded and consistent international global media coverage and demonstrated third-party support on the fisheries subsidies issue and WTO negotiations.

Success Indicators

a. Number, reach, and content of media stories and coverage. The initial objective was to generate at least 25 unique stories, including in key international outlets such as the *Financial Times*, the *International Herald Tribune/New York Times*, and the *Wall Street Journal*.

b. Number and quality of third-party groups and/or opinion leaders that are recruited and take action. The objective was to establish awareness and knowledge of the fisheries subsidies issue within at least 15 key country delegations. Key third-party targets included former officials, subject matter experts, and people affiliated with major international organizations such as United Nations entities, the International Union for Conservation of Nature (IUCN), and the World Economic Forum.

c. Inclusion of and/or action on fisheries subsidies in other international forums.

- Objective 2: The U.S. government and relevant constituents publicly demonstrate to the international community, by the end of 2011, the importance of a strong outcome in the WTO fisheries subsidies negotiations.

Success Indicators

a. Public statements by senior administration officials that clearly identify a desire for fisheries subsidies reforms as essential to the larger WTO trade negotiations.

b. Actions by the U.S. Congress that express the issue's importance as part of a WTO trade agreement.

c. Public displays of support (statements, letters, etc.) from relevant U.S. constituencies, including trade, business, and environmental proponents.

- Objective 3: By the end of 2011, generate public visibility and political support in Brussels, Belgium (considered the EU capital), for fisheries subsidies reforms and the WTO negotiations.

Success Indicators

a. Number and content of European media stories related to the European Union and fisheries subsidies negotiations.

b. Public statements of support by members of the European Parliament, European Commission, and officials in EU member states.

COMMUNICATION

Oceana created a story line and life-sized mascot called "Finley the Fish" to establish a recognizable brand and make the issue more accessible to lay audiences.

- Finley made appearances at the WTO in Geneva, Switzerland, and on Capitol Hill in Washington, DC, and was a popular photo op with key audiences.

- Finley was featured in eight outdoor advertising campaigns in Geneva, Switzerland; Washington, DC; and Ottawa, Canada.

- A series of outreach materials were produced and distributed showcasing Finley. These included cartoons, magnets, and a snow globe containing Finley surrounded by fishing boats, floating fishhooks, and money "confetti."

- Branded outreach kits were created, including backgrounders, fact sheets, press releases, key news stories and opinion pieces, third-party letters and testimonials, policy and science briefs, infographics, and photos.

Media Relations

- Oceana and a major business association published an op-ed in the *Financial Times* and issued a letter to the WTO director-general to demonstrate how fisheries subsidies reform is in the best interest of both business and the environment, and they are not incompatible.

- Oceana took advantage of the first United Nations–declared World Oceans Day on June 8, 2009, to generate statements by major trade leaders advocating the reduction of fisheries subsidies. These trade statements received top billing by key wire services and other international outlets. World Oceans Day became an annual news hook for issue advocacy, particularly from a business and trade angle.

Third-Party Outreach and Grassroots Advocacy

- Oceana organized a letter signed by 125 scientists from 27 countries to the WTO director-general and country delegations that detailed the gravity of the fisheries subsidies issue and called for the elimination of harmful subsidies. The letter was referenced in a *New York Times* editorial on the subject. A separate issue advertising campaign was conducted in Geneva, Switzerland, featuring billboards with the message "Stop Overfishing Subsidies."

- Oceana presented scientific papers and organized events on fisheries subsidies at major conferences, including the World Fisheries Congress and the World Conservation Congress of the International Union for Conservation of Nature.

- Oceana coordinated a letter from four former U.S. trade representatives to President Obama urging action on fisheries subsidies.

- Oceana worked with Mission Blue, an initiative of the Sylvia Earle Alliance, and international conservation organization the World Wildlife Fund to generate support from 77 thought and opinion leaders, who called on the president to renew U.S. leadership on WTO fishing subsidy reform.

Events

- Oceana created an art exhibit, *The Deep: Life on the Deep Sea Floor*, which was displayed in the lobby of the WTO in Geneva for three months. This exhibit was custom designed by French author and curator Claire Nouvian, and featured stunning images of deep sea life from Nouvian's acclaimed exhibit at the Natural History Museum in Paris.

- Oceana created a program featuring Ted Danson with the Economic Club of Toronto, one of Canada's most prominent public affairs forums. The appearance generated major national, regional, and local media coverage about fisheries subsidies throughout Canada. Danson's speech was published by Toronto's *Globe and Mail*. Oceana also held a similar event at the National Press Club in Washington, DC.

Government Relations

- Oceana conducted outreach and advocacy and offered technical assistance to educate WTO about fisheries subsidies and generate strategic action by countries in the negotiations. More than 500 meetings were conducted with approximately 40 WTO country delegations.

- More than 175 meetings were conducted with the U.S. executive branch and congressional offices.

- Oceana conducted outreach to more than 150 offices in the U.S. Senate and House of Representatives, including nearly all of the members on the committees with jurisdictions over international trade and environment matters.

EVALUATION

In 2007, the WTO produced a first-draft agreement on fisheries subsidies that addressed, and surpassed in some cases, all of Oceana's conservation recommendations. The WTO fisheries subsidies negotiations, however, were never completed due to issues unrelated to the reform of fishing subsidies. Subsequently, a much-expanded group of countries continued to pursue fisheries subsidies reforms at the WTO, and have successfully advanced measures in other international organizations and bodies. Nine countries presented proposals in the WTO fisheries subsidies negotiations that reflected Oceana's conservation priorities.

Oceana generated nearly 500 unique news stories. These stories produced more than 1,200 media placements, resulting in 586 million impressions in 86 countries. The coverage included front-page stories in the *Financial Times*, the *International Herald Tribune*, and the *Wall Street Journal*, two editorials by the *New York Times*, and television pieces by BBC and CNN. There was also extensive coverage by international wire services.

Don't let Finley be the last fish in the ocean.

Reducing fisheries subsidies is the single most significant action that can be taken to address global overfishing. The WTO has a historic opportunity to make new trade rules that will turn the tide for the world's fisheries and the communities that depend on them.

- Fish is a primary source of protein for nearly a **billion** people.
- Leading scientists project that the world's commercial fish populations could be **beyond recovery** within decades if current trends continue.
- **Subsidies** promote overfishing, pushing fleets to fish longer, harder, and farther away than would otherwise be possible.
- Destructive fisheries subsidies are estimated to be at least **$20 billion** annually—an amount equivalent to approximately 25 percent of the value of the world catch.

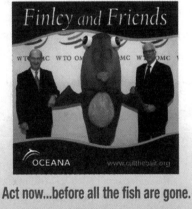

Act now...before all the fish are gone.

For more information, please contact Courtney Sakai at csakai@oceana.org, +1 202 833 3900

OCEANA
www.cutthebait.org

Source: Oceana. Reproduced with permission.

A media analysis of the period 2005 through 2011 found that as the Cut the Bait campaign progressed, Oceana emerged as both a trusted media resource and an influential participant in the negotiation process. In 41% of the press coverage, at least one quote came from an Oceana spokesperson, and in 45% of the stories, the press featured one or more of the organization's messages. The analysis also concluded that Oceana was well respected among WTO participants, high-profile international politicians, journalists, and other environmental advocates based on the high number of neutral-to-positive stories around its efforts.

Both houses of the U.S. Congress passed resolutions calling for U.S. leadership in the WTO negotiations to reduce harmful fisheries subsidies. A bipartisan group of 12 congressional trade leaders from the powerful House Ways and Means Committee called on the United States to make the successful outcome of the negotiations a trade priority.

Oceana's seemingly light treatment of a serious subject was found by many post-campaign interviewees as creative, nonthreatening, and effective. The nonthreatening aspect of the campaign was seen as important because WTO delegates and the organization are not used to aggressive tactics. For example, a number of interviewees observed that negotiators from countries opposed to ending fisheries subsidies were nonetheless in the queue to have their picture taken with Finley the Fish.

Beyond Finley the Fish, the campaign benefited from the use of other new tactics. Basic collateral like magnets and snow globes were a huge hit with WTO negotiators, some of whom sent stacks of materials to their home country offices. The campaign's choice of celebrities, especially Ted Danson, was particularly effective. The audiences had high affinity and affection for Danson and found compelling his personal story and long commitment and involvement in protecting the oceans.

Finally, Cut the Bait received numerous awards, including accolades for best campaign and excellence in global communications, speeches, and public affairs from the International Public Relations Association and the Public Relations Society of America.

RACE PIT STOP

Discussion Questions

1. Unlike most of the case studies in the book, this campaign called for a multiyear effort. What are the advantages and disadvantages of such a long campaign?

2. How might a communicator interest Americans who do not live near an ocean in this issue?

3. What do you think are the unique challenges in working to persuade an international organization through a communications campaign?

4. Research Oceana.org. What campaigns is the organization currently involved with? Which one resonates the most with you? Why?

5. The "objectives" listed in this case study read more like strategies. How might you turn them into true objectives?

Trendlines

The International Public Relations Association published a "thought leadership" essay in 2013 that remains relevant to this day.[7] In it, the author identified four trends in global advocacy:

1. The instant and permanent possibility of being in dialogue with individuals as well as large interest groups with a single mouse click, making traditional media more or less redundant

2. The great interest and potential for activation among all levels of society beyond parties and established democratic structures

3. The growing involvement of celebrities

4. The rising importance of public–private partnerships

Could Oceana have made better use of any of these four trends to make its campaign more effective? Why or why not? Furthermore, based on these trends, what additional research could Oceana have done, and how could that have made the campaign even more successful? Finally, what are the advantages of using a character "celebrity" such as Finley the Fish instead of a former political celebrity such as Kofi Annan? What are the disadvantages?

REFERENCES

1. Hidden harvest: The global contribution of capture fisheries. (2012, May). *World Bank*. Retrieved from http://documents.worldbank.org/curated/en/515701468152718292/pdf/664690ESW0P1210120HiddenHarvest0web.pdf

2. Green economy in a blue world: Synthesis report. (2012). *United Nations Sustainable Development Knowledge Platform*. Retrieved from https://sustainabledevelopment.un.org/index.php?page=view&type=400&nr=656&menu=1515

3. Pauly, D., & Zeller, D (2016). Catch reconstructions reveal that global marine fisheries catches are higher than reported and declining. *Nature Communications, 7.*

4. Bene, C., Barange, M., Subasinghe, R., Pinstrup-Andersen, P., Merino, G., Hemre, G.-I., & Williams, M. (2015). Feeding 9 billion people by 2050: Putting fish back on the menu. *Food Security, 7*(2), 261–274.

5. The state of food insecurity in the world. (2015). *Food and Agricultural Organization of the United Nations*. Retrieved from http://www.fao.org/3/a-i4646e.pdf

6. How to feed the world in 2050. (2009). *Food and Agricultural Organization of the United Nations*. Retrieved from http://www.fao.org/wsfs/forum2050/wsfs-forum/en/

7. Meyer, L. (2013). A new approach to advocacy: Four trends. *International Public Relations Association*. Retrieved from https://www.ipra.org/news/itle/a-new-approach-to-advocacy-four-global-trends/

Source: Oceana. Reproduced with permission.

FOR IMMEDIATE RELEASE

October 17, 2007

Who's That Fish?

Gills and Fins Advocate Comes Out of Water to Stop Overfishing Subsidies

Source: Oceana. Reproduced with permission.

Source: Oceana. Reproduced with permission.

GENEVA—Today, Geneva city center is buzzing as Oceana's Finley the Fish emerged from the depths to increase awareness for a true special interest—stopping the massive subsidies provided by many countries to their fishing industries that are causing the oceans to be fished to death.

Finley the Fish has come to Geneva to rally support for the negotiations currently under way as part of the Doha round at the World Trade Organization. Unfortunately, governments underwrite their nations' foraging fishing fleets to the tune of an estimated $30 to $34 billion a year, pushing fleets to fish longer, harder, and farther away than would otherwise be possible.

"Finley the Fish is here to shake fins and make friends," said Courtney Sakai, campaign director at Oceana. "Overfishing is one of the world's greatest environmental challenges, and we must act now to stop destructive fisheries subsidies, before all of the fish are gone."

The vast majority of global fisheries subsidies increase fishing capacity, which in turn drives overfishing. Government subsidies have helped to produce a worldwide fishing fleet that is up to 250% greater than that needed to fish sustainably. The European Union, Japan, and China are among the world's largest subsidizers of their fishing sectors.

This massive subsidization comes at a time when the world's fisheries are in crisis. An international team of leading fishery scientists projects

Source: Oceana. Reproduced with permission.

that all commercial fish populations will be in permanent collapse within decades (by 2048) if current overfishing trends continue.[1]

In addition to his policy work and media interviews, Finley is appearing in an Oceana advertising campaign throughout Geneva. The advertisements show money raining down on numerous fishing boats with Finley in the ocean, imperiled by baited hooks.

"The Doha round negotiations represent the single best opportunity to address the fisheries subsidies issue on a global scale," said Sakai. "The question is if the WTO will seize this opportunity to leave a lasting legacy for the protection of the world's oceans."

For more information, please visit www.cutthebait.org.

###

Oceana campaigns to protect and restore the world's oceans. Our teams of marine scientists, economists, lawyers, and advocates win specific and concrete policy changes to reduce pollution and to prevent the irreversible collapse of fish populations, marine mammals, and other sea life. Global in scope and dedicated to conservation, Oceana has campaigners based in North America (Washington, DC; Juneau, Alaska; Portland, Oregon; Boston, Massachusetts; Los Angeles, California), Europe (Madrid, Spain; Brussels, Belgium), and South America (Santiago, Chile). More than 300,000 members and e-activists in over 150 countries have already joined Oceana. For more information, please visit www.Oceana.org.

Media Contact

Dustin Cranor

Oceana

+1 (202) 341-2267

dcranor@oceana.org

[1]Worm, B., Barbier, E. B., Beaumont, N., Duffy, J. E., Folke, C., Halpern, B. S., . . . Watson, R. (2006, November 3). Impacts of biodiversity loss on ocean ecosystem services. *Science, 314*(5800), 787–790.

A STRATEGIC VIEW: JAZZ WITH THE STARS: FUNDING OF K–12 MUSIC CELEBRATED IN DC

Mike Fulton, Director of Public Affairs and Advocacy, Asher Agency

THE CHALLENGE

The National Association of Music Merchants (NAMM) conducts an annual Washington, DC, gathering for its members to advocate on Capitol Hill for continued policies and

Senator Joe Manchin ✔
@Sen_JoeManchin

[Follow] ⌄

Proud 2 be honored by @NAMM @vh1savethemusic @NAfME for #MusicEducation w/ @VanessaCarlton @RHCPchad & @bw51official

1:04 PM - 20 Mar 2013

13 Retweets 2 Likes

◯   ⇄ 13   ♡ 2   ✉

Tweet your reply

Source: Twitter/@Sen_JoeManchin.

funding to support music education in K–12 public schools. The California-based nonprofit organization sought ways to enhance its advocacy efforts to motivate members of Congress, solidify the music industry, and secure media coverage for this worthy cause.

NAMM works closely with other music industry partners, including the VH1 Save the Music Foundation and the National Association for Music Education. The effort is backed by grants made nationwide by the VH1 foundation for public schools to purchase musical instruments for talented, financially challenged students. In 2013, the VH1 Save the Music Foundation invited one of its grantees—the Shepherdstown (West Virginia) Middle School Jazz Ensemble—to perform on Capitol Hill. National celebrities Chad Smith, drummer for the Red Hot Chili Peppers; Bernie Williams, New York Yankees champion and Grammy-nominated jazz guitarist; and Vanessa Carlton, singer-songwriter, helped educate Congress and conduct media interviews and performed with the young musicians.

To help coordinate this DC event and secure comprehensive media placements, NAMM sought public relations and marketing firm Asher Agency as a partner because of its presence in both the nation's capital and West Virginia, as well as its government relations, event planning, and media relations expertise.

THE RESPONSE

Agency representatives recommended a conference call of all music industry groups (lobbyists and association executives) and their respective public relations firms to ensure assignments were understood and task timelines were set. Communications and legislative staff for West Virginia's senators and its state commissioner of culture and history were excited about the opportunity to mix constituents and celebrities together to help West Virginia rebuild its school music programs. Close coordination was essential to achieve the client's media and advocacy objectives.

Agency team members in Washington, DC, and Charleston, West Virginia, edited the national press release, customizing it for West Virginia dissemination. They secured a list of the 35 West Virginia schools in 30 counties where grants, totaling $1.05 million, were awarded by the VH1 Save the Music Foundation. Asher Agency staff suggested that one of the senators might issue a statement in the *Congressional Record* about the awards as well as the musical presentation. Senator Joe Manchin III came through, ensuring a possible keepsake for the students, their parents, and music industry leaders.

THE RESULTS

Asher Agency blanketed the public policy and West Virginia media with news articles about the event and facilitated complimentary press outreach for the two senators and commissioner. Client reaction to a WHAG-TV (Hagerstown, Maryland) story, which aired only hours after the performance, was short and to the point: "This piece is beautifully done! All of the messages are completely on point. Bravo!" *Politico, The Hill*, the *Washington Examiner*, the *Huffington Post, Rolling Stone*, and the *Washington Post* also carried the story, as did the Associated Press, resulting in multiple West Virginia placements and others in Seattle and Houston. West Virginia publications the (Martinsburg) *Journal* and the *Shepherdstown Chronicle* published articles and photos, and so did the *Charleston Gazette-Mail,* which is located in the West Virginia state capital. Notably, Senator John D. Rockefeller IV did a "one minute" video message on his website about the project and his commitment to music education. To date, VH1 Save the Music has donated $52 million worth of new musical instruments to 1,964 public schools in 233 school districts around the country, impacting the lives of 2.6 million public school students. All 55 counties in West Virginia have benefited from this generosity, one of the few states to receive statewide support.

6

HEALTH COMMUNICATION

Among the specialties in public relations, health communication is one of the most rapidly growing. This area can encompass communication for a variety of organizations within the health care industry—from a government organization such as the Centers for Disease Control and Prevention to pharmaceutical companies or even a hospital or nonprofit advocacy organization. While some advocacy and nonprofit organizations only focus on one major health concern (e.g., cancer), others, such as pharmaceutical companies and hospitals, have a broader focus, and they may be expected to be well versed about more than one health issue.

Health communication also touches other communication specialties such as investor relations and community relations. Thus, practitioners may find themselves performing several different public relations functions with an emphasis on health. Within this chapter, there are case studies with various areas of focus within health communication: the Mental Illness Fellowship of Australia executed a campaign to raise the visibility of mental health issues across the country; the American Heart Association's Cedar Valley chapter put together the "Go Red for Women" campaign to raise awareness and money to fight heart disease; and the final case study in this chapter examines advocacy on behalf of a rare disease.

USING THE LIVED EXPERIENCE AS A POWERFUL ADVOCACY AND AWARENESS STRATEGY IN AUSTRALIA

Charles R. Harman, Chief Development Officer, National Alliance on Mental Illness

David Meldrum, Former CEO, Mental Illness Fellowship of Australia

SITUATION

MENTAL ILLNESS
FELLOWSHIP
of Australia Inc

Source: Mental Illness Fellowship of Australia Inc. (MIFA).
Reproduced with permission.

The Mental Illness Fellowship of Australia (MIFA) is a federation of like-minded service providers operating in most parts of Australia. Combined staffing is around 2,000—including 1,500 trained volunteers—accessible at more than 150 locations. While MIFA has a wide range of programs and clients, its core focus is individuals and families affected by severe mental illness. Both the national body and all of the member organizations have been operating for more than 30 years. "Lived experience" is highly valued, in both the volunteer and paid workforce of MIFA members, with up to 50% of the paid workforce having a mental illness and/or caring for someone who does. The National Alliance on Mental Illness (NAMI) is the largest grassroots organization for people living with mental illness and their families in the United States. There are more than 900 NAMI-affiliated organizations throughout the country and nearly 200 NAMI affiliates at U.S. colleges.

While there is widespread support for people with major diseases including cancer, heart disease, and AIDS, there is significant evidence that the stigma surrounding mental illness has resulted in discrimination toward individuals living with diseases such as depression, bipolar disorder, and schizophrenia. Mental illness does not enjoy the same level of positive visibility, awareness, or acceptance as other illnesses. Australia is seen as a global innovator of mental health research and services, but it is not immune to negative opinions about people who live with mental illness. The consequences of these negative stereotypes result in a decreased willingness by people experiencing a mental illness to seek appropriate help, ultimately resulting in untreated illness and, in some cases, suicide. A lack of public interest in mental illness also contributes to governments being less willing to allocate resources to the care and treatment of people living with these conditions. Therefore, MIFA wanted to increase public awareness of mental illness and change inaccurate perceptions. The organization also advocated for more assistance from the government for mental illness treatment and services.

The 2014 report of the Australian National Mental Health Commission, *Contributing Lives, Thriving Communities*, set out a 10-year plan for reforms that would deliver effective help to all Australians dealing with challenges to their mental health. The report called for a variety of initiatives, including a renewed approach to suicide prevention, a digital mental health gateway, an integrated approach to youth mental health, and improving services for people with severe mental illness.

The federal government, which had commissioned the report, remained silent about its intentions for more than six months after it received the report, until it was leaked to the press. This lack of action by the government caused growing unrest among mental health advocates. In addition, challenges included Australia's geography, which can make it difficult to involve individuals and build an advocacy movement. The country is approximately the same size as the United States but has a population of only 23 million people (compared to the 323 million in the United States). The majority of the population lives on either coast and is separated by thousands of miles of Australian outback.

RESEARCH

As a nongovernmental organization with a not-for-profit mission, MIFA was limited in terms of resources for primary research. Nevertheless, the organization employed various forms of research to guide the campaign planning process. A national survey by SANE Australia (a national charity devoted to helping those with mental illness) revealed that 80% of Australian mental health consumers believed that inaccurate or insensitive portrayals of mental illness had a negative effect on them. This was consistent with similar surveys in Australia at both state and national levels in recent years, and with European and U.S. evidence.

MIFA also took the following steps:

- Used data and information in government reports to substantiate the mental health need. Independent estimates of great unmet need from the *National Mental Health Service Planning Framework* (2014), the *Survey of High Impact Psychosis* (2010), and the report from the Productivity Commission (2012) all supported the conclusions of the National Mental Health Commission.

- Spoke with politicians from all major parties, finding remarkable consensus around the need to act on the report.

- Surveyed MIFA's own networks of service providers to confirm the extent of unmet need and broad agreement with the commission's recommendations.

From this research, MIFA knew that the direct voice of consumers and caregivers had enormous potential influence with politicians if it combined authentic stories drawn from personal experience and offered productive ideas on how to improve mental health care.

ACTION PLANNING

Using these research findings, MIFA decided in February 2015 that it was time to take a new stand against stigmatizing mental health and to use the direct voice of the lived experience to influence politicians. The organization settled on the creation of the "It's time to act NOW on mental illness" campaign. The campaign's objectives were as follows:

1. Organize and empower mental health advocates to tell their own stories to legislators by holding training sessions in four cities by the end of May 2015 with a minimum attendance of 100.

2. Create a national and regional media strategy focused on the government's inaction following the report by the National Mental Health Commission that resulted in at least one national radio broadcast and one print placement or radio talk/news segment in Sydney, Melbourne, Adelaide, and Townsville by the conclusion of the training.

3. Use the power of personal messages and media exposure to successfully advocate for the government's adoption of the recommendations from the report of the National Commission on Mental Health.

To help implement these strategies, MIFA contracted with Media Key, an Australian public relations agency. Media Key was tasked with ensuring extensive media coverage to bring these issues to the attention of Australian lawmakers and their constituents. Next, MIFA collaborated with NAMI, the largest mental health patient advocacy organization in the United States. NAMI had a strong history of successful advocacy in state legislatures and on Capitol Hill. The organization also had experience in advocacy training through its NAMI Smarts program that builds knowledge and skills to help advocates engage in effective meetings with legislators. The curriculum teaches participants to prepare for and secure meetings with politicians and deliver short, compelling personal stories that include an "ask."

Planning efforts with MIFA, Media Key, and NAMI led to the development of a series of trainings throughout Australia for people living with mental illness and their families. The key message was "It's time to act NOW on mental illness" (by supporting the commission's two-year plan). A secondary message was that "The report offers hope to me." The goal was to equip these individuals with skills and confidence so they could speak directly with Australian legislators. Participants would be taught to develop a personal communications strategy that would be effective in a one-on-one interview with a politician.

Great care was taken to include a rich mixture of diverse cultures and ethnic backgrounds among the participants. The workshops required travel and accommodation subsidies for many of the participants to ensure that people from every state and territory in Australia had a voice. This included men and women, young adults and people in their 70s, people from multiple ethnic backgrounds, and indigenous Australians. The trainings were planned to coincide with two highly visible mental health campaigns in Australia: Schizophrenia Awareness Week and World Mental Health Week. These two annual events are well established in Australia, building in profile for more than 25 years, with a good baseline of media awareness already established.

COMMUNICATION

The campaign slogan, "It's time to act NOW on mental illness," reflected both urgency and a call to action. This theme was embodied in the work with key stakeholders, training participants, and the media. Daylong workshops were held in Sydney, Melbourne, Adelaide, and Townsville, with participation by more than 100 advocates with lived experience of severe mental illness, representing every Australian state. The trainings were conducted by NAMI's national director of strategic alliances and MIFA's national CEO. Components of the training included background on how to approach legislators and the development of key messages that were consistent with MIFA's agenda of implementing government policies that supported mental illness treatment, but were also personalized to the individual. Participants were given ample opportunity to practice what they learned. Each training session also included an active or retired national politician who gave his or her perspectives on the type of advocacy that was most effective, and they participated in role-playing exercises.

Two press releases about the trainings were distributed to 200 newspapers and 100 radio stations across Australia. In each of the cities where the trainings were held, Media Key secured media opportunities for the trainers. These spokespeople appeared on the top-rated shows of the national and local networks of the Australian Broadcasting Corporation. They also appeared on Sky News, as well as several top-rated radio programs. NAMI's representative appeared live on *Life Matters*, the morning show that is Australia's version of the *Today* show in the United States.

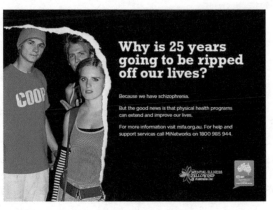

Why is 25 years going to be ripped off our lives?

Because we have schizophrenia.

But the good news is that physical health programs can extend and improve our lives.

For more information visit mifa.org.au. For help and support services call MiNetworks on 1800 985 944.

MENTAL ILLNESS FELLOWSHIP Australia Inc

Source: Mental Illness Fellowship of Australia Inc. (MIFA). Reproduced with permission.

EVALUATION

This groundbreaking campaign was successful in a number of ways. First, the goal of participation by 100 advocates in the trainings was met. More than 90% of participants reported that the training was helpful. The second campaign objective was met: through media placements in major TV and radio networks and print media that reached potential audiences of several million people. Third, MIFA's efforts overall were instrumental in securing the endorsement of the report by the Australian government.

Most importantly, "It's time to act NOW on mental illness" provided mental health consumers with the impetus for telling their own stories and developing confidence in their efforts to form a citizen lobby to support better responses to mental illness. As some training participants noted about the training sessions:

- "I feel very excited and motivated."

- "The workshop gave me a good chance to network with others. There is strength in numbers."

- "Great workshop and feeling supported knowing that I can contact someone with my prepared script and ask with my key issues."

- "Useful advocacy skills for any situation."

An unexpected side effect came from the participants' feedback on which messages were, and were not, easy to understand. The focus was responding to a report from the National Mental Health Commission of Australia, to which the government had made no response at the time of the workshops. MIFA had proposed to the workshop participants that their key message for politicians be "act now on mental illness," followed by a number of points drawn from the report's recommendations. However, participants found some of the lengthy document's recommendations confusing and complex, and instead suggested that the focus be simply "get on with implementing this report."

MIFA accepted this advice, and used this approach in all its advocacy around the report. The impact was profound. In a major television speech at the National Press Club in Canberra, Allan Fels, chairman of the National Mental Health Commission, quoted a portion of MIFA's key messages that had been developed and used in the workshop trainings. His speech was one of the key factors that led to the government enacting most of the report's recommendations. He said of the report:

> It's not perfect. I could argue with some of the detail. But my own experiences with mental illness and the mental health services tell me that it seems to be about right on all the big issues. Most importantly, it gives us all a framework that we can get started on as the first part of a 10-year plan. Let's argue the detail *after* we get started on implementation. . . .
>
> Please do all you can to have the report of the National Mental Health Commission adopted as the 10-year plan Australia needs. We have waited too long to let this great opportunity be lost.

This advocacy campaign was effective, and it was largely the product of the workshop participants' efforts. The government's subsequent adoption of many of the report's recommendations was heartening, but perhaps more importantly, the overall framework of the report now shapes most of the debate about the next reform steps.

Despite the enthusiasm recorded at the completion of the workshops, only a dozen of the more than 100 participants actually secured and attended a meeting with the politician of their choice. A few signaled in the workshops that they would not be doing this, even though they got a lot from the experience. One participant said she would not be able to cope with the stress, and did not want to put her mental health at risk. Others said they would think about going with a friend to give them support. Some later reported that they shared these concerns, but did not want to speak up. A few wrote to politicians but got no reply. MIFA was understanding and respectful of the impact of mental illness on each participant and how that factored into his or her decision to participate further.

While MIFA considered the effort a success, it had three reflection questions to explore how it could have been more effective. First, were its expectations of many of the participants unrealistic, in terms of participants securing and then conducting face-to-face advocacy with a high-profile politician? Second, should MIFA have provided additional resources and followed up with participants after the workshop? Third, would the creation of a digital community for this population have been utilized to maintain the momentum raised in the workshops?

RACE PIT STOP

Discussion Questions

1. This case study mentions that Australian geography presented a significant challenge toward building an advocacy movement. How was the communications team able to overcome or adapt to this challenge?

2. MIFA partnered with NAMI during this campaign. What was the strategic benefit of this partnership? How did the partnership aid in the achievement of the campaign's objectives?

3. While the campaign succeeded in meeting its objectives overall, the authors note that many of the workshop participants did not follow through on meeting with politicians. What do you think the communications team could have done differently to encourage more participants to meet with legislators?

4. Think about what types of audiences the campaign focused on engaging. What additional audiences could be engaged in future iterations of this campaign?

Trendlines

According to the National Institute of Mental Health[1] and the World Health Organization,[2] about 43 million Americans and more than 400 million people worldwide are affected by some type of mental disorder. Despite the sizable population impacted by mental health issues, there is still a stigma attached to mental disorders in many societies. Additionally, health coverage plans do not always cover mental health care to the same degree as physical health ailments. Both of these issues can create significant barriers to treatment for those experiencing mental health disorders. Public relations can play a significant role in educating the public and reducing the stigma associated with these types of issues.

With this is mind, do some research about local mental health issues. If you were to create a public education campaign for your locality, could you follow the approaches that MIFA and NAMI took in Australia? What different strategies and tactics might you employ? Which audiences would you target?

REFERENCES

1. Mental illness. (2015). *National Institute of Mental Health.* Retrieved from https://www.nimh.nih.gov/health/statistics/prevalence/any-mental-illness-ami-among-us-adults.shtml

2. Mental disorders affect one in four people. (2001). *World Health Organization.* Retrieved from http://www.who.int/whr/2001/media_centre/press_release/en/

EXAMPLE OF ADVOCATES' TAKE-HOME MATERIALS

The Ask

(the key things you ask at the start and again at the end of your visit)

Act Now on Mental Illness

Commit to implementing the report of the National Mental Health Commission.

Late in 2013, the government asked the National Mental Health Commission to undertake a full review of the right way forward for Australia in tackling mental health and suicide prevention. For more than a year, the commission consulted widely and researched extensively. Hundreds of face-to-face meetings were held in dozens of cities and towns across Australia, and more than 1,800 written submissions were received.

During 2014, virtually all requests for policy directions or funding were met with the response, "We are waiting for the report of the National Mental Health Commission before we make any major decisions in mental health." We all accepted that, and waited patiently. On December 1, 2014, the report was handed to the government. In the next five months, the only thing we heard from the government is that it was not going to implement one of the recommendations, and that was only because the report was leaked.

This report, which sets out a 10-year plan for achieving better outcomes, deserves more respect than this, as do the thousands of people who contributed, the hundreds of thousands of people living with debilitating mental illnesses, and the millions of Australians who care about mental health as a national priority.

Australia can do better, and it is not all about more money, as the report makes clear. Services can be better organized to get them talking to each other. The confusions about the National Disability Insurance Scheme and its impact on mental health funding can be clarified. Suicide can be reduced if we apply all the best evidence from here and overseas.

There have been dozens of reports about mental health in Australia, including several big ones in the last few years. For all sorts of reasons, these seem to have little impact.

This one should be different, because it was commissioned by the government, generally supported across all parties, and repeatedly described by the government as the report that would point the way forward on mental health.

It's not perfect. We could argue with some of the detail. But our own experiences with mental illness and the mental health services tell us that it seems to be about right on all the big issues. Most importantly, it gives us all a framework that we can get started on as the first part of a 10-year plan. Let's argue the detail *after* we get started on implementation.

We hope all our legislators can commit to helping to see a start made on implementing the report. We know Australia has budget constraints, and that not all of this will be easy to implement as soon as we would like. What we want is all politicians' commitment to use their influence to make sure we are doing all we can to get started. We don't want to hear about referrals to committees, expensive consultants, or "experts" to consider the report until we have a commitment from the government that it will use the report as the agreed framework to start tackling reform. Commitment from the other parties as well would be even better.

We hope politicians do all they can to have the report of the National Mental Health Commission adopted as the 10-year plan Australia needs. We have waited too long to let this great opportunity be lost.

CEDAR VALLEY AMERICAN HEART ASSOCIATION "GO RED FOR WOMEN" SPECIAL EVENT

Gayle Pohl, Associate Professor, University of Northern Iowa

Jeffrey Brand, Associate Professor, University of Northern Iowa

SITUATION

Cardiovascular diseases and stroke are major causes of death. One in three women dies each day from heart disease. The American Heart Association (AHA) is diligently trying, through medical research, to reduce the number of heart-related deaths in the United States. As the nation's oldest and largest voluntary organization dedicated to fighting heart disease and stroke, AHA is committed to eliminating heart disease as the leading cause of death for Americans and reducing its impact on lives and businesses. The Cedar Valley branch of the American Heart Association decided to pursue a campaign to mobilize women in the fight against heart disease.

RESEARCH

For 90 years, heart disease has been the number-one reason we lose our loved ones. Who is at stake? All women, especially those who smoke; have diabetes, high blood pressure, or high cholesterol; lack regular exercise; and/or are overweight. High blood pressure, obesity, and physical inactivity are on the rise across all age groups, yet each year the AHA is only able to fund approximately half of the research grant requests that are classified as "highly meritorious" or "meritorious," leaving possible breakthroughs unfunded. Still, risk factors can be managed.

One in three Americans lives with high blood pressure. That is almost 80 million people. Of those 80 million people, approximately 40 million have controlled their high blood pressure with diet, exercise, and/or medication. The other 40 million have not controlled their high blood pressure, living with an increased risk for a stroke or heart attack. From 2001 to 2011, high blood pressure–related deaths increased by 13%. It is the silent killer because it has no symptoms.

A high intake of sodium can also increase your risk for a heart attack and/or stroke. The average daily salt consumption is 3,500 milligrams (mg). The recommended intake is 1,500 mg per day. Sodium is sneaky. It is in foods that you do not think about. Natural foods, such as fruit, contain sodium. A small slice of watermelon contains 8 mg of sodium; a small apple has 1 mg of sodium. Processed foods contain a large amount of sodium, and restaurants are notorious for adding salt liberally. Reducing sodium intake helps reduce blood pressure and weight, which assists in living a heart-healthy life.

Working to improve the availability of lower-sodium foods, the "Healthy for Life" message was designed to improve 10 billion meals over the next five years, by improving food choice standards for food supply and manufacturing, governments and contractors, work sites, schools and child care, and individuals and families. The goal is to pass strong laws and policies for lowering sodium in foods. If the AHA succeeds, then more than 31 million kids could cut 300 mg of sodium a day by 2018, and 5.5 million employees will have a healthier workplace by 2020.

ACTION PLANNING

The goal of the organization is simple: to build healthier lives free of cardiovascular diseases and stroke. Cardiologists and medical researchers need funding to accomplish this goal. Since heart disease is the number-one killer of women, and because more women are lost to heart disease than men each year, "Go Red for Women (GRFW)" was created.

The primary audiences were women 40–80 years old and women outside of that age range who have risk factors for heart disease such as high blood pressure, high cholesterol, obesity, smoking and smoking-related issues, poor diet, high sodium intake, and a lack of heart health information.

Some of the key messages disseminated by the campaign's communications committee included the following:

- Heart disease is a silent killer, claiming more lives than all forms of cancer combined. But women can't be silent any longer.

- Heart disease is no match for women's voices, and sharing your story is just one way you can increase awareness about heart disease and demand change.

- For more than 10 years, women have been fighting heart disease individually and together as part of the GRFW movement. More than 650,000 women's lives have been saved, but the fight is far from over.

Objectives for this campaign included the following:

- Raise $10,000 in sponsorship sales in association with a GRFW special event; accomplish this by October 1, 2015.

- Through the GRFW special event, raise $50,000 gross to support the AHA's fight against heart disease and stroke by November 6, 2015.

COMMUNICATION

The GRFW luncheon was an afternoon tea/luncheon event (1:00 p.m.–4:15 p.m.). The rationale was women could come from work to the event and then go home or to an after-work activity. Food at the "high tea" is plentiful enough for a full meal or a heavy snack, depending on the amount a person consumes. Nine months before the 2015 AHA tea, communication professionals volunteered their time to work on a communications committee. The committee operated with a zero budget that depended on donations and sponsorships. The committee pursued the following tactics:

A fundraiser for the American Heart Association.

Source: Emily Hummel. Reproduced with permission.

1. Developed a four-minute survivor video for the luncheon presentation that featured survivors of heart attacks and strokes. The video featured stories like (a) a mother giving CPR to her infant son as he lies in her arms having a heart attack, (b) a middle-aged workaholic who refuses to stop for a heart attack, and (c) a panicked husband with tears running down his face as his wife of 45 years is ripped from his arms and whisked to the hospital. The video emphasized that anyone, no matter age, race, ethnicity, or socioeconomic status, can have heart disease or a stroke.

2. At the event, there was a booth where attendees could video stream their message of "My Life Is Why." For example, a My Life Is Why message may be "I live and work for my children" or "I live because I survived a quadruple bypass heart surgery and my family depends on me."

3. Designed event collaterals, including the following:

   a. "Save the date" postcards that announced the date of the tea

   b. Invitations (and reply cards) that personally invited each individual

   c. Event signage and posters that were disseminated over the entire Cedar Valley, which encompasses a 100-mile radius

   d. Worked with a local newspaper to create and publish a four-page foldout explaining the event sponsors and all event activities

   e. Designed artwork, auction tables, and a PowerPoint presentation for the event itself

   f. Worked closely with all traditional and social media partners in highlighting local survivors

   g. Worked with traditional and social media sponsors and vendors to promote the AHA and the Cedar Valley GRFW event through print, TV, radio, online, and social media

EVALUATION

The 2015 AHA GRFW tea/luncheon raised $51,374, surpassing the objective. Of that figure, $34,000 came through sponsorship sales.

Other evaluations included the following:

- On the day of the luncheon there were 300 attendees.
- The event received approximately 100 Facebook likes (AHA attendees have a history of not liking Facebook posts after an event, so this is not always a reliable measurement).
- Qualitatively, the most positive remarks were about the quality of items available at the silent auction. Positive comments were also made about the types of vendors at the event. However, many negative comments were made about the speaker in 2015; attendees found that speaker dry and rambling. This showed in the "Open Your Heart" donations where we asked attendees to give money at the event. The donations were down by 40% from the previous event.

The primary audience for this event comprised women ages 40–80; while baby boomers are not afraid of social media and often embrace it, they like the way an invitation looks and feels in their hands. They may not think about looking at Facebook for an event date because they are expecting a tangible invitation. So when the AHA decreased the mailing of invitations to the GRFW luncheon and relied on social media, the attendance numbers dropped slightly. Audience preferences for receiving information need to be constantly kept in mind.

RACE PIT STOP

Discussion Questions

1. The primary audiences for this campaign were women between the ages of 40 and 80. What other audiences might this campaign have targeted?

2. The campaign used personal testimonials from heart attack and stroke survivors to communicate campaign messages. What is the strategic benefit of using these testimonials?

3. The outcome of the campaign is discussed in the evaluation section. Based on the results discussed, do you think the campaign was a success? Why or why not? What areas could be improved upon?

4. This case study was very focused on one particular event. What could be some complementary strategies and tactics that would still tie back to the goal and objectives listed in the case study?

Trendlines

The Centers for Disease Control and Prevention[1] indicates that heart disease is the top cause of death of females in the United States, accounting for 22.3% of deaths, followed by cancer at 21.6% of female deaths. When the statistics are broken down, however, heart disease falls to the second leading cause of death for Asian or Pacific Islander and Hispanic females. With these two groups, cancer is the leading cause of death. While heart disease is still a critical issue for these groups, these statistics illustrate that different groups may have different health priorities. Compounding these factors is the issue of access to health care. In 2016, 12.8% of people under the age of 65 lacked health insurance,[2] which limits the type of health care these people can receive. Other factors like socioeconomic status and location may also have a significant impact on the type of health care women receive and how often they go to the doctor.

While the American Heart Association is one of the largest charities in the United States and has significant resources, understanding how to speak to all these different types of audiences could be a big challenge. What type of audience research could you conduct to understand the most effective ways to communicate with the different types of audiences the AHA would want to reach with its messages about heart disease prevention?

A fundraiser for the American Heart Association

Spend all day in downtown Cedar Falls to take advantage of great deals offered by local businesses: merchandise discounts, buy one-get one half deals, specialty drinks and more.

Friday, November 12th 11AM-10PM

Community members are invited to purchase punch cards giving them access to deals at many Community Main Street Businesses on November 12th. A $25 punch card provides access to any 15 deals whereas a $35 punch card provides access to all 30+ participating businesses. There will also be live music from 11AM-7PM.

PAINT THE TOWN RED **Sponsorship Opportunities**

- **$250 level** includes
  - company name listed at refreshment stations
  - mention in press releases

- **$500 level** includes
  - company name listed on access punch cards
  - mention in press releases

- **$1,000 level** includes
  - company logo on access punch cards
  - company logo at refreshment stations
  - mention in press releases and public relations materials

To sponsor or for more information, visit
cedarvalley.red

Source: Emily Hummel. Reproduced with permission.

REFERENCES

1. Leading causes of death (LCOD) in females United States. (2014). *Centers for Disease Control and Prevention*. Retrieved from https://www.cdc.gov/women/lcod/2014/index.htm

2. Health insurance coverage. (2017, January 20). *Centers for Disease Control and Prevention*. Retrieved from https://www.cdc.gov/nchs/fastats/health-insurance.htm

WORKING WITH A DIFFICULT CLIENT: EXAMINING THE TENSIONS EXPERIENCED WHILE DEVELOPING THE HALO SYNDROME CAMPAIGN

Lindsey B. Anderson, Assistant Professor, University of Maryland–College Park

Melanie Morgan, Associate Professor, Purdue University

Shavonne Shorter, Assistant Professor, Bloomsburg University

Brian C. Britt, Assistant Professor, South Dakota State University

SITUATION

Halo USA (a pseudonym) is a nonprofit organization that was founded by parents of children who have Halo syndrome (a pseudonym). Halo syndrome is a rare genetic disorder, and children with this disease may have a range of symptoms, including learning disabilities, motor skills deficiencies, slow muscle growth, immune and digestive systems problems, and a form of epilepsy that tends to resist current seizure treatments.

Halo syndrome is classified as an orphan disease—a disease that affects fewer than 200,000 individuals around the world. Since orphan diseases are extremely rare, they are underresearched; small market demand makes it unprofitable for pharmaceutical companies to pursue treatments. Worldwide, there are only about 50 known cases of Halo syndrome.

Developing a public relations campaign about an orphan disease comes with many unique challenges. How do you identify important publics beyond those few individuals who are personally connected to a child with the orphan disease? How do you build identification and arouse emotion with those publics when most individuals will never encounter someone with Halo syndrome? How do you persuade those publics to donate to your organization when there are so few known cases of the disease? We sought to answer these questions when serving as pro bono public relations consultants for Halo USA. In this role, we designed a campaign intended to help our client increase awareness about this disease among multiple publics with the hope of raising funds for continued research.

As the campaign began, we soon realized that we had an unexpected challenge to attend to—learning how to work with a difficult client. During the course of our campaign, we encountered multiple dilemmas associated with fulfilling our responsibilities to the organization. One of the most challenging was board members' resistance to advice. Because the board was made up of parents with children affected by Halo syndrome, they were extremely emotionally involved in the organization and project, making it challenging to move the campaign through its various stages.

Client relationships can be fraught with difficulties like poor communications and lack of client understanding of public relations. The public relations team working for Halo USA (a pseudonym) attempted to overcome such problems by seeking clarity with the Halo board.

Source: Photo by Free-Photos, https://pixabay.com/en/workplace-team-business-meeting-1245776/, licensed under CC0, https://creativecommons.org/choose/zero/.

RESEARCH

In order to prepare for this project, we researched campaigns designed for other orphan diseases, but they did not fit the context of our case. For example, we found that certain orphan conditions are related to specific chromosomes that are shared by several other conditions; this allowed for some campaigns to address more than one condition, allowing for a more effective combined message. However, because Halo syndrome is so rare, combining forces with several other diseases was not a possibility.

With that said, we faced significant challenges in developing research to support this campaign. The parents who served on the board were knowledge gatekeepers, and they only shared what they thought we needed to know. Since Halo syndrome is a rare disease, knowledge is limited, and published research on the syndrome is scarce. There is a small amount of medical literature on the disease, but it is dense and was not appropriate for framing this campaign to all of the key publics—doctors, researchers, and families of diagnosed children. Therefore, we were extremely dependent on the information board members were willing to share; we read through the literature they provided and interviewed each of the board members.

The interviews primarily served as a mechanism for the families to describe their experiences of dealing with Halo syndrome on a daily basis. The parents used the interviews as a way to share their stories, highlight their children, and humanize them. From these interviews, we were able to collect stories and examples of the caregiving challenges and successes and setbacks each of the families faced. This was helpful in creating documents for newly diagnosed families, but failed to provide a more extensive background of the syndrome that would allow us to create other documents.

Then, early in our relationship with the board, we encountered members who proposed using two logos for the organization. Of course, we were concerned that this approach would dilute the organization's branding efforts. So, we turned to research on branding and logos to bolster our position. Based on this research, we were able to achieve support from a board member who convinced the other members to abandon the two-logo idea.

By using research to justify our position and display credibility, we were able to establish our legitimacy as consultants. It seemed after this issue was resolved we had less trouble convincing the client that we knew what was best for the organization—at least in terms of public relations.

ACTION PLANNING

The campaign's main goal was to raise awareness about Halo syndrome among key publics (e.g., doctors, researchers, and families of diagnosed children). With this goal in mind, we developed three measurable objectives. First, we wanted 100 people to attend the fundraising dinner held in early May 2012. Second, we wanted to collect 50 items for the accompanying auction. Finally, we wanted to raise $50,000 for Halo USA following the fundraising dinner.

As previously mentioned, the campaign focused on reaching members of the medical community, including doctors and researchers. The reason these publics were targeted was because of their ability to encourage families of diagnosed children to donate blood samples to biobanks that facilitate research related to Halo syndrome. In addition, we targeted families of diagnosed children in order to create a community that can advocate for Halo syndrome research.

COMMUNICATION

During this stage, we ran into another difficulty: Poor communication from our clients made our consulting experience difficult. We were contracted to complete several deliverables, including creating informative brochures, redesigning the website, developing a social media strategy, and facilitating a fundraising event. Pressure points appeared here relatively quickly. We started by producing a brochure targeted toward the medical community. One of the goals of this brochure was for doctors to persuade their Halo syndrome patients to donate blood samples to a research data bank, the Consortium Network of Genetic Biobanks (a pseudonym). These biobanks are the major source of biological samples used in research on this disease. However, an additional data bank, located at a specific European hospital, had been created for medical providers to track medication therapies for Halo syndrome. The board also wanted to encourage physicians to contribute to this database and utilize it when formulating treatment plans. Unfortunately, no one had ever informed us about the second database, and the Halo USA board was irritated that the information was not in the brochure we created.

We soon faced another hurdle; one board member wanted to make T-shirts that said "Cure Halo Syndrome" because it was catchy. However, there is no cure for Halo syndrome. While treatments may be developed that address the symptoms of the syndrome, the very nature of Halo syndrome as a genetic disease makes finding a cure impossible. One of the defining goals of the campaign was to communicate accurate information about the disease to the community. By making and distributing these T-shirts, we would be spreading misinformation. It took some effort to explain to the board why the T-shirts would be ineffective, but we believe our earlier, persuasive "one-logo pitch" helped us gain credibility on this issue. The board ultimately voted down the T-shirt per our recommendation.

On a more positive note, we developed profiles of various children with Halo syndrome in collaboration with the board members. These children were featured at the fundraiser with oversized photo posters and a corresponding narrative. We documented family stories from parents and siblings to create a "day in the life" narrative to use at the event. Parents and the board were very appreciative and loved the way their children were highlighted at the event. Parents had the opportunity to edit their children's narrative, and we co-constructed what was eventually presented at the dinner.

The final pressure point was managing the consultant–client relationship, which began on a pleasant note but eventually soured. During the project, board members were asking campaign members to complete errands that were not tied directly to the public relations campaign. As such, it became difficult for the team members to balance their responsibilities with the demands placed upon them by the board. Our consulting team leader was eventually forced to tell the board to stop asking the group to complete any additional tasks. In retrospect, roles and expectations should have been better communicated at the beginning of the campaign.

EVALUATION

Our evaluation techniques centered on meeting the client's expectations in terms of creating audience-centered materials about Halo syndrome and planning/promoting a fundraising event, which we completed successfully. We gauged the effectiveness of our campaign through the number of attendees at the fundraising dinner, items garnered for the silent auction, and money earned at the event, all of which met or exceeded our expectations. Specifically, 150 people attended the fundraising dinner. The attendees were able to bid on 50 donated auction items, and as a result, we earned over $50,000 for Halo USA.

Moreover, we used the feedback we received from the client to evaluate our campaign and make decisions about what we would do if we found ourselves in a similar situation in the future.

While the campaign was a success, raising over $50,000, there were tensions that created turning points throughout the process. Information on Halo syndrome was limited, and our team had to rely on the client for research on the subject, but we were still able to use our own public relations expertise and research to justify our recommendations when we were questioned.

The Halo USA board members also did not provide us with all of the information they wanted us to include in their brochure, so our initial draft failed to meet all of their expectations. We also discovered that clients may resist the advice of their consultants in favor of self-destructive plans or products. In short, although the Halo USA board members were not always forthcoming with their expectations and initially resisted our recommendations, we were able to work through those problems by drawing on our expertise and persuasively arguing for the most important aspects of our work. Once we had developed a climate of trust, our client saw the merits of the products we developed. Although some of our communication challenges persisted through the end of our project, the client still grew to recognize the value of our services and made use of all our recommendations. Our interactions were difficult at times, but by tackling those challenges head-on, we were ultimately able to ensure that our work served the client's needs.

RACE PIT STOP

Discussion Questions

1. A major challenge for this campaign was convincing people to pay attention to a disease that only affects a very small portion of the population. Do you think the public relations team successfully overcame or solved this problem? Are there other approaches the team could have taken?

2. The public relations team members indicated that they encountered a client who resisted taking their advice. This is a situation that is not at all uncommon. Think about how the team members in the case study handled the situation. Do you agree with the way they handled it? Is there anything they could have done differently?

3. How did the public relations team go about building client trust and enhancing the consultant–client relationship?

4. The public relations team members conducted interviews with the board members as a major component of their research for the campaign. Do you think that was sufficient? Was there other research that could have been conducted?

5. In this case, the client wanted to use two logos for the campaign. Why did the public relations team discourage the client from doing this?

Trendlines

Learning how to work effectively with clients is a key skill for public relations practitioners. Many clients may be easy to work with and clearly understand the realities of public relations. However, a number of factors can complicate a campaign for a public relations team. Robert Wynne, a public relations professional and contributor to *Forbes*, notes that client issues usually stem from impatience, being uninformed, a tendency to bully, being disorganized, and ego.[1] More specifically, clients may not accurately understand the public relations function or have unrealistic expectations, particularly when it comes to media placements. In the case of the Halo USA organization, the main problem stemmed from the client being too close to the cause—the board members were unable to look at the situation from an outsider perspective, which gave them unrealistic expectations for the campaign.

After reviewing the Halo case, list attributes of a difficult public relations client. How would you handle the issues you have raised? Are there any that would be severe enough for you to fire the client?

REFERENCES

1. Wynne, R. (2015, October 8). Handling nightmare public relations clients. *Forbes*. Retrieved from https://www.forbes.com/sites/robertwynne/2015/10/08/the-public-relations-nightmare-clients-from-hell/#72d0af44583d

A STRATEGIC VIEW: THE HALO CAMPAIGN AND BUILDING A POSITIVE CLIENT RELATIONSHIP

Lindsey B. Anderson, Assistant Professor, University of Maryland–College Park

Melanie Morgan, Associate Professor, Purdue University

Shavonne Shorter, Assistant Professor, Bloomsburg University

Brian C. Britt, Assistant Professor, South Dakota State University

The Halo syndrome campaign that immediately precedes this Strategic View required both knowledge of communication processes and information about the disorder itself. We employed a two-pronged approach, which framed our expertise as public relations scholars and allowed the client to serve as the content expert in order to take advantage of the unique skill sets that all involved parties possessed. Together we crafted a multimedia communication campaign to provide multiple avenues through which awareness of the orphan disease could be increased.

This initial strategic move helped to encourage a positive consultant–client relationship at first, but we soon found ourselves entrenched in an "us versus them" mentality. This division stemmed from the insular nature of the organization and the perception that we, as outsiders, could not fully understand the impact of the disease. As a result, our client distrusted our campaign advice. With that said, we sought to counteract this growing conflict by fostering mutual respect between

The HALO public relations team members used research and listening effectively to encourage a better relationship with their client.

Source: Photo by Free-Photos, https://pixabay.com/en/office-meeting-business-partners-336368/, licensed under CC0, https://creativecommons.org/choose/zero/.

the client organization and ourselves. While we acknowledged that we could not fully empathize with those affected by Halo syndrome, we attempted to showcase the ways in which our expertise could contribute to the client's goals by using the following primary tactics.

First, we relied on our own research about Halo syndrome and our communication knowledge to provide a rationale for our decisions in order to mitigate the effect of knowledge on the client's gatekeeping and to justify our own competence to work in this domain. Second, we used communication to remind the board about explicitly defined expectations for the tasks that we could complete in the contract period as well as the messages that should be used in the final campaign materials. We also attempted to preserve client relations by being accommodating by performing unrelated tasks, even those that fell outside of the scope of our campaign (e.g., collecting silent auction items for the Halo syndrome fundraiser), and were overtly responsive to questions and critiques of the communication materials the team delivered.

One final consideration: It is possible that the status of our team as a group of pro bono consultants contributed to board members being critical of the advice and products we offered. It is not uncommon for clients to be concerned about the quality of work they are receiving when they do not pay for it.

A STRATEGIC VIEW: DONATE LIFE OHIO CAMPAIGN: SAVE A LIFE. BE A DONOR

Michele E. Ewing, Associate Professor, Kent State University

Source: Donate Life Ohio. Reproduced with permission.

More than 3,000 people await organ or tissue transplants on any given day in Ohio. Yet millions of eligible Ohioans remain unregistered organ donors. Donate Life Ohio, a coalition of the state's organ, eye, and tissue recovery agencies, partnered with the Second Chance Trust Fund and an Ohio public relations agency to determine how a communication campaign could motivate Ohioans to become registered organ donors. They created a "Do It Now" college competition to engage college students.

A team of public relations students at Kent State University in Ohio competed with teams from 12 universities in the statewide Do It Now initiative. Each team had a specific target number of new registrants based on population within its respective regions.

With limited resources, the students needed to create a difficult behavioral change among thousands of Ohio residents in a short time frame. It was a daunting challenge; however, the students were inspired by the worthy cause and the opportunity to use their communication skills to help save lives.

Through secondary and primary research, the Kent State team gained insights about obstacles:

- Lack of awareness about need. Audiences may have been aware of organ and tissue donation, but they did not understand the dire need for organ donors.

- Sensitivity. Typically, people are approached at the local bureau of motor vehicles in an impersonal manner regarding this serious subject.

- Misconceptions. Some people believe their religious beliefs restrict organ donation, even though all major religions support it. Others thought that individuals who designate as organ donors could risk less thorough treatment by medical professionals.

- Uncomfortable conversation. People thought registering to become an organ donor was the "right thing to do," but they do not want to think or talk about their mortality.

Source: Courtesy of Michele Ewing.

The team developed objectives to increase awareness about the need for registered organ and tissue donors and sought to register 10,750 new donors.

Primary audiences included the Kent State community, African Americans who attend church, and Kent State Recreation and Wellness Center members. Secondary audiences or influencers were identified as organ donor recipients, families of donors, medical professionals, clergy, and registered donors.

Key campaign strategies included the following:

- Emphasize the feeling of doing the right thing. The campaign needed to communicate that organ donation is more about *being a hero and saving a life and less about someone dying.*

- Rely on credible sources and personal stories to overcome misconceptions and motivate audiences to register. Create a dialogue about organ and tissue donation. Encourage registered donors and donor recipients to communicate with family members and friends.

- Involve and engage key publics in face-to-face communication at existing events and programs.

The team created a "hero" campaign theme to quickly convey key messages about how registering to be an organ donor is a heroic act. Almost 100 student volunteers helped spread the campaign's hero message and register new organ donors at residence halls and other campus locations, Kent State basketball games, area churches, YMCAs, and campus and community events.

This campaign also integrated a "flash mob" on campus, class presentations, and story ideas for media and bloggers. A photo and caption of the flash mob was featured on the Reuters board in New York City's Times Square, the largest digital sign in the world.

Based on the circulation numbers of the media and social media outlets, the campaign's messaging reached more than 2.1 million people. The Kent State team exceeded its registration goal by adding more than 12,500 new organ and tissue donors to the Ohio Donor Registry.

7

CRISIS COMMUNICATION

Crisis communication is one of the most recognizable functions of public relations. While not all crises reach a nationwide or worldwide level of visibility, they can still have a high level of positive or negative impact on an organization depending on the extent that the crisis directly affects its stakeholders or the community it operates within. Successful recovery from a crisis with the brand untarnished and stakeholders feeling positively about the organization is the ultimate goal of any crisis communication professional. Additionally, it is important to remember that not all crises occur over a finite amount of time, and some industries are in a constant state of crisis due to political, economic, or other factors.

In this chapter, you will read about crisis communication case studies from a variety of organizations. One case study focuses on Whitesville, West Virginia, which was faced with a long-term crisis as a result of the decline of the coal industry, while another demonstrates how the Louisiana Office of Tourism sought to draw visitors back to the area in the wake of the BP oil spill. Still another case study discusses how a school district in Omaha, Nebraska, dealt with a budget reduction that had implications for the local community. These case studies explore a variety of crises and how they are handled, and further illustrate how not all crises can be managed with the same approach.

BOOSTING PRIDE IN THE FACE OF A DOWNTURN IN WHITESVILLE, WEST VIRGINIA

Geah Pressgrove, Assistant Professor, West Virginia University

Julia Daisy Fraustino, Assistant Professor, West Virginia University

SITUATION

The town of Whitesville, West Virginia, is located about an hour south of the state's capital, Charleston. Once a bustling hub of social and economic activity, as of 2010 only about 500 residents called Whitesville home. By 2015, the town was on the verge of collapse due to a major loss of jobs, with more than 800 layoffs between the shutdown of mines and consolidation of local schools in the year prior. The coal industry's deterioration brought hard times to the town and its members, not only economically but also emotionally. The morale around the community was steadily dropping, with some residents giving up faith in the town's future. In an effort to reverse the tide and improve community morale, a team of faculty leaders, undergraduate senior strategic communication capstone students at West Virginia University, subject matter experts, and community partners worked together to develop a campaign that encouraged a sense of community and a vision for the future.

RESEARCH

As a first step in this process, the campaign assembled a branding committee of key community stakeholders (e.g., nonprofit leaders, educators, and community business leaders). This group revealed that Whitesville primarily attracts residents from surrounding communities who travel to the town for necessities, work, and leisure. Committee members and townspeople explained that the main community image is based on its coal history and mountainous nature. Nearby cities with greater resources (e.g., Charleston and Beckley) present clear competition as they offer more opportunities for dining, shopping, and accommodations.

Next, because there are few Whitesville residents, the team chose to interview 13 key residents who were heavily involved in the community, region, or area and lived within a 30-minute drive. Among the findings:

> *Feels like home.* The majority of respondents described Whitesville as unique in that the town felt like "home," whether they lived in the town proper or in an unincorporated area along Route 3. Many residents described a "warmth" or "aura" about the town not found elsewhere.

> *Hospitable host.* Business owners, residents, and the area's elected leaders prided themselves on making every person's visit the best it could be. In fact, many respondents stressed that the town's greatest quality is customer service and friendly hospitality.

> *Events attract.* Almost every interviewee spoke highly of town events, including the Christmas Parade. Respondents also commented on a variety of outdoor activities at the river, such as fishing.

Additionally, 66 individuals who live in Whitesville or the surrounding region completed surveys about the attractiveness of Whitesville. When asked why visitors might come to the area, the most common response was community outdoor-themed events such as fishing tournaments, festivals or fairs for families, and heritage events. Two focus groups with community residents also found that outdoor recreational events were important for bringing visitors. These focus groups emphasized the need to stress that Whitesville was a friendly, family-oriented town and that Whitesville's leadership needed to look beyond its history with coal to portray itself as an attractive destination.

ACTION PLANNING

The overall goal of the campaign was to brush the coal dust off of Whitesville and to reveal its attractiveness to audiences in the region and beyond. The overall strategic message was to portray Whitesville as part of a Route 3 region, a scenic winding road dotted with unincorporated communities connecting two population centers in the state. Along this path, people can reconnect with natural beauty.

Campaign planning centered on these key messages directed to these key audiences:

- Bikers/drivers: The Route 3 region offers motorcyclists and car enthusiasts mountainous, waterfront views ideal for quaint, peaceful, off-the-grid travel.

- Outdoor enthusiasts/history buffs: From hiking the West Virginia mountains, to paddling down the Big Coal River, to physically touching pieces of history, the Route 3 region presents adventure enthusiasts with a vast variety of options for exploration.

- Whitesville residents: Whitesville is a place that "feels like home."

Objectives included the following:

- Increase community pride by 10% in the Whitesville community measured by pre- and post-surveys of the residents.

- Increase community involvement among Whitesville residents by 30 people.

- Drive 50 site views for the website as measured by Google Analytics.

COMMUNICATION

To help support the brand launch, the team created two official logos—one represented the town of Whitesville, and the second highlighted the Route 3 regional partnership. The tagline "Feels Like Home" was used for the campaign. A billboard was placed at the entrance to town celebrating the Feels Like Home image and Route 3 affiliation.

The campaign created a special Family Adventure Night to kick off a summer series of family-friendly events. The event was promoted through flyers, email blasts, and social media, as well as at local schools. Prior to the event, residents had nominated people for community pride awards; nominees were recognized with a branded, insulated picnic basket. The campaign also unveiled the new community website at the event.

Community beautification (e.g., de-littering, mural painting, and flower and vegetable planting) events were held as well.

The campaign also supported events designed to attract visitors. Supporting a trout rodeo, public relations team members helped coordinate stocking of the river and a raffle for a kayak. At the centennial of the little red caboose at the community park, team members developed coloring pages, secured a former conductor to take children on tours, and took pictures of children to help them remember the occasion.

The campaign used several tactics to support these efforts. It developed separate email templates for outdoor, heritage, educational tourism, and community announcements. A website hub of information included an interactive map, stories of the town, an archive of historical photos, an events calendar, and a job resource database. Media kits, feature story ideas, and invitations to community events were sent to regional media outlets, including print, broadcast, and radio, as well as bloggers.

EVALUATION

Success for the first objective associated with increasing community pride was measured by a post-campaign survey. Responses to questions associated with community pride showed a full-point improvement above the average response of the pre-brand launch survey. Although this numerical improvement was below the stated objective, open-ended questions asking residents to describe their town were centered on messages of hope, a dramatic improvement over prior sentiments like "dying" and "dead." Post-event survey responses also revealed that

Source: www.whitesvillewv.com. Reproduced with permission.

78% of respondents strongly agreed that they would attend other community events and 87% agreed or strongly agreed that there should be a focus on continuing to create opportunities for family to enjoy the community. This area ranked as most improved in the post-event survey.

Success concerning community involvement was measured by the number of people who volunteered at events or attended the brand launch. This objective was far exceeded, as 165 children helped to paint the mural, 20 volunteers helped during cleanup projects, 20 youth helped with the planting event, and 170 residents were added to the contact database.

Additionally, in the two weeks following the brand launch, the new website garnered 2,589 site views originating from 589 unique users. Site visitors spent an average of about three minutes on the site. Using the targeted databases provided by the convention and visitors bureau (CVB), 870 unique individuals were sent targeted emails based on their interest for four of the campaign initiatives (trout rodeo, community cleanups, etc.). These emails were opened by no less than 30% of addressees.

The Route 3 initiative was added to the most recent motorcycle trail guide distributed by the regional CVB. In addition, the community has sustained the email blast tactics to promote its events, resulting in greater attendance at family-friendly community activities. And the original community branding committee has expanded and made outdoor adventure a regular focus, even producing a new water trail map and creating brand signage to install at water access points. Yet persistent attention from public relations, branding, and strategic communication experts for a more sustained time period could enhance Whitesville's likelihood for long-term regional success. For example, since this campaign, the community was unable to identify volunteers with the time and capability

Source: www.whitesvillewv.com. Reproduced with permission.

to maintain the newly developed website and event calendar; without individuals fulfilling that role, the website has begun to fall behind. Ultimately, the attempt to manage Whitesville's crisis through enhancing wider stakeholder awareness is experiencing many of the rewards and pitfalls common to volunteer initiatives with limited budgets.

RACE PIT STOP

Discussion Questions

1. Why was it important to speak with key stakeholders before beginning to plan the communication campaign? Were there any key insights that could have been overlooked by not meeting with them?

2. Since a key component of the campaign centered on planning events to attract people to the town, can you think of any other types of events that could be planned to attract local visitors? What about events that may attract regional or national visitors?

3. .As the authors indicate, a key component of the continued success of the communication campaign for Whitesville depends on recruiting volunteers to help with all public relations efforts. What strategies, tactics, and messages might help with recruiting volunteers to help with the town's communication efforts?

Trendlines

The decline of some industries in the United States has resulted in people leaving certain areas in favor of cities or other rural areas with better job prospects. For the coal industry, in particular, 2016 marked the lowest production levels since 1981.[1] Many communities in these situations are struggling with how to attract both people and jobs to their areas. Communities across the country have tried different methods of combating this situation including attracting new industries and attempting to increase tourism to the area.

The success of different approaches the communities have taken depends on a number of factors, such as the state and community business climate, proximity to more densely populated areas, and types of attractions in the area. In thinking about these types of factors, discuss the long-term success of the communications strategy for Whitesville. Do you think this strategy can continue to be successful for the community? Are there additional advantages that could be leveraged by Whitesville, and if so, what are they, and how could they be communicated? As you craft your response, do some research on the community, attractions, and demographics of the town and region.

REFERENCES

1. Krauss, C. (2016, June 10). Coal production plummets to lowest level in 35 years. *New York Times*. Retrieved from https://www.nytimes.com/2016/06/11/business/energy-environment/coal-production-decline.html

REGAINING TRUST AMID A CRISIS: LOUISIANA OFFICE OF TOURISM AND THE BP OIL SPILL

Dedria Givens-Carroll, Associate Professor, University of Louisiana at Lafayette

John Deveney, President, Deveney Communication

SITUATION

The British Petroleum (BP) oil spill disaster negatively affected the tourism industry in several Gulf Coast states; however, Louisiana's situation was unique in that the state was still reeling from the devastation left by the 2005 hurricanes Katrina and Rita. This case study looks at how public relations (funded through a BP grant) reached out to special publics—particularly, tourists and seafood lovers—in an effort to help the recovery of Louisiana's tourism industry.

When the Deepwater Horizon oil spill occurred on April 20, 2010, the crisis brought with it a sense of instability and miscommunication to the entire Gulf Coast. The Louisiana Office of Tourism (LOT) understood the crisis could negatively influence and reduce the amount of tourism to the state, especially at the height of the travel season. Tourism is a major influence on Louisiana's economy. In 2010, the state hosted 24.1 million visitors, generated $9.4 billion for the tourism industry, collected $864 million in tax revenue, and employed 200,000 people. Deveney Communication, a New Orleans–based public relations agency that handles the LOT account, was charged with developing a response to the crisis.

RESEARCH

Tourism-related activity directly employs about 8% of the Louisiana workforce, accounting for nearly 3% of Louisiana's gross domestic product (GDP).[1] Closely tied to tourism is the seafood industry; it affects 1 out of 70 jobs and has a $2.4 billion economic impact on the economy. More than one in four Louisiana citizens employed by the tourism industry are connected to dining establishments and venues; dining accounts for roughly 30% of all visitor spending.

The Deepwater Horizon well leaked a total of 185 million gallons of oil into the Gulf of Mexico by the time the wellhead was finally capped on July 15, 2010. As a result, Louisiana's seafood industry, a primary attraction for many Louisiana tourists, suffered a large blow when fishing areas affected by the spill were closed down indefinitely. Even though there was never a lack of safe seafood available from the Gulf of Mexico, there remained a large aversion to Gulf seafood across the nation, and with it came the fear of a decrease in Louisiana's tourism, especially in New Orleans.

"We are fortunate that 100 percent of reports have shown Gulf seafood to be safe to consume from approved waters," said Ralph Brennan, a famous New Orleans restaurateur, in his U.S. congressional testimony in the summer of 2010. Still, he said, "visitor perception is key to decisions about where to vacation. . . . The overall numbers of tourists are down; restaurant guests and sales are decreasing; product cost is increasing; and jobs are in jeopardy as already-thin margins precariously slip away."[2] By the end of 2010, Louisiana lost approximately $32 million in visitor spending and $247 million in leisure visitor spending, though $216 million in business spending related to the spill offset some of these decreases.

The LOT conducted audience research. Surveys revealed that, nationwide, respondents had negative perceptions of Louisiana in May and August 2010, and that visits to the state were lost as a result of the crisis. About a third of respondents in the survey indicated that they had canceled or postponed trips to Louisiana due to the oil spill.[3] Many respondents believed that Louisiana's prized seafood was contaminated. Of leisure travelers nationwide, 87% were familiar with and following the oil spill story; 79% of travelers believed the oil spill would affect Louisiana for at least five years; and a majority were not certain that seafood in Louisiana restaurants was safe.

ACTION PLANNING

The LOT embarked on a "regaining trust" public relations campaign that was focused on the broader goals of diminishing adverse economic impact and encouraging the public to continue to see Louisiana as a viable vacation destination.

The targeted audiences/publics included the following: 1,100 industry partners and stakeholders, as well as news media, including print, radio, television, and online travel and tourism trade publications. The most valuable stakeholders were visitors coming from the surrounding Gulf Coast of the United States. They have an equal stake in the overall recovery of the Gulf Coast and make up the majority of Louisiana visitors.

The campaign focused on these key themes:

- *Come hear the music. Come taste the cuisine. Come enjoy the pristine outdoors. Come experience every aspect of Louisiana's unique culture.* Most of the campaign's key messages included the crucial word *come*. The LOT reminded its target audiences and stakeholders that 92% of the state waters remained open, and all 20 of the state parks were open 365 days a year.

- *Come to Louisiana and help.* This second key theme was that the recovery process required assistance. This campaign message encouraged visitors to come help

Louisiana recover by making a visit and eating Louisiana's seafood. This essential theme focused on the fact that tourism is the foundation of Louisiana's economy and that the most effective and fun way for people to contribute to a fast cleanup and recovery from the spill is to make a personal visit.

Research drove the formulation of the following objectives: (1) to provide accurate and timely information during the initial crisis response to all targeted publics by using the one-voice method, (2) to demonstrate the LOT's genuine concern for the safety of tourists visiting Louisiana, (3) to safeguard the public's perception of tourism in Louisiana, and (4) to keep the public's perception of Louisiana tourism positive and show that it is a desirable place to visit. The goals of protecting Louisiana as a tourist destination were intrinsically tied to Louisiana's popular seafood industry.

COMMUNICATION

Deveney Communication distributed a daily messaging document to 1,100 partners, stakeholders, spokespersons, and media contacts. Information about the oil spill was available to their publics and was updated regularly on the LOT's website (www.louisianatravel.com). The website also hosted several interactive features, including the "top 100 reasons to visit Louisiana," an interactive personal online space for prospective tourists to get inspired by and plan for events happening in Louisiana during their trip.

Louisiana Travel ✔
@LouisianaTravel

(Follow) ⌄

Help build the Top 100 Reasons to visit Louisiana! To mark 100 days of oil tragedy, tweet ur reasons for visiting Louisiana using #LaTOP100

8:14 AM - 28 Jul 2010

3 Retweets   🔵 🟠 🟢

Source: Twitter/@LouisianaTravel.

The LOT also focused and expanded its social media outreach by developing several sites and keeping those updated with the latest developments about the oil spill. On Facebook, individuals could show their support by liking the LOT's fan page and requesting daily updates on the news feed. Twitter followers received multiple up-to-the-minute news updates. Also, on YouTube, the LOT shared video updates, including interviews of influential individuals across the state (domestic and international leisure and business travelers, state officials, etc.), and posted feature news stories and travel videos from across Louisiana. Flickr allowed the LOT to share an assortment of Louisiana photographs. The LOT also used Blip.fm—internet radio that allowed prospective tourists to easily search for, play, and discover free music from Louisiana that was recommended by state residents. Finally, the video hosting site Vimeo allowed Louisiana residents to share their creative work, along with intimate personal moments of their everyday lives, via video sharing.

The LOT's website provided daily updates on the available areas for sport fishing, promoted 400 of Louisiana's annual festivals, and reminded prospective tourists that Louisiana's coast is made up primarily of wetlands, not beaches, and that a trip to Louisiana can be experienced without any interference from the cleanup efforts in the

Gulf of Mexico. The website provided links and information on how visitors could register to volunteer to help local, regional, and national organizations with the recovery. Additionally, the "top 100 reasons to visit Louisiana" campaign, leveraging the 100th day of the oil spill, asked participants to share their favorite Louisiana experiences on social networking sites using the hashtag #LATOP100.

Other tactics included showcasing the low costs of overnight accommodations in Louisiana during summer travel. Key spokespersons were ready to speak on behalf of the state, including top chef Tom Colicchio and others willing to vouch for Louisiana's seafood. However, most of the media relations tactics consisted of satellite media tours,

Source: www.louisianatravel.com.

opinion/editorial pieces, letters to the editor, media familiarization tours, and an online media center, which was developed as a one-stop shop for all information.

EVALUATION

Within the first two weeks of its response to the crisis, Deveney Communication realized more than 3 million impressions. Additionally, the "top 100 reasons to visit Louisiana" campaign received coverage on MSNBC.com, NBC 33 News Morning Edition (Baton Rouge), and a variety of evening broadcasts across Louisiana. Within its first 24 hours, the #LATOP100 element of the campaign delivered more than 100 mentions on various social networking sites (on average, a mention regarding the topic every six minutes), resulting in more than 37,400 impressions.

In the subsequent weeks, media coverage was also secured in such major publications as the *Chicago Sun-Times*, the *Martha Stewart Living* blog, the *Atlantic*, *Southern Living*, and SeriousEats.com. Letters to the editor appeared in the *New York Times*, the *Palm Beach Post*, the *Seattle Times*, the *Cincinnati Enquirer*, and the *Fresno Bee*. Overall, this publicity achieved more the 78.5 million impressions, including hits on ABC News, CNN's *American Morning*, Fox Business, *The Situation Room With Wolf Blitzer*, and the *Today* show, as well as in *USA Today* and the *Wall Street Journal*. The seafood industry and New Orleans were featured in *Southern Living*'s November food guide issue. From November 1 to 7, 2010, the campaign achieved 107 national, regional, and state television and print articles related to the spill, which was significant as a lead-up to the White House Commission's hearings on November 8, 2010. By the end of this campaign, Deveney Communication helped the LOT achieve 667.5 million impressions.

Source: www.louisianatravel.com.

Perceptions that Louisiana would be significantly affected by the oil spill for at least five years declined by 19% by January 2011, and regionally, perception regarding the extent of the devastation was less than previously expected. Hotels boasted nearly a 13% increase in occupancy in 2010 compared with 2009, and today New Orleans has the eighth-highest hotel occupancy rate among the top 25 markets. Entertainment and recreation spending in New Orleans increased by 11% in 2011 over 2010, and restaurant spending increased by 4.3% over the same time period. In 2011, visitor spending went beyond $10 billion for the first time since 2004.

Finally, New Orleans' tourism industry welcomed 8.78 million visitors in 2011, a 5.6% increase over 2010, spending a record-breaking $5.47 billion. First-time visitors to New Orleans in 2011 were 40.6% of those figures. As of 2015, visitor spending in the state has increased to $11.5 billion, with $7.1 billion of this total spent in New Orleans.

From this case arose some important lessons. First, anticipating the topics and questions from stakeholders was vital, because this allowed us to identify the most credible spokespeople and also gather the most accurate information to train and prep them for adequately managing situations and issues. Another lesson was that messages should be exhaustive and inclusive. Beyond the state and city tourism stakeholders, the campaign included other industries such as commercial fishing and health care. This, at times, was particularly challenging as differences in geographies, industries, and leaders often complicate collaboration.

RACE PIT STOP

Discussion Questions

1. Research played a big role in this particular campaign. How did the research conducted inform the approach of the campaign?

2. The campaign targeted very broad audiences. What other audiences could have been targeted? Are there any secondary audiences that should be considered? Also, this campaign lacked numerical objectives. What could have been reasonable numerical objectives?

3. The Louisiana Office of Tourism made extensive use of particular social media and online platforms throughout the campaign. What other online and social media outlets could the LOT have strategically utilized?

4. Based on the figures presented in the evaluation, do you agree that the campaign was a success? What other ways might the campaign have been evaluated?

Trendlines

Industrial accidents such as the BP oil spill in the Gulf of Mexico can have far-reaching consequences for more organizations than just the company responsible for the leak. For example, the 2014 Freedom Industries' spill of chemicals into the Elk River impacted the water supply for nine counties in West Virginia. Similarly, the Belle Fourche oil pipeline leak in North Dakota in 2016 spilled at least 176,000 gallons of oil into the Ash Coulee Creek.[4] Though neither of these examples received as much media attention as the BP oil spill, they also affected a number of groups, particularly the local communities. From a communications perspective, successfully recovering from an industrial accident calls for a great amount of transparency regarding the cleanup efforts and can require a significant amount of coordination among affected organizations and stakeholders.

While not all communities affected by an industrial accident have a significant tourism industry,

Louisiana and the neighboring states do. Do some research into how the neighboring Gulf Coast states such as Alabama, Florida, and Mississippi handled their communications efforts in the aftermath of the BP oil spill. Did they take the same approach as Louisiana? Were their campaigns more or less effective? Also, do some research on the Elk River and Belle Fourche spills. How did the communication approaches for those campaigns differ from the LOT's approaches regarding the BP oil spill crisis?

REFERENCES

1. The 2011 tourism satellite account: An update. (2011). *Louisiana State University*. Retrieved from http://www.crt.state.la.us/Assets/Tourism/research/documents/2012-2013/2011Louisiana TSA-Final.pdf

2. New Orleans restaurateur Ralph Brennan urges focus on tourism industry impact in BP oil spill recovery. (2010, July 27). *National Restaurant Association*. Retrieved from http://www.restaurant .org/Pressroom/Press-Releases/New-Orleans-Restaurateur-Ralph-Brennan-Urges-Focus

3. The impact of the BP oil spill on visitor spending in Louisiana: Revised estimates based on data through 2010 Q4. (2011). *Tourism Economics*. Retrieved from http://www.crt.state.la.us/Assets/Tourism/research/documents/2011-2012/Oil_Spill_Impacts_201106.pdf

4. Dalrymple, A. (2017, March 23). Oil spill in creek originally underestimated, making it one of the largest in North Dakota history. *Bismarck Tribune*. Retrieved from http://bismarcktribune.com/news/state-and-regional/oil-spill-in-creek-originally-underestimated-making-it-one-of/article_93c58fa0-3d22-554c-a1ae-cfb08b248aee.html

TRANSPARENCY IN THE MIDST OF A BUDGET REDUCTION

Peggy M. Rupprecht, Assistant Professor, Creighton University

SITUATION

Westside Community Schools is a small urban public school district with roughly 6,100 students located in the heart of Omaha, Nebraska. During the 2015–2016 school year, Westside administrators announced the district would face an anticipated budget shortfall of approximately $5 million for the upcoming school year, and announced they would need to make nearly $4 million in spending reductions. Some of those reductions would come through the elimination of staffing and programs.

Some of the proposed cuts included the elimination of programs such as elementary foreign language, replacing the teaching positions with foreign language software programs. Also slated for elimination were enrichment summer school and a culminating research project for Westside High School seniors. Transportation for some students would be reduced; students would now need to live two or more miles from their school to be eligible for free transportation. Several other positions were planned for elimination, including an instrumental music teacher, a drug and alcohol counselor, two school custodians, and one of the high school librarians.

RESEARCH

Research found that in previous years the district balanced its budget primarily by renegotiating vendor contracts, reducing spending on non-salary items, and drawing from cash reserves. The district also eliminated central office administrative positions, cut employee overtime, and reduced substitute teacher costs. However, annual expenses continued to increase, including salaries, health insurance, transportation, and utility costs. Given that 80% of the district's budget consisted of salary and benefits, cuts would need to be made in those areas.

A small team of administrators used a decision-making model to develop strategic objectives on how they would reach budgeting decisions. Some of the priorities included minimizing the impact on instructional programs, limiting the impact on instructional technology, and avoiding adversely affecting the recruitment, hiring, and retaining of quality staff. The district shared these objectives with other administrators along with teachers, staff, parents, and community members. The district asked these groups if the administration had missed anything important, but no other recommendations came from this process.

As the district drew closer to decisions about the proposed budget reductions, the superintendent walked building by building to meet with staff members. At these meetings, he once again outlined the funding challenges and asked teachers, administrators, and other staff members to offer their ideas on ways to reduce district spending, yet maintain quality within the classroom. Some of the ideas that emerged among the various groups—the elimination of elementary foreign language, the elimination of the senior project, and the reduction of infrastructure costs, such as printing and transportation—became part of the proposed budget reductions.

Westside also used the district's historical funding data to build a case for the proposed reductions. Among other things, property valuations, a source of revenue for the landlocked school district, had remained flat for a six-year period. This, coupled with increases in expenses mentioned earlier, resulted in a budget shortfall.

ACTION PLANNING

The goal for this campaign was to educate stakeholders about the district's financial challenges and to involve them in the decision making about budget reductions. Once the district announced the proposed reductions, the leadership wanted to create ample opportunities for public dialogue. Westside Community Schools sought to build trust with its stakeholders through transparency. The district wanted to engage parents and other community members in a two-way conversation, to solicit input, and to make final budget decisions based on that feedback. The administration and board of education (BOE) wanted stakeholders to know the district was hearing them and thoughtfully considering what they had to say.

The district was committed to providing timely information to its stakeholder groups, particularly internal stakeholders (teachers, administrators, and staff) and BOE members. The timeliness, in part, was out of necessity. Decisions about any budget reductions needed to happen by late March/early April. By law, if the district planned to reduce teaching positions, it needed to inform those educators of that decision by mid-April.

Ultimately, the district's communication focused on two key objectives:

- By February 2016, the school district leadership would increase awareness among stakeholders about the funding challenges.

- By March 2016, the district would expand opportunities for community members to provide feedback on the proposed budget cuts.

Additionally, the district would continue its ongoing efforts to share information about the investments the school district was making to enhance the value of a Westside education. Included in those conversations was information about some of the offerings that made the school district unique, and perhaps costlier, such as neighborhood schools, modular scheduling at Westside High School, and the district's K–12 1:1 initiative, which provided laptops for all students in Grades 8–12 and iPads for all students in Grades K–7.

COMMUNICATION

Through an internal newsletter in October 2015, well in advance of any official announcements, the superintendent informed employees that the district would look at staffing as it considered budget cuts. In that piece, he said, "These are not easy discussions and I realize that we are talking about people. However, I need to take a long-term view and maintain a balanced budget for the long-term health of our District."

When the time came to announce the budget reductions in February 2016, the superintendent, finance director, chief financial officer, and communications director met with a reporter from the *Omaha World-Herald* newspaper for an embargoed story on the budget. In the ensuing weeks, the district would work with other journalists, including local affiliate television stations KETV, WOWT, KMTV, and KPTM. High school journalists working at the *Lance* student newspaper and *Westside Wired* online contributed stories about the reductions. The superintendent gathered the district's leadership team to inform them of the proposed reductions; some of these administrators met with employees whose positions were directly impacted by the proposed cuts. At a subsequent public meeting, the Westside administration walked members of the BOE through the proposed cuts.

Following the February BOE meeting, the superintendent sent three email messages through an automated communication system—one to staff, one to parents, and one to key communicators (business leaders and community/opinion leaders)—informing them of the proposed budget reductions and urging them to go to the website for more

Forums with community members were essential to helping with discussing budget reduction information.

Source: Photo by MariSmithPix, https://pixabay.com/en/audience-speech-speaker-1677028/, licensed under CC0, https://creativecommons.org/choose/zero/.

information or to share their feedback. The next day, the superintendent sent a communication to employees, informing them of an informational meeting the following afternoon. Given that the district had roughly 1,000 employees, the superintendent met first with staff and teachers at the secondary level at Westside High School, then with elementary staff and teachers at Westside Middle School. The district sought to assure employees that it would make every attempt to handle staffing reductions through retirements and attrition.

During this time frame, elected BOE members also received many emails and phone calls from constituents, some angry or frustrated by the perception that the district and the board had been hiding budget challenges. To combat this misinformation, the district's communication team provided board members a budget question-and-answer sheet, news articles highlighting past budget reduction discussions throughout the years, and archived meeting minutes in which BOE members addressed the budget issues.

The district also held two forums, one in the morning and one in the evening, for community members to have their questions addressed. Audience members wrote their questions on note cards, the director of communications read the note cards, and the superintendent answered the questions. Audience members were encouraged to write their names and email addresses on the cards; district administrators promised to use those cards to respond to community members if they had unanswered questions.

In terms of digital communication, Westside Community Schools placed a feedback form on the website where community members could share their questions, comments, or concerns. The school district's communications department also used its social media channels—Twitter and Facebook—during the budget discussions, primarily to announce meetings or forums. The superintendent ended the budget discussions with a blog addressing the final reductions and discussing the ways in which the district would move forward. Similar information was shared with employees through the district's employee newsletter.

EVALUATION

The management of this crisis was measured in several ways:

Two months following the budget reduction discussions, Westside Community Schools conducted a communications survey with district parents. The district discovered its message about funding challenges resonated with them. In this 2016 survey, when asked an open-ended question

Message from the Superintendent...

March 25, 2016

The past three weeks have given us an opportunity to reflect on our District as we announced approximately $4 million in budget reductions for the 2016-2017 school year. Following public comment during our Board of Education meetings, question/answer sessions during two town hall forums, and feedback from hundreds of emails submitted through Let's Talk, we announced our budget decisions during the March 21 Board of Education meeting.

As a result of community feedback and further internal discussions, we decided to reinstate the K-12 instrumental music position. With the help of local music leaders, we will take the next school year to study our program as we look for ways to boost enrollment. We also heard concerns from our educators about the use of foreign language instruction software in our elementary classrooms. While we are eliminating elementary

foreign language, we will not replace it with instructional software, as we previously discussed. The other outlined budget reductions remain in place. As a gesture of support and commitment, our senior leadership team also offered to freeze their salaries for a year.

Going forward, we must work very hard to increase our revenue streams by working with the Nebraska Legislature, protecting our commercial property values, and developing partnerships with the Westside Foundation and other community stakeholders. We cannot solve our financial issues through budget reductions alone and must continue to look for ways to generate and increase our revenues.

We hope the outlook will improve through our work with the Nebraska Legislature. As I shared with you a few weeks ago, we are following LB 1067. LB 1067 would eliminate the common

levy for the Learning Community and fund open enrollment students as option enrollment students, similar to the rest of the state of Nebraska, beginning in the 2017-18 school year.

While we must reduce expenses, we cannot stagnate as a District. We must remain competitive with our District's salary and benefits. Research tells us that strong classroom teachers and strong building administrators provide the foundation for academic success. We will do all we can to attract and retain the best and brightest.

Westside has long been known for its excellence and innovation. Whether through personalized learning, authentic problem-solving, or technology integration, we are

Continued on page 2......

Source: Courtesy of Peggy M. Rupprecht and Dr. Blane McCann. Reproduced with permission.

about the biggest challenges facing the school district, 37% of parents who responded to the question used words such as *budget, budget cuts, financial concerns, funding, resources,* and *money* as part of their answer. This compared to 11% of parents who answered the same open-ended question in 2015.

Early in the crisis, parents, students, staff, and community members emailed 270 questions, comments, or concerns through a feedback form on the website. Throughout the month-long budget conversations, feedback from these emails and heavily attended public forums provided the district's communications team valuable insights and allowed the team to evaluate and refine its communication. For instance, when parents emailed with specific concerns about class size, transportation, and the loss of certain programs, the district responded with additional information on its website and through face-to-face conversations with stakeholders.

The in-person and online forums also provided district administrators with information from their stakeholders regarding the proposed budget cuts. As a result of feedback from staff, parents, and community members, some of the initial budget plans were scrapped, such as the proposed elimination of an instrumental music teacher. Stakeholders were also against the purchase of foreign language software, which had been initially suggested as a way to continue an elementary foreign language program; the administration chose to eliminate this elementary program entirely. Through this engagement, district administrators listened to stakeholders' feedback and responded accordingly.

Following the announcement of the final budget reductions at the end of March, the flood of questions and comments to the online feedback form reduced to a trickle. The district received eight questions/comments following the final budget decision; five of them were sent by the same stakeholder.

Ultimately, the district was able to reduce staffing through retirements or attrition. A commitment to communicating and receiving feedback with transparency helped minimize disruption to stakeholders' lives and to the mission of the school district.

RACE PIT STOP

Discussion Questions

1. Throughout all steps in this campaign, the school district tried to involve multiple stakeholders in the decision-making process. How was this transparency beneficial to the district when it came to the communication aspect of the campaign?

2. The campaign was mainly evaluated by comparing the responses to an open-ended

question in 2015 and 2016 about problems the district was facing and the number of queries the district received about the budget. What other ways could the district have evaluated the success of the campaign?

3. The school district determined the campaign to be a success by openly communicating with the community about its funding challenges. Do you think this approach would have been successful in other types of

(Continued)

(Continued)

organizations (e.g., a public corporation or a nonprofit organization) facing either a budget shortfall or decreasing revenues? Why or why not?

4. Organizations engaged in a campaign to manage a crisis tend to have difficulty articulating numerical objectives. Why might this be so? What can public relations people offer as approaches for considering numerical objectives early in a crisis management campaign?

Trendlines

School districts across the country are facing situations similar to those discussed in this case study. Districts from Los Angeles, California, to Austin, Texas, have faced increasingly tight budgets over the last few years. In some cases, these crises come as a result of decreasing support from various state and federal organizations, while in others they might come as a result of a decreasing local population, or decreasing property values and taxes, or the budget funds being diverted elsewhere. For example, the Los Angeles Unified School District in 2017 called for layoffs based on anticipated cuts to federal anti-poverty aid (Title 1) and the costs of expanded health benefits to part-time employees,[1] while Baltimore city schools have seen layoffs each year since 2014 due to continued budget deficits despite the city and state government increasing aid.[2] Regardless of the reason, the districts are forced to make difficult decisions such as laying off teachers and staff or limiting the number of programs or afterschool activities available to students.

Do you think the approach used in this case study would be as effective in a significantly larger school district such as Los Angeles Unified, which has around 60,000 employees and more than 500,000 students? Would the strategies and tactics change? What additional research might be needed?

REFERENCES

1. Blume, H. (2017, June 20). More than 120 layoffs proposed in L.A. school district budget. *Los Angeles Times*. Retrieved from http://www.latimes.com/local/lanow/la-me-edu-los-angeles-schools-layoffs-20170620-story.html

2. Prudente, T. (2017, May 12). Baltimore schools chief proposes up to 300 layoffs to balance district budget. *Baltimore Sun*. Retrieved from http://www.baltimoresun.com/news/mary land/education/k-12/bs-md-ci-city-schools-layoffs-20170512-story.html

A STRATEGIC VIEW: "HURRY UP, THEN WAIT": OLD DOMINION UNIVERSITY'S CRISIS COMMUNICATION RESPONSE TO CRUDE MOVE-IN DAY BANNERS

Brendan O'Hallarn, Lecturer in Communications, Old Dominion University

Giovanna M. Genard, Assistant Vice President for Strategic Communication and Marketing, Old Dominion University

Families dropping students off for the 2015–2016 school year at Old Dominion University (ODU) in Norfolk, Virginia, were greeted by banners offering a welcome that would not ever be found in a higher education public relations manual. Students in off-campus housing hung bedsheets from a balcony with painted messages such as "Freshman daughter drop-off" and "Go ahead and drop off mom, too." The students, who belonged to a fraternity, set off a firestorm of publicity that engulfed the university during the first week of classes.

Banners with crude slogans are not a new occurrence on campuses, and have been dismissed as juvenile pranks. But in an era of social media connectivity, they spread virally. So we took several steps within hours of their discovery. We issued statements from administrators reinforcing ODU's

Source: Old Dominion University. Reproduced with permission.

zero tolerance for sexual assault, denouncing the students' actions, and reaffirming that any student found to have violated the ODU code of conduct would be subject to disciplinary action.

Even before we received news media calls, ODU's Student Government Association released a video on ODU's social media channels, suggesting that the banners reinforced the need for a student-led initiative called "Monarchs Rising Up," empowering students to speak up against sexual harassment and assault in all forms. Viral sharing of the banner photographs and university response reached local television news. The video spread nationally. Because of the amplifying effect of social media sharing—and the way the story prompted curiosity and conversations—the images went around the globe on Facebook, Twitter, and Instagram.

These actions were part of the "hurry up" portion of this crisis response. Soon, our office was flooded with media inquiries and requests for interviews. With each inquiry—from outlets ranging from *Cosmopolitan* to the BBC, CNN, and the *Washington Post*—journalists were directed to ODU's zero tolerance statement. Two days after the banners were discovered, the national fraternity whose students had created the signs suspended its ODU chapter and released this information to the press.

Still, the story spread. Using media monitoring tools, we counted more than 1,000 stories about the banners on Monday through Wednesday following the incident. It became the top trending topic on Facebook. We looked at each media mention, reaching out to journalists who had disseminated incorrect information. Interestingly, by the second day, the tone of the coverage had shifted from outrage about the banners to a broader discussion of this type of behavior on college campuses. Because of ODU's "hurry up" prompt response, some critics questioned whether there had been an overreaction to what those critics perceived as a "dumb joke." In contrast, other regional and national op-ed columnists wrote about sexual harassment and rape culture on college campuses. Other observers suggested ODU was attacking freedom of speech.

This is where the "wait" portion of our crisis response was executed. Each new piece of information provided would create another round of news stories. Instead, we referred reporters to our original statements of response and waited for the story to run its course. Indeed, as news cycles can change quickly, four days after the banner story broke, a shooting of two journalists in southwest Virginia led local newscasts and dominated social media feeds. News media mentions of the banners dropped by 99% in two days (from over 1,000 mentions to fewer than 10).

The value of a few key aspects of crisis communication response was demonstrated in this incident. With a proactive and coordinated response to the discovery of the banners, we were better able to provide material to journalists that reflected the exact tone the university wanted to convey. The value of discretion was also underlined as providing new information was likely to give this story more viral momentum. Media analytic tools were also invaluable, allowing ODU public relations staff to conduct crisis scanning, gauge sentiment, and debunk misinformation before it spread. This was not the way any of us wanted to start the school year. But the collective feeling after the furor over the incident subsided was that its impact could have been greater had we not acted quickly and then deliberately— hurrying up to respond, and then waiting for the story to run its course.

Good morning Monarchs. President John R. Broderick sent the following letter to our campus community on Saturday. Please feel free to share it with the ODU community.

"Dear Colleague:

I am outraged about the offensive message directed toward women that was visible for a time on 43rd Street. Our students, campus community and alumni have been offended.

While we constantly educate students, faculty and staff about sexual assault and sexual harassment, this incident confirms our collective efforts are still failing to register with some.

A young lady I talked to earlier today courageously described the true meaning of the hurt this caused. She thought seriously about going back home.

But she was heartened, she explained, when she saw how fellow students were reacting to this incident on social media. She realized this callous and senseless act did not reflect the Old Dominion she has come to love.

The Student Government Association has recently developed the "Monarchs Raising Up" campaign educating our students on prevention of sexual and relationship violence, bystander intervention, and off-campus responsible behavior. Through video, online and in-person content, we layer education on these topics for all of our students throughout the year. All new freshman just received education this weekend on preventing discrimination and sexual assault in sessions we call "First Class."

Here is a link to a video from our student leaders responding to this event-- just one example of how Old Dominion University students take a stand every day in regards to respecting each other and promoting responsible behavior: https://youtu.be/NC72ruvRtdY

I said at my State of the University address that there is zero tolerance on this campus for sexual assault and sexual harassment. This incident will be reviewed immediately by those on campus empowered to do so. Any student found to have violated the code of conduct will be subject to disciplinary action.

Sincerely,
John R. Broderick
President"

Source: Facebook/@Old Dominion University (2015). Reproduced with permission.

A STRATEGIC VIEW: CONTRASTS IN A CRISIS: FACT-BASED TRADITIONAL MEDIA VERSUS EMOTION-LADEN SOCIAL MEDIA IN THE MIDST OF AN EMPLOYEE STRIKE

Maureen Schriner, Communications Consultant, 531 Media

In my work as a communications consultant, I served as media liaison and spokesperson for a coalition of five Minneapolis–St. Paul health systems that own 14 hospitals with unionized staff. The coalition of hospitals jointly negotiates labor contracts with registered nurses through the Minnesota Nurses Association (MNA) union and with service workers, such as hospital room cleaners, through the Service Employees International Union. The hospitals' approach to communications contrasted sharply with the MNA labor union's approach. This case study of contrast provides an opportunity to assess the strengths and weaknesses of organizations in using traditional and social media during times of crisis. It also offers insight into the influence of messaging, and how groups isolated on social media can develop hostile media perceptions and false consensus effects.

My consulting for the hospitals began in May 2010, as the crisis was transitioning from an internal issue to external publicity. The 14 hospitals renewed union contracts with MNA-represented nurses every three years. Two previous contracts had settled quickly and quietly. But, by 2010, MNA had affiliated with a different national union. The preeminent demand by the MNA for a new contract, advocated by the national union, was for strict nurse-to-patient ratios, based on a law passed in California. The hospitals opposed the ratios as unnecessary added costs, arguing that California hospitals had not improved in quality of care since that state's hospitals needed to hold down costs.

Contract negotiations reached an impasse; by June, MNA members held a one-day strike, involving over 12,000 nurses, which garnered international media attention. In media channels, MNA relied heavily on social media. Its public Facebook page had hundreds of postings by users, most of whom had pseudonyms and self-identified as nurses. MNA also used a blog, Twitter, YouTube, and live-streaming video. News media attended MNA press conferences and followed MNA social media. The messaging approach by MNA emphasized emotions. For example, nurses told tear-filled stories of being unable to care for patients, and the patients suffering as a result. News media initially covered the "horror stories," but stopped when the MNA could not produce actual patients, or family members, to interview.

While the Minnesota Nurses Union relied heavily on social media during a strike, the Twin Cities Hospitals used traditional media to good effect.

Source: Twin Cities Hospitals. Reproduced with permission.

The Twin Cities Hospitals chose to not use Facebook or other social media platforms. Instead, the hospitals' communication focused on traditional media channels: newspaper and radio advertisements, letters and calls to community key influencers, and traditional media relations, with press releases, press conferences, or one-on-one interviews with me as a key spokesperson for the hospitals. We took a fact-based approach; my role in each media interview was to emphasize key messages: that the hospitals were offering nurses generous contracts and opposing strict nurse-to-patient ratios as costly and unnecessary. Messages to media were tailored, based on their needs and requests. For example, television stations were provided a visual graphic showing that Minnesota hospitals, compared to other states, ranked high in quality and safety. The newspaper media, particularly editorial writers, needed more detailed, extensive information, such as full copies of studies on nurse–patient ratios. While TV reporters were seeking brief interviews, the editorial writers engaged in hours-long conversations and information gathering, which involved extensive explanation about labor contracts, hospital policies, and government regulations.

Numerous indicators showed the media agenda, on social and traditional channels, was dominated by the hospitals' messaging. While national and international news media covered the one-day strike by the MNA, they focused on facts offered by the hospitals. On the day of the one-day strike, both the Minneapolis and St. Paul daily newspapers published editorials supporting the hospitals' position. As the hospitals' position continued to dominate media conversations in both traditional and social media, the MNA's communications director disparaged traditional news as being irrelevant and biased, at one point stating, "We don't need the mainstream media to tell our story. We built our whole campaign around social networking—10,000 fans on Facebook and the MNAblog.com gets 8–10,000 hits a day. It's not 1988 anymore." The attacks garnered support on MNA's social media from nurses who shared the hostile media perceptions, but put local reporters on the defense.

When the MNA called for a longer, open-ended strike in July, support from union members began to erode. Hospitals were hearing internally about nurses who planned to cross picket lines. An opposition blog, called "No Strike for Nurses," was started by a registered nurse. The blog garnered news media attention and supportive comments from nurses. As the July open-strike date neared, the MNA suddenly dropped its controversial nurse-to-patient ratios demand and agreed to settle the contract.

In a post-crisis assessment with the hospitals' management teams, we discussed several possible reasons the hospitals' communication approach was successful. In terms of media channels, traditional news and advertising had a broader reach and stronger influence than MNA's social media. The state's largest daily newspaper, the *Star Tribune*, had a weekday circulation of almost 300,000 and Sunday circulation of 1.88 million, compared to the MNA's Facebook page with about 11,000 "likes." News media could readily report the hospitals' fact-based messages, but couldn't confirm the nurse union's emotion-laden stories of patients. The hospitals' ads reinforced our messages.

In sum, the case indicates three lessons of media during crises: First, traditional media still has a powerful reach and influence in advertising and news. Second, fact-based news is easier to report by news reporters than emotion-laden stories. Finally, consistent messaging, tailored to fit media needs, can shape the media agenda on traditional and social media.

8

FURTHER VIEWS IN PUBLIC RELATIONS STRATEGY

Outside of the areas covered in the previous chapters, there are several arenas where public relations operates. This section offers further views on some of those areas including promotion, employee communications, business-to-business communications, public service messaging, and measurement. These efforts reveal that, while not all public relations campaigns necessarily follow a RACE (research, action planning, communication, and evaluation) format, public relations operates best when it is approached in a strategic manner that centers on how the needs and desires of stakeholders must be of the highest consideration.

MAKE 90 SECONDS LAST A MONTH: THE STORY OF THE 84 LUMBER SUPER BOWL COMMERCIAL

Steve Radick, Vice President, Director of Public Relations, Brunner Inc.

SITUATION

Founded in 1956, 84 Lumber Company, headquartered southwest of Pittsburgh, Pennsylvania, is the nation's largest privately held supplier of building materials, manufactured components, and industry-leading services for single- and multifamily residences and commercial buildings. 84 Lumber operates more than 250 stores, component manufacturing plants, custom door shops, custom millwork shops, and engineered wood product centers in 30 states, representing the top 130 markets in the country. 84 Lumber was named one of *Forbes'* Best Midsize Employers in America in both 2016 and 2017 and one of *Forbes'* Largest Private Companies in America in 2016.

For 84 Lumber and its competitors in the building supply industry, sales are driven by the relationships they have with their professional builder customers. To get those professional sales, the company needs to hire people who know the industry. Despite having more than 250 stores across the United States, 84 Lumber's brand awareness was very low outside of southwestern Pennsylvania, where its headquarters is located. Traditional employee recruiting tactics (ads in the classified sections of local papers, posting on job boards, etc.) had been used for years, but if 84 Lumber wanted to attract more top talent to its stores, it had to do something different—something that would attract candidates who may have never considered a career in the industry before. And if you are looking to make a big splash, what better way to do it than on the world's biggest stage? The Super Bowl.

RESEARCH

In January 2017, an annual tracking study was done to understand audience awareness of 84 Lumber and its competitors and better gauge perception and purchase behavior among builders, remodelers, and homeowners. We found that builder material suppliers, such as 84 Lumber, have the lowest national awareness across the board when compared to local lumberyards and big-box do-it-yourself retailers (e.g., Lowe's and Home Depot). We learned that awareness of 84 Lumber was extremely low, especially among our target audience of millennial men. However, our competitive analysis also revealed that 84 Lumber's primary competitors were doing very little marketing, and even less branding. No one outside of the industry even knew who these massive homebuilding supplier companies were. With this information in mind, we viewed the Super Bowl commercial as an opportunity to disrupt the industry.

Many meetings were held with the entire 84 Lumber leadership team to identify the company's needs and risks in this situation. From these meetings, we learned the following:

- The building material category was highly fragmented. The industry needed disruption and new thinking to drive change, ultimately leading to more homebuilding and homeownership.

- The challenge from the client was clear: "I want everyone in the country to know 84 Lumber's name."

- Beyond the high cost and rarity of a 90-second Super Bowl spot, another risk involved in creating such an ad was that, if we were going to tell our story so publicly, we had to anticipate and mitigate criticism from the homebuilding industry, as well as perhaps from the advertising community and consumer public.

ACTION PLANNING

With a budget of about $15 million, the goal of the campaign was to increase brand awareness and position 84 Lumber as an employer of choice. Specifically, our objectives were as follows:

- Increase awareness of the 84 Lumber brand on a national scale by more than 20% within a year of the ad's airing.

- Within 60 days of the ad's airing, increase 84 Lumber employment applications by more than 20,000.

- Within 60 days of the ad's airing, achieve 80 million impressions of the 84 Lumber website.

Our primary advertising target audience was male millennials (ages 20–32). We were looking for people who were not satisfied with their current jobs and were looking for a *career* with training and development to help them succeed. The hope was that this high-profile ad would help create a halo effect, where people at all levels and across all industries began to look at 84 Lumber as an employer of choice. If we were going to launch a recruitment campaign, we knew we had to first explain who 84 Lumber was and what the company stood for. We needed to do something big to put the 84 Lumber name on everyone's radar so that the direct call-to-action recruitment campaign to follow would be effective.

One of the major images of 84 Lumber's Super Bowl ad "The Journey Begins" was a border wall.

Source: M. J. Brunner, Inc. Reproduced with permission.

Figure 8.1 shows the messages for the campaign and the Super Bowl ad "The Journey Begins," which were designed to appeal to our key audiences.

COMMUNICATION

84 Lumber gave final approval on the concept on December 9, 2016, just 44 days before the final commercial had to be sent to Fox for pre-air screening. We did not have the luxury of time or resources; we had only two public relations people working on the account at the time. Our approach had to be focused, agile, and efficient. Therefore, we chose to spend our time on the top-tier media outlets in each of our target categories—marketing trade publications, human resources trade publications, mainstream nationwide news media, and the nearby Pittsburgh news media—and then use the coverage of the ad in those outlets to drive additional coverage elsewhere. For example, we broke the story that 84 Lumber was doing its first ever Super Bowl commercial in *Ad Age* on January 10. That story was then picked up by other marketing trades, involving no additional media

FIGURE 8.1 ■ 84 Lumber Pre–Super Bowl Message Map

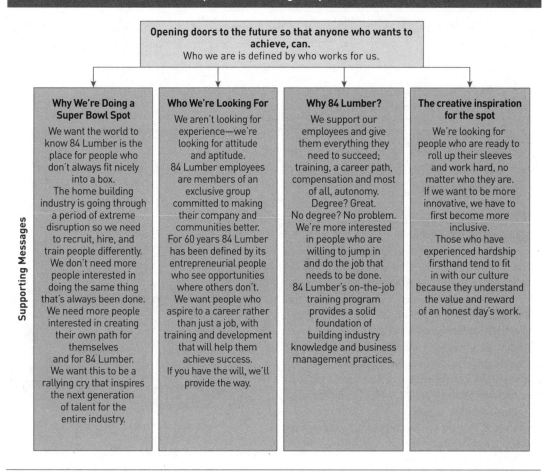

Source: Adapted from M. J. Brunner, Inc. Reproduced with permission.

relations work from us or our client. We then used that article as the primary hook when pitching the story to the Pittsburgh media and the human resources trades. We leveraged this approach throughout the campaign, spending the vast majority of our time working one-on-one with individual reporters and editors at outlets we knew would drive substantial syndication and additional coverage, including such outlets as the *Wall Street Journal*, the *New York Times*, and *Good Morning America*.

A week later, on January 17, *Campaign* magazine broke the story that Fox had rejected our initial ad idea: a concept that included a border wall along Mexico. We knew that we would have to adjust our messaging. We knew that in three short days, President Donald Trump would be inaugurated and that 100% of the media would be focused on that. We chose to ride that wave and become the example for how brands could/should advertise in this highly partisan environment. For the next week, we were portrayed as one of the few brands to run headlong into the political controversy rather than playing it safe. This helped set up 84 Lumber's role as a "disrupter brand."

This was also the time where we began running brand and nonbrand ads for people conducting internet searches for such things as "Super Bowl commercials," "Super Bowl commercials 2017," "best Super Bowl commercials," and similar search terms. We used ad copy to inform searchers about our upcoming commercial as well as who 84 Lumber is, and we took these searchers to our press release about the spot.

The week before the Super Bowl, we achieved two big earned media drivers—articles in the *Wall Street Journal* and the *New York Times*. The *Journal* article appeared on January 31 and focused on the business objective behind the commercial, while the *Times* article, published the next day, included the first leak of the ad's content. We chose to leak the commercial to the *Times* knowing it would drive coverage across all mainstream outlets. Those two articles led directly to articles in *Variety*, *USA Today*, and *Rolling Stone* and, ultimately, to coverage on *Good Morning America*.

Verbiage from the "Journey Begins" advertisement highlights a theme from 84 Lumber's Pre–Super Bowl Message Map: "If you have the will, we'll provide the way."

Source: M. J. Brunner, Inc. Reproduced with permission.

Knowing that we succeeded in driving anticipation for the spot, we leaked the full film to the editors of *Adweek* the Friday before the Super Bowl. Based on their prior coverage, we knew they had a very positive impression of what we were trying to do, so we gave them exclusive access to tell the full story behind the ad as soon as it aired.

EVALUATION

Key evaluation outcomes for the ad included the following:

Brand Awareness

Our own research shows that brand awareness went up more than 25%, and advertising awareness more than doubled. Among those who said they have actually seen the ad, positive sentiment was 63%. Among those who say they are familiar with the brand but have *not* seen the ad, positive sentiment for 84 Lumber was only 42%. This gap suggested that the ad itself had a positive impact, while the *controversy* surrounding its content did not.

Recruitment

In the first 90 days following the Super Bowl, 84 Lumber received more than 35,000 applications: a 191% increase in the number of individuals joining its online talent network where job seekers receive 84 Lumber job updates. In those first three months, 84 Lumber made more than 750 new hires across its network. According to 84 Lumber's human resources department, there has also been a noticeable difference in the types of candidates applying at 84 Lumber since the Super Bowl. Management trainee candidates are consistently more experienced and educated. Recruiters say they no longer have to explain who 84 Lumber is when they are at job fairs. Instead, prospective employees are seeking the company out, not only to apply for a job, but to explain exactly why they are looking for a career at 84 Lumber.

Website Traffic

Ad web analytics included the following:

- 90 million+ impressions
- 337,000+ clicks
- Drove 17% of 84 Lumber's total website traffic from February 2 to 6, 2017

Message Prominence

- *AdWeek* rated 84 Lumber's ad the number-one ad of Super Bowl LI.
- The company's Net Tonality Score (the overall sentiment rating associated with the brand) was up 28%.
- The ad received the number-two Share of Voice among Super Bowl advertisers (second only to Budweiser).
- The ad's 14,000+ media placements were shared more than 150,000 times.
- The ad was the number-one trending video on YouTube during the Super Bowl.
- The ad was the number-four trending topic on Twitter during the Super Bowl.
- The ad received more than 17 million video views across platforms.

The ad received many key industry awards, including the Bronze Lion at the Cannes International Festival of Creativity, the Design and Art Direction Pencil Awards for Cinematography and Editing for Film Advertising, and the 2017 Creative Industries Award for Communications.

RACE PIT STOP

Discussion Questions

1. When considering a major ad buy or campaign, it is important to assess not only competitors, but also the political, economic, societal/cultural, and technological landscape or environment in which the ads/campaign will take place. (This is often referred to as a PEST analysis.) Depending on the current climate, audiences may perceive the brand/company/organization differently than they would otherwise. Given the short amount of time 84 Lumber had to create and promote its Super Bowl ad, do you believe the company did adequate research beforehand? Why or why not? If you had been

assigned to this account and had more time available for research, what else might you have done, and why?

2. How did the media relations campaign help extend the reach and awareness of 84 Lumber? Google or find the media coverage via LexisNexis through your school's library. Were the key messages identified in Figure 8.1 on page 146 apparent in the coverage? Would you assess the overall tone/sentiment of the media coverage toward 84 Lumber as positive, negative, or neutral?

3. Although the 84 Lumber Super Bowl ad garnered impressive evaluation metrics, the cost of the 90-second spot airtime (not counting production) was estimated to be nearly $15 million. If you were asked to defend the ad's return on investment in both the short and long terms, what would you say?

Trendlines

Political campaigns—particularly long presidential ones—can heighten and intensify people's emotions about issues, and the 2016 Donald Trump–Hillary Clinton contest, in which candidate Trump vowed to build a wall with Mexico to keep out illegal immigrants, was no exception. Conduct a Google search to find (a) coverage of the 84 Lumber Super Bowl ad controversy, (b) the Super Bowl ad itself, and (3) the company's "Complete the Journey" video, which completed the ad characters' story. Do you think 84 Lumber's approach may have alienated some of its intended target audience? Is the story line consistent with the company's key messages and values?

If the company had been publicly—rather than family—owned, what additional considerations would have come into play regarding (1) airing a Super Bowl ad and (2) employing this creative concept?

ONE COMPANY'S QUEST FOR QUALITY: FROM BALDRIGE TO LEAN SIX SIGMA

Koji Fuse, Associate Professor, University of North Texas

George Bowden, Senior Marketing Strategist, Freese and Nichols Inc.

Freese and Nichols Inc., headquartered in Fort Worth, Texas, had provided a variety of services to plan, design, and manage public infrastructure projects since 1894. The centennial celebration of its founding, however, occurred in the midst of declining profits throughout the early 1990s. The population of Texas had been growing rapidly, attracting national engineering companies to move into the lucrative market. But Freese and Nichols was doing business as usual: Managers were making questionable decisions to pursue projects unrelated to its core services, and the company was operating as a group of independent engineering consultants without a unified focus on its overall profit success. As a result, the company suffered its first financial loss in 1995 and laid off about 50 of its 300-plus employees. This incident shook employees' confidence in the survival of the company.

Encouraged by its younger owners' insistence on remaining independent, however, the Freese and Nichols management rejected a merger offer and decided in 1996

Freese and Nichols engages its employees in optimizing facilities and operations for clients, such as Dallas Water Utilities' Influent Pump Station, the largest of its kind in the world.

Source: Freese and Nichols. Reproduced with permission.

to embark on a long continuous-improvement journey to earn a prestigious Malcolm Baldrige National Quality Award. The Baldrige Award (inspired by the Japanese Deming Prize given to organizations and individuals worldwide for their contributions to total quality management) has been given to U.S. organizations since 1987 to recognize their achievements in quality improvement. Chief Financial Officer Cindy Milrany recalls that Freese and Nichols' continuous-improvement journey was based on "listening to the voices of our clients and employees, and measuring ourselves against industry benchmarks." After identifying employees and clients as the most important target publics, the company management demonstrated its commitment to continuous improvement through its actions and communications. Employees received a variety of training through an in-house training program called FN (Freese and Nichols) University, heard about the company's financial performance during monthly Quality Day lunch meetings, and strove to achieve their specific individual and team goals accompanied by incentives. Clients benefited from taking FN University's classes and having expert employees as their "trusted advisers." The company also revamped its website to provide clients with more interactive features and service-specific blogs with employee-published postings, used an intranet to allow daily updates and encourage employee feedback, and maintained strong social media presence among clients and industry peers.

All those efforts paid off. The employee turnover rate went lower than average, and both employee and client satisfaction increased. In fact, the company grew to more than 500 employees and enjoyed double-digit growth in revenue and profits from 1997 through 2010, even during a recession. In 2010, Freese and Nichols became the only engineering/architecture company to receive the Baldrige Award.

Of course, Freese and Nichols' quest for quality is here to stay. Continuous improvement, which is the English translation of the Japanese word *kaizen*, does not know its end. It is a philosophy of never-ending searches for process improvement because no such thing as perfection exists. The company is currently implementing the Lean Six Sigma, a method to eliminate waste and thus boost efficiency through statistical control, with the specified defect rate of 3.4 per one million. In August 2015, Freese and Nichols took an analytical approach to understanding negative project variances, which accounted for 7.9%, or $6.7 million, of the firm's overall budget. A negative variance—the difference between the budgeted and actual revenues or costs—can negatively impact the company's profitability. Based on the results obtained by analyzing more than 2,300 projects spanning 2010 to 2015, the company's Lean Six Sigma team developed specific countermeasures that focused on such issues as how to assign team members to projects, develop new project fees, and manage the overall project life cycle. Milrany said the Lean Six Sigma team will communicate a specific path forward to employees as the plan is rolled out.

Freese and Nichols continues to expand its business territories and services, not only across Texas but also into North Carolina, Oklahoma, and Georgia. Looking back, Robert F. Pence, president and CEO between 2002 and 2016 and current chairman of the board, says, "1995 was probably the best thing that ever could've happened to this company." As is the case with successful public relations, Freese and Nichols' continuous improvement journey has used ongoing communication with employees and clients to positively affect employee morale and performance and client service. In 2017, *Fortune* ranked Freese and Nichols as number 10 among the "100 Best Medium Workplaces" in the country and as a "Best Workplace for Millennials."

ADDRESSING INTERNAL COMMUNICATION AT THE U.S. EMBASSY IN KIGALI, RWANDA[*]

Bond H. Benton, Associate Professor, State University of New York–Fredonia

One of the most compelling opportunities I have had in my career was the chance to work with the U.S. State Department on improving internal public relations from 2005 to 2014. The most challenging dimension of this project was work I did with the U.S. Embassy in Kigali, Rwanda, in its attempts to display American support for the country after the 1994 Rwandan genocide. This slaughter resulted in the deaths of an estimated 800,000 people with over 500,000 dying in fewer than 100 days. The primary cause of the genocide was ethnic tension between the Hutu and Tutsi groups.

The United States was singled out for its alleged apathy during this crisis, with observers noting that the country had evacuated its embassy at the onset of the mass killing of Tutsis. After the genocide, and with the support of international forces, the U.S. government invested heavily in an effort to help Rwanda rebuild and reconcile. These efforts culminated in the building of a new multimillion-dollar U.S. Embassy in Kigali, which opened in 2008. The facility, which houses consular services and outreach programs, also serves a symbolic function, suggesting permanence and vigilance in the American relationship with the country.

A key element of the U.S. initiative in Rwanda was staffing. U.S. diplomatic posts employ large numbers of local employees to assist American officers in creating programming appropriate for local populations. Internal divisions and tensions among staff (the local workforce included Hutu and Tutsi employees), however, had compromised the success of this project. Beyond internal ethnic and tribal tension, cultural differences and

---

[*]Portions of this essay appeared in the October 2016 edition of the Public Relations Society of America's *Tactics* publication.

President George W. Bush visiting dancers at the opening of the new U.S. Embassy in Kigali, Rwanda, in February 2008.

Source: www.whitehouse.archives.gov.

mistrust created serious difficulties between the Rwandans and their American supervisors. Given the public face the embassy presents for Rwanda, these tensions risked undermining U.S. efforts to promote reconciliation.

Through anonymous online surveys of staff, I discovered that misunderstandings were frequently the source of perceived hostility and incompetence. For example, the American tendency to ask, "How are you?" without showing interest in the reply was a source of much confusion for Rwandan staff. Another source of internal tension was the frequency with which various Rwandan groups requested days off to attend family funerals. I found out from Rwandans that if a third-cousin-twice-removed dies, one is required to attend the funeral and offer assistance to the family. Failure to do so could mean the community would implicate you as *being the reason the person died!*

To attempt to address misunderstandings between constituencies, I developed a series of open communication sessions comprising local staff and American officers. These regularly scheduled sessions allowed for safe exploration of existing grievances and provided a starting point for ongoing conversations about openness, inclusion, and teamwork. Then, I assisted in the development of a program that included each of the following:

- *Client Service Simulations:* I constructed a series of role-play events based on the public relations activities of the embassy. The simulations were based on the cultural tendencies of both Americans and Rwandans. Americans, for example, generally want information to be explicitly given and business to be transactional. Rwandans, however, generally want communication to be less direct and client communication to be more relational. Adapting these role-play activities based on cultural preferences improved understanding of internal communication.

- *Together Towers:* In symbolic reference to the newly built U.S. Embassy, we created diverse teams and gave them each a roll of adhesive tape and cotton swabs. With only these materials, teams were instructed to build the tallest "tower" possible. The exercise encouraged the collaboration and transparency necessary for cohesive public imaging of the embassy's mission.

After completing these sessions, internal evaluation from 50 participating employees revealed an overall 3.8 on a 4-point effectiveness scale. Unfortunately, subsequent performance evaluations in the months after the program showed no sustained improvements due to lingering issues related to organizational and cultural communication.

A clear implication is that cultural tensions, especially those as pronounced as Rwanda's, are not likely to be remedied by a program with limited duration and scope. Additionally, while there was much initial enthusiasm for the better understanding of cultural differences, building on that understanding appears to have been difficult. Further compromising program effectiveness was the power imbalance of participating members. My immediate supervisors in this project were high-ranking American staff. They had requested the chance to participate in group activities and in open communication sessions. I concurred with their wishes despite serious concerns. By placing American supervisors in open communication sessions with the very people they supervised, the openness of the communication sessions was likely compromised.

The lesson learned was quite clear—I had probably overpromised in my attempt to secure the contract for services. In both my heart and my head, I knew that such profound cultural differences were not going to be mitigated with audits, discussion sessions, and group activities. Yet I wanted the opportunity to participate in the program and, therefore, overstated the effectiveness of such activities to secure this opportunity for the State Department. Keeping client expectations reasonable, especially when you *really* want to work with a specific client, is a lesson that public relations practitioners should continue to reflect upon.

Ultimately, the key takeaway from working on a multinational public relations project is the need to be realistic about *time*. Cultural and logistical issues cannot be managed quickly or tidily. Organizations need to consider time and create clear expectations for all constituencies. Budgeting for time, and allowing for a more substantial period of adjustment, must be part of all international public relations activities.

TENNECO BUILDS EMPLOYEE ENGAGEMENT THROUGH RECOGNITION

Keith Burton, Principal, Grayson Emmett Partners

We live in a time when people are simply too busy—overwhelmed with work, gagging on data, and starving for information. We multitask while taking conference calls, race through emails, or use a text or voice message as our proxy when a face-to-face discussion is more important. Not surprisingly, in 2014, Tenneco Inc.—a company that designs, manufactures, and distributes products and technology solutions for cars, commercial trucks, and off-highway equipment—looked at employee survey results and found that employees were concerned about receiving recognition. Tenneco wanted to get a better understanding of employees' concerns. Over three months, it conducted focus groups with more than 1,000 front-line managers and hourly employees, and one-on-one interviews with 40 executive leaders and plant managers in 18 global locations in the Americas, Europe, and China (facilitators used a common discussion guide and led the interviews spoken in the native languages). In most locations, lack of employee recognition at all levels rose to the surface as a global theme, especially valuing employee contributions and acknowledging employees who go above and beyond the expectations of their jobs to deliver for their employer. Tenneco launched an employee communication campaign, called TEN10, that was designed to do the following:

- Create a unified global recognition program involving all Tenneco employees.

- Celebrate those who embody Tenneco's Shared Values.

- Incentivize performance and instill a sense of pride.

- Build the reputation internally for a credible, authentic program that could be sustained.

Kicked off in April 2015, with a total budget of approximately $275,000, the campaign encouraged employees to nominate their coworkers for embodying one or more of Tenneco's 10 Shared Values. The "TEN10 Program Package"—a tool kit featuring an overview of the program, key messages, a timeline of activities, a PowerPoint presentation for leaders, a "frequently asked questions" guide, and communication templates for use in plants and offices—was distributed to senior leaders and managers. More than 7,000 nominations were submitted. Local leaders reviewed these nominations to identify 1,000 local winners for the first phase of recognition, who were honored during the global Month of Celebration held at approximately 100 plant and office locations in September 2015. During this month, facilities focused on Tenneco's growth, history, legacy, and shared values; the celebrations were publicized in the local communities through events held in plants and offices where employee nominees were recognized.

For the second phase of recognition, facility leaders selected an individual or team to represent their facility. Then, regional human resource directors reviewed the names to identify 60 semifinalists. Next, individual members of the Executive Strategy Group provided their recommendations for the top 10 winners, with the final decision made by Tenneco's chairman and CEO. These 10 individual winners, along with a top team winner, were unveiled on a global all-employee town hall webcast, and the winners were honored in their locations. As part of the celebration plan, the company's chairman and CEO then visited the work location of each of these honorees so as to recognize winners in front of their families and peers. The diverse group of winners included individuals from China, Spain, South Africa, Poland, Mexico, the United States, and India, ranging from front-line workers to managers.

Source: Tenneco Inc. Reproduced with permission.

Tenneco employees recognized in India as part of the TEN10 campaign.

Source: Tenneco Inc. Reproduced with permission.

TEN10 has met every objective the company set: It has proven to be a successful employee recognition program involving Tenneco employees worldwide, celebrating those who embody the company's shared values, and providing education and reinforcement of these values in ways that celebrate local cultural needs and language requirements. As a peer-driven program, TEN10 has also increased overall employee engagement levels, with close to 25% of the employee population being nominated as part of the program.

BEATING THE "BIG THREE": PUBLICIZING FOX TV NETWORK'S 1987 DEBUT

Jack Breslin, Associate Professor, Iona College

How do you publicize the launch of a new TV network of small, upper-channel broadcast stations covering less than 75% of the nation's TV households against the established "Big Three" networks, ABC, CBS, and NBC?

That was the challenge a small group of veteran network publicists and energetic public relations newcomers tackled in the spring of 1987 to debut the fledging Fox Broadcasting Company. Crammed into Trailer 761 on the 20th Century Fox movie lot in Los Angeles, we combined traditional publicity campaign strategies with a lot of energy, creativity, and plain luck.

As I tell my students, the secret to job hunting is networking. A former NBC colleague just hired at Fox pitched me to his boss. Having handled the first three years of NBC's *Late Night With David Letterman*, I was hired to publicize Joan Rivers's late-night show.

Meanwhile, the Fox public relations team focused on the launch of five Sunday night shows and four Saturday shows by generating media attention for the shows, the stars, and the Fox network brand. No one had successfully launched a new TV network since ABC some 30 years ago, so there were no case studies or campaign models to follow.

Fox's approximately 80 affiliates were mostly small, upper-channel operations that struggled against stronger ABC, CBS, and NBC stations. With established stars and seven-night lineups, the "Big Three" giants enjoyed more than 200 affiliates each and larger publicity staffs in New York and Los Angeles.

In addition to Fox's unknown young talent were three established stars: George C. Scott, Patty Duke, and Chuck Connors. While they generated substantial publicity for their shows' debuts, would older stars attract and hold Fox's younger target audiences?

Fox quickly realized that we needed to establish our own younger stars identified with our brand. Along came the first three Fox sensations—actor Johnny Depp of *21 Jump Street*, the Bundys of *Married . . . With Children*, and Bart Simpson of the animated series *The Simpsons*.

Depp's growing popularity, especially among key young advertising demographics, led to several high-profile media breaks. At a December promotional event, "Fox Feeds the Homeless," thousands of screaming teenaged girls nearly shut down the Sherman Oaks (Los Angeles) Galleria over Depp and the other *21 Jump Street* cast members.

A typical advertisement announcing the arrival of the new Fox television network in 1987, this one featured Tracey Ullman.

Source: Photo uploaded by Alan Light, https://commons.wikimedia.org/wiki/File:Tracey_Ullman_-_rehearsal.jpg, licensed under CC BY 2.0, https://creativecommons.org/licenses/by/2.0/deed.en.

Spun off from *The Tracey Ullman Show* (Fox's first Emmy winner), *The Simpsons* debuted in December 1989 with a much-needed midseason publicity blitz, including newsmagazine covers.

In addition to pitched media interviews, our early publicity efforts capitalized on events, such as the Sunday night launch party, the Television Critics Association press tour, affiliate-generated cast appearances, and a multicity integrated communications campaign called "The Fox Tune-In Tour."

Fox's top publicity coup was totally unexpected, however. On March 2, 1989, the *New York Times* ran an inaccurate front-page story about a Michigan woman who allegedly convinced "several of the nation's largest advertisers" to pull their spots from the Fox comedy series *Married . . . With Children.* The resulting national media feeding frenzy gave the show saturation publicity exposure—and ratings.

What did we learn? What would we do differently today? As one colleague, now a network public relations executive, remembered, "It was all trial and error. It still is. I would not trade the experience for anything."

Another colleague, now a merchandising executive for TV and film, recalled what he would do differently: "We were changing hubcaps at 85 miles an hour. I wouldn't have been so damn concerned with what the talent, colleagues, management thought about anything—and I definitely would have 'hung up' more often on the talent's arrogant outside public relations counsel."

What can a public relations student learn from Fox's launch publicity experience? "How to become a 'maverick marketer,'" said this merchandising executive, who emphasized being "creative, determined, and contrarian."

MY PRESS NEEDS CHALLENGE: CREATING A BRAND IN A MATURE MARKET

Allison Weidhaas, Assistant Professor, Rider University

SITUATION

The clamshell is a press that derives its name from its clam-like function. When the press closes together, the force of the machine allows it to perform a die cut or press foil onto a flat material to create a high-impact design. Based on the clamshell's ability to complete many different types of jobs, U.S. factories purchased these presses in record numbers from the 1950s to the 1990s. As technology advanced, industry experts forecasted that the clamshell press would become obsolete. Today, however, most facilities that perform die cutting still own at least one clamshell, and some larger manufacturing plants literally have lines of them.

MY PRESS NEEDS LLC
Reliability backed by integrity. Guaranteed.

As a relatively new player in an established industry, My Press Needs LLC of Tampa, Florida, wanted to build a brand in a highly competitive market segment with its high-quality clamshell at a higher price point. By building a quality press, this company intended to address two needs of people who cut products: (1) quicker productivity per job run so as to increase revenues and (2) a better ability to cut a wide range of hard materials, like plastics.

Manufacturing plants in a variety of industries purchase the Crest Clamshell, a machine capable of die cutting, foil stamping, and embossing a variety of materials. The Crest Clamshell can cut out decals, apply shiny foil to a birthday card, cut out a life-sized action figure to display at a movie theater, or cut out the plastic loyalty tags many people attach to their key chains.

The challenge is that a clamshell, a press technology that closes like a clam, represents older technology, while newer machines that feature lasers tend to get more attention by both consumers and the media. My Press Needs, a small business with a high-end clamshell press, needed to build a brand and create awareness for the benefits of its product versus other clamshell-style presses that sold at half the price.

RESEARCH

It is not uncommon, especially in a business-to-business public relations case, for a public relations practitioner to learn an entirely new industry in a relatively short period of time. To better understand the client's public relations needs, we used a "Listen, Watch, and Read" approach to gathering information.

Listen

This started by listening to the company's goals. What would the company consider a success? Its main focus was to grow a business. Similar to many small businesses, the managers focused their attention on activities that directly affected the organization's bottom line because they needed sales to survive as a small business. The management team set the goal to double the previous year's sales.

When public relations people listen to a company's plans, this conversation only gives the public relations person one side of the story. Public relations people also need to listen to what customers want and find a way to marry the two needs. To learn what customers needed, we spoke with people who bought the Crest Clamshell and asked: Why did you buy the Crest? Does the press do anything different from similar-style presses? What other types of machines do you own? Would you buy another Crest, and why? We found the following:

- Customers bought the Crest because it fulfilled a need, such as reducing their setup times; cutting more difficult materials than their previous press could handle; or updating older, unsafe equipment, and because they were impressed by the heavy-duty construction of the Crest.

- Customers cited the primary difference between this and other presses was this machine's ability to handle more difficult jobs that required either more precision or, in many cases, more tonnage to cut through difficult materials, such as plastics.

- Many of the customers owned other manufacturers' clamshell presses, and they reported they were satisfied with their Crest purchase and, if the need presented itself, would consider buying another Crest.

Watch

To better understand how people use the product in a production environment, we watched how people used this type of machine to determine what challenges they ran into. We found that the process is time intensive. The Crest, and other clamshell presses, requires an operator to physically hand-feed and cut one sheet at a time. By watching the entire process from start to finish, someone can learn that while the cutting action appears simple, an operator can often spend several hours getting a machine to cut the material just right.

People purchase a clamshell-style press because it offers faster setup times than alternative methods, which makes the clamshell press ideal for the short- to medium-run jobs frequently found in today's fast-paced, just-in-time environment. By watching the number of jobs moving onto and off of a press, one also learns the target market for a clamshell: customers who run jobs of between 100 and 2,500 sheets. These jobs can include decals, customer loyalty cards, and many other products that people need in smaller quantities, while alternative-style presses, such as hydraulic and roll feed presses (and even some laser presses), target larger job runs, such as cereal boxes or other mass-marketed consumer goods.

Since customers use the clamshell press for many jobs within a single workday, the ability to quickly set up this press is an important selling feature. Yet, even within the clamshell press segment, setup times vary widely based on the type of job, the operator's experience, and the quality of the press. For example, Crest customers report an average of 10- to 15-minute setup times, while other low-cost presses can easily take over an hour on even a simple job with a trained operator.

Read—Surveying Industry Publications

We reviewed magazines and journals, including the *Specialty Graphic Imaging Association (SGIA) Journal* and *Paper, Film & Foil Converter*, to understand better each of the different industry segments (graphic overlay, labels, etc.) that could use the Crest Clamshell. We also reviewed competitors' websites to examine their key messages. Several competitors included an inexpensive, clamshell-style press in their product portfolio, but often highlighted their other technologies. Additionally, from this information, we determined that (1) many of the articles discussed the time and effort required to get a press ready to run and (2) several of the competitors touted price, often termed as "value," rather than focusing on the capabilities or benefits of their products.

ACTION PLANNING

How do we increase the sales of a high-priced item that, to some, may appear dated? The answer was to communicate that a higher-priced item fulfills some unmet need. In this case, the research showed clamshell press operators spent a significant amount of time setting up the lower-priced or old, worn-out presses. This process, referred to as "make ready," costs a company time and money. Specifically, *make ready* refers to the process of adjusting or preparing the press to run the job. For example, if an operator needs to "kiss cut" decals, the operator must adjust the press to gently "kiss" through the decal portion, but not cut through the back lining. This requires adjusting the depth of cut, and the amount of time this adjustment takes depends on both the operator's skill and the quality of the machine. The process, which in some cases can take several hours, costs a company money both in the time spent by the operator to fine-tune the adjustment and in ruined material.

Objectives

- Increase sales for the Crest by 100% by the end of October 2007.

- By 2007–2008, increase brand awareness by 30% among our target audiences that Crest is a "No More Make Ready" clamshell.

- Businesses always want more opportunities to get in front of customers. In this case, the company wanted 130% growth in customer inquiries. It is important to recognize that not every inquiry results in a sale, but by increasing the number of inquiries, we increase the number of potential sales.

The job above was "kiss cut" on the Crest Clamshell. The top board, known as a die, includes the rubber and knife needed to cut the job. The press must cut through the adhesive layer but leave the backing intact so that one can later remove decals from the sheet. This job requires a specific amount of force that must be applied delicately, known as kiss cutting.

Source: My Press Needs LLC. Reproduced with permission.

Strategies

To meet the objectives, we focused on two distinct audiences:

Primary Target Audience

- *Die Cutters of Plastics:* While customers use the Crest to cut a wide range of substrates (i.e., a layer of material that rests under another layer), we focused on those who cut plastics because that substance is one of the most difficult to cut on a clamshell, and the Crest excels in this area. We decided to highlight the Crest's ability to kiss cut decals (or half cut—cutting through the decal, but leaving the liner or backing intact). We used the key message of "No More Make Ready."

Secondary Target Audience

- *Current Crest Customers:* We needed these individuals to champion our product and discuss the benefits. We emphasized our partnership with our customers, how we worked to support their needs.

COMMUNICATION

The tactics included the following:

Case Studies: One of the tactics that naturally flowed from our research included creating online case studies that highlighted how individuals used the Crest Clamshell to achieve results. By setting up a simple format of problem, solution, and results, we told a story of how individuals used these presses to solve a problem. The case studies allowed us to exhibit real-world applications and helped to humanize a large, impersonal machine.

Media Relations: We specifically targeted publications read by people who purchase and use clamshells. We developed press releases and also pitched bylined articles to position our company leaders as experts in the clamshell market. Articles that ran in these publications helped us gain third-party credibility as industry experts for clamshells. For example, an article that ran in the *SGIA Journal* titled "No More Make Ready" allowed us to offer usable tips to any clamshell press operator, establishing credibility for our statement about eliminating make ready, and positioning My Press Needs' founder as an industry leader.

Dave Mussi (right), a clamshell service provider, conducts operator training on the Crest Clamshell. A public relations campaign helped increase its sales by 300%.

Source: My Press Needs LLC. Reproduced with permission.

Advertising: We developed a timeline advertisement that showed the company's commitment to the clamshell across the years—this appeared in the International Association of Diecutting and Diemaking/Foil & Specialty Effects Association (IADD/FSEA) Odyssey trade show materials, in publications *The Cutting Edge* and the *Printing Equipment Guide*, and on our website. The timeline emphasized longevity, leadership, and the organization's exclusive focus on developing clamshell products.

Industry Events: An important part of this campaign also included gaining credibility by participating in industry events. During this campaign, we exhibited at SGIA and the Odyssey show, events that attract those interested in both die cutting and foil stamping. Prior to the shows, we pitched the idea that our company spokesperson could discuss "No More

Make Ready." At the SGIA show, My Press Needs' founder spoke in a lecture-style environment with pictures and props to explain key points. At the Odyssey show, the founder also offered a live demonstration of the Crest Clamshell where attendees learned how to reduce make ready while setting up a complicated job to cut decals. Attendees watched the demonstration from a packed row of bleachers, and a video camera taped the entire process.

EVALUATION

Often the best gauge of a communication plan's success is whether or not the company achieves its goals. In this case, the company wanted to double its sales. In the year we started this campaign, sales for the Crest Clamshell tripled. In 2006, My Press Needs sold five Crest Clamshells. In 2007, it sold 19 presses, almost four times the number of Crests sold the year before.

We also developed increased awareness for the Crest as a "No More Make Ready" Clamshell. We achieved our goals, which we measured by increased product inquiries. Product inquires typically came from trade shows, phone calls, and the internet. Initially, our key message of "No More Make Ready" was received with skepticism. People asked if the Crest could reduce their make ready. These customer inquiries showed (1) we reached our target audience (their responses showed they heard our message) and (2) we properly identified a need.

Customers helped us by offering their feedback on the reasons they selected the Crest, and we forged ongoing relationships with these customers. These relationships benefit both parties because companies and public relations practitioners must constantly stay engaged to understand evolving needs and trends. It helps customers because it starts a conversation and often means that customers talk to us about challenges with new materials or trends in their business, such as an increase in large-format jobs. Now, 10 years later, we find that customers went beyond saying they would purchase another Crest; we estimate that about 30% of Crest customers own more than one machine, some with as many as five Crests on their production floor. This proves that customers will purchase a high-quality item, if the company communicates to the right audiences with messages that address their needs.

RACE PIT STOP

Discussion Questions

1. As a business-to-business campaign, this case study emphasized a significant amount of research. Why would research be especially essential for this kind of campaign?

2. While this campaign provided several objective measurables, the evaluation section did not specifically address data points for each one. Take a look again at all the objectives for this campaign. How would you propose measuring each one?

3. In an increasingly online world, individuals can now send invitations and cards via emails or social media. What kind of challenges does this present for My Press Needs? What

(Continued)

(Continued)

would you recommend the company do to meet these challenges?

Trendlines

Business-to-business (B2B) public relations presents some particular challenges. Edelman public relations advises that the best B2B public relations focuses on "authentic engagement" that emphasizes "customers' shared values." The firm goes further by pointing out that a company engaged in B2B communications must "go beyond the functional benefits and tap into emotional storytelling."[1] These observations appear to be a good fit for small businesses engaged in B2B public relations; the public wants to believe in small businesses. A 2017 Gallup poll revealed that 70% of Americans have confidence in small businesses, the highest number among 14 major institutional groups (labor, church, banks, etc.).[2] Still, the country still sees 80% of all new small businesses fail within one year.[3] How could Edelman's observations about engagement and meaningful storytelling help small businesses engage in effective B2B and reduce their risk of going out of business?

REFERENCES

1. B2B marketing. (2018). *Edelman*. Retrieved from https://www.edelman.com/expertise/b2b-marketing

2. Newport, F. (2017, June 26). Americans' confidence in institutions edges up. *Gallup*. Retrieved from http://news.gallup.com/poll/212840/americans-confidence-institutions-edges.aspx

3. Dishman, L. (2017, June 30). This is the state of small business failure in the U.S. *Fast Company*. Retrieved from https://www.fastcompany.com/40435072/this-is-the-state-of-small-business-failure-in-the-u-s

A STRATEGIC VIEW: #WHATIDIDINSTEAD: A SOCIAL MEDIA RATHER THAN SOCIAL NORMS APPROACH TO CURB TEEN DRINKING

Kimberly Field-Springer, Assistant Professor of Communication, Berry College*

In the spring of 2016, Floyd Against Drugs (FAD), a nonprofit located in rural northwestern Georgia, approached a public relations cases and campaigns class and requested

**The author acknowledges the work of Nicholas Fischer, Jessica Bozeman, Allyson Cole, Travis Helton, and Mackenzie Ross.*

assistance with campaign planning aimed to discourage underage drinking. FAD received a $625,000 grant from the White House Office of National Drug Control Policy. FAD, in order to satisfy criteria for the grant, was required to research, develop, implement, and sustain a "positive social norms" media campaign with the collaboration of local partnerships (e.g., schools, businesses, and governmental agencies). A positive social norms approach aims to increase already held attitudes among both teenagers and their parents who believe that drinking is not a socially acceptable behavior or the norm. A typical positive social norms message, for example, would report that 9 out of 10 students do not need alcohol to have fun.

The only problem was that one of the stakeholders, from the Council on Alcohol and Drugs, imposed restrictions upon the campaign research process. Rather than offering teenagers a space to share their own experiences about what messages might be successful, the class was asked to test preexisting positive social norms messages relying on traditional print media for dissemination. Contributing to the problem was the hiring of a new FAD director who came from law enforcement, not public relations. The new FAD director, however, wanted to know directly from local youth what messages they felt would work to persuade their peers to refrain from underage drinking. In

Source: Courtesy of Mackenzie Ross and Kimberly Field-Springer. Reproduced with permission.

this case, students in the class were answerable to two stakeholders who held conflicting opinions about how to plan, implement, and sustain a campaign.

In order to meet the needs of both stakeholders, the class designed three traditional posters with positive social norms messages (e.g., "92% of you have fun without alcohol") but included #WhatIDidInstead, an interactive, social media campaign component. Additionally, a focus group, consisting of six local teens ranging from 13 to 18 years old, was conducted. Three of the participants were male, and three of the participants were female. The participants were asked to review the posters and circle what they liked with a blue pen and circle what they did not like with a red pen.

Three out of the six participants circled the positive social norms messages with the red pen. When asked to elaborate why they did not like the message, students said, "I don't really believe this part is true. Peer pressure is real"; "These are the same facts/statistics we've been hearing. It has become mundane and it doesn't resonate with me at all"; and "But the other [percentage who drink] are really loud and open about all the fun they've been having [while drinking]. They seem like the majority." There was an overwhelming negative response to the positive social norms statistics. One teenager even commented, "It doesn't deter me from making bad decisions. It makes me want to have fun [by drinking]." Four out of the six participants circled the #WhatIDidInstead social media component with the blue pen. When asked to elaborate about why they liked the social media component, students said, "I think the hashtag can promote a healthier way to have fun"; "It would be cool to see people tweeting this"; and "If you want to reach teenagers, you have to use social media."

Following the focus group, the class recommended listening to the voices of local teenagers by creating a programmatic campaign utilizing a social media platform. Students in the cases and campaigns class recommended scheduling, in advance, at least three social media posts per week led by a FAD employee or volunteer student leader selected by FAD. They also suggested assigning an administrator from FAD to monitor the feed in case of a crisis because of the uncontrolled nature of social media platforms. Students also encouraged posts to include a combination of text, photos, and/or videos of local teenagers having fun without the use of alcohol. Each post should contain the Twitter hashtag specific to the campaign and employ other social media platforms like Instagram to increase cross-promotion.

In order to measure success, FAD teenage representatives can organize and measure social media reach, impressions, and engagement by recording the number of views, number of posts, and number of likes, comments, shares, and retweets. This information can be recorded using or creating a social media management system. Since our work with FAD, its board cut ties with the outside agency that originally placed constraints upon the campaign planning process. The new FAD director used the feedback we collected from local teens, and is getting ready to launch the social media campaign, #ItsNotJustAFAD.

A STRATEGIC VIEW: DRIVING BEHAVIOR CHANGE THROUGH PUBLIC RELATIONS: HOW EARNED MEDIA LEAD CONSUMER DECISION MAKING ABOUT MEDICARE

Mark Weiner, CEO, PRIME Research Americas

One of the most vexing challenges facing marketing and communications executives today is planning, managing, and quantifying return on investment (ROI). However, when it came to the Medicare Open Enrollment (OE) season, the Centers for Medicare and Medicaid Services (CMS) research team, working with PRIME Research, set out to deliver high returns from a campaign that combined both paid and earned media (or publicity) by

- planning for ROI from the beginning;

- setting objectives that were meaningful, reasonable, and measurable;

- deploying strategic investments through tactical channels with the highest potential;

- quantifying a solid rate of return based on how the target audience behaved as a result of the message.

Source: www.cms.gov.

In this way, the CMS team overcame territoriality and disjointed marketing communication to become one of very few organizations to successfully link communications output with behavioral outcomes and meaningful business results.

CHALLENGE/OPPORTUNITY

Each year during OE season, CMS encourages Medicare beneficiaries to review and update their health and prescription drug plans for the coming year. However, beneficiaries encounter a complex task when they select their Medicare coverage during OE. These choices can influence the doctors they see, the types of drugs they receive, and the costs of their medical care for the coming year. All of this can have a significant impact on their health and financial situation. In addition, Medicare consumers are frequently bombarded with conflicting messages from multiple sources, including health insurance companies (whose television ad campaign expenditures dwarf that of CMS), friends and family members, doctors, and pharmacists—each and all of which increase the likelihood of misunderstanding and confusion. It is no wonder that many beneficiaries often choose the path of least resistance by doing nothing.

The Centers for Medicare and Medicaid Services and PRIME Research worked to measure how Open Enrollment season messages were effectively communicated to seniors.

Source: www.cms.gov.

Furthermore, because the government agency needed to display cost efficiencies, it was vital that CMS determine the effectiveness of its outreach and learn which efforts best motivated consumers to respond to the primary call to action: comparing and reviewing their plans during OE.

The campaign challenge/opportunity was to develop a research program that could gauge such standard metrics as the following:

- Opportunities for beneficiary exposure to OE communications compared to previous years' totals

- Target audience awareness of paid television compared to previous years

- Beneficiary knowledge of OE

- Earned media coverage compared to previous years

- The relative impact of paid and earned media tactics to determine which most efficiently communicated key CMS messages

OBJECTIVE

The CMS team's objective was to design and implement a research program to create and ensure key messages broke through the clutter and impacted consumer behavior during a brief OE period (October 15–December 31) in 2010. But more importantly, the research program had to measure the relative impact of paid and earned media tactics to determine which most efficiently communicated key CMS messages, and do so within the confines of standard tools for data collection.

STRATEGY

The key research strategies were communication and collaboration. Too often, research teams craft tracking studies without thoughtful consideration of whether or not the surveys accurately gauge all elements of campaign outreach. Similarly, traditional, social, and digital media monitoring and analysis tools tend to reside independently of marketing evaluation approaches. So, before any research began, the CMS team discussed how we could best work together to develop a holistic set of key metrics.

EXECUTION

The Centers for Medicare and Medicaid Services conducted telephone tracking studies immediately prior to the campaign in November 2010 ($N = 1,019$) and immediately following the campaign in January 2011 ($N = 1,034$). Through a partnership with PRIME Research, CMS obtained media analyses from early October through the end of December 2010. Once all research concluded, CMS and PRIME Research explored how to combine the data into one data set. Thanks to the team's planning at the start of the campaign, data linkage at the regional level was simple and straightforward.

RESULTS

Despite the unique challenges facing the OE campaign, post-campaign evaluation research confirmed that it successfully achieved a quantifiable outcome among its target audiences. Specifically:

- Beneficiaries' exposure to OE communications increased 11% over 2009, with 64% reporting they had seen, read, or heard information about OE, and there was a threefold increase of OE knowledge from pre- to post-campaign assessment.

- Awareness of the OE television ads increased by 6% compared to the previous year over the same time period.

- Those aware of the OE television ads were more likely to have either reviewed their Medicare plans for changes or compared their plan with others. Among those who recalled OE ads, 68% reported having reviewed their coverage.

- By the end of the campaign, almost 88% of respondents were aware that Medicare has an OE period.

The earned media results were also positive:

- The combined earned media impressions reached nearly 3 billion for print, social, digital, and broadcast clips, far surpassing previous campaign totals.

- News coverage and social media conversations during the campaign were overwhelmingly positive and factual.

Most importantly, the post-campaign evaluation program was able to show that exposure to both paid and earned media significantly improved the odds of taking the desired behavioral actions (reviewing/comparing plans) during the OE period, and the effects of earned media were found to be particularly robust. Even after controlling for exposure to paid media and a variety of demographic and decision-making variables, beneficiaries who reported exposure to public relations through earned media coverage about OE were 2.3 times more likely to adopt the campaign's primary call to action.

APPENDIX

CONSULTING 101

Robert S. Pritchard and Cylor Spaulding

Whether or not they know it, most people have acted as a consultant in their personal lives. Think about the last time you gave advice to a friend or family member. Whether it was making dating suggestions to your friends or advising them on how to work with a challenging coworker, you were fulfilling the role of consultant. Your friends came to you with a problem they needed to solve, and you provided strategic advice on how to handle the situation (and hopefully solve the problem) based on your own expertise. After you provided your friends counsel, they made the decision to either accept or disregard the advice. This process is similar to how a professional consultant operates.

On the most basic level, a client facing a problem (or opportunity) will hire a consultant based on the client's perception of the consultant's expertise and abilities to help address the client's goals and needs. The consultant will then conduct research and analyze the situation before formulating a plan to solve the problem or achieve the goal. After presenting the proposed plan, the client can decide to either accept or reject the advice. Depending on the client, consultants may be asked to do more than advise and be tasked with executing the plan they are proposing. There are three ways that public relations consultants interact with clients. The first is to be hired on staff with an organization. Second, consultants can operate as part of a firm like Edelman or Weber Shandwick that specializes in the communications field, or they can join the communications team within a firm that operates across industries and expertise (e.g., firms like Accenture and Deloitte). Finally, consultants can also operate on a small scale as solo practitioners or as part of a network or partnerships.

Consulting can be quite a bit more than just providing clients with advice. According to organizational behavior professor Arthur Turner, the role of a consultant should encompass any or all of these purposes:

1. Providing information to a client

2. Solving a client's problems

3. Making a diagnosis, which may necessitate redefinition of the problem

4. Making recommendations based on the diagnosis

5. Assisting with implementation of recommended solutions

6. Building a consensus and commitment around corrective action

7. Facilitating client learning—that is, teaching clients how to resolve similar problems in the future

8. Permanently improving organizational effectiveness[1]

In many cases, clients may not have the experience or resources within their on-staff public relations team to execute the consultant's proposal. Thus, consultants may be asked to help enact the plan. Many larger consultancies are full service, with teams that can execute all aspects of the recommended communications plan. For example, Edelman has industry-specific practice areas as well as subsidiaries that specialize in event coordination, research and measurement, social media engagement, and several other areas. In order to compete with these full-service firms, successful solo practitioners will need to have a network of vendors that they can leverage if the client wants the recommendations to be executed and to effect organizational change to any significant degree.

CONSULTING ADVANTAGES AND DISADVANTAGES—ON-STAFF VERSUS PUBLIC RELATIONS FIRMS

Many companies have an internal public relations person or department. Being on staff for a company presents several inherent advantages, but also some troublesome disadvantages, points out a leading textbook in public relations.[2] One of the largest advantages is that the practitioner is normally readily available, oftentimes in the same business location as the client. Not surprisingly, the on-staff practitioner is customarily seen as a member of the team, who has extensive knowledge of the organization's business practices, culture, and office politics. Such organizations also tend to perceive that, if the on-staff professional is giving good service, his or her counsel is preferable to hiring outside consultants (who charge by the hour, while the on-staff practitioner is salaried).

However, on-staff public relations consultants also face several disadvantages. For one, they are closely aligned with the day-to-day happenings and imperatives of both their supervisors and their peers and, therefore, potentially suffer from a lack of objectivity that could allow them to better see public relations challenges and opportunities. Second, they face the very real threat of being dominated by powerful players or units within the organization (e.g., legal or financial departments), which can lead to the self-censoring of needed public relations counsel. Lastly, in-house public relations people may find that clients and peers confuse their public relations role with responsibilities that belong to others—for example, being required by a top executive to review and balance the marketing unit's budget, or being asked by human resources to lead training on effective management of employees.

Acting as a counselor while employed by an outside firm also provides distinct advantages and disadvantages.[3] While staffers employed by the client may exhibit bias that is greatly informed by being a part of the corporate culture, the public relations firm employee brings objectivity and prior experiences that can benefit the client. Firms can also offer a team of counselors who can meet the varying needs of clients—expertise can vary from crisis communications, to research, to graphic design and social media. Public relations firms also offer a wide geographical reach through branch offices or affiliation agreements with other firms, a valuable network for corporations who have a national or international presence.

Counselors working from within firms also face several challenges when dealing with clients. From within the client's organization, they can face resistance about advice from outsiders, skepticism about the service offered and the costs required, and, at times, outright conflicts of personality between them and their client contacts. Other problems encountered are client unavailability and a superficial understanding of the public relations counselor's role (although it can be argued that an on-staff public relations counselor can face the same problems).

CONSULTING ADVANTAGES AND DISADVANTAGES—THE SOLO PUBLIC RELATIONS PRACTITIONER

All public relations practitioners have dreamed at one time or another of being their own boss. The lure of making money while working in sweats and fuzzy slippers and being able to take/pick up the kids from soccer, baseball, or ballet has been a siren song for many a professional and caused many a career shift into independent practice.

Quality of life can be a huge advantage of solo public relations consulting. A 2008 Public Relations Society of America (PRSA) Study of Independent Practitioners found that 100% of public relations consultants said the most important factor in becoming an independent practitioner was "control of work life," which also accounted for a 96% satisfaction rating of the arrangement. The second most important and satisfying aspect of consulting, indicated by 90% of respondents, was "more time with family."[4]

Karen Swim's blog offered nine advantages of independent consultancy that will likely resonate with those looking for the independent life:

- You get to be the boss of you.
- No "calling in sick," or a measly 10 days of vacation time.
- No dress code.
- No commute.
- No soul-sucking assignments—you have the power to choose your clients, and can select only projects that interest you.
- You focus on what you do best, with no bureaucracy.
- Work where you want, when you want.

- No trying to look busy when you're not.

- No dread of Sunday evening, knowing that another unsatisfying work week lies ahead.[5]

Two other advantages worth mentioning were offered by Arik Hanson of ACH Communications. The first is "You can always say 'no.'" No matter how wonderful one's position might be in an organization (corporate, nonprofit, agency, etc.), the employee still works for somebody else, so having the ability to say no to work is freeing for many. The second point Hanson made is the creative freedom one gains from being independent. Many enjoy the complete autonomy inherent in being a consultant. The client might have "great ideas," but the actual solution offered is the consultant's alone. Clients appreciate this, as the consultant's ideas and approaches are not locked into doing it "the way we've always done it."[6]

Of course, with everything in life, there are disadvantages to being a solo practitioner as well. First is the lack of human interaction. There's no company water cooler or colleagues "dropping by" to visit. It is not unusual to spend days on end without any face-to-face conversation. Accordingly, it can be difficult to find a way to bounce ideas off others and get good advice in return. Such sounding boards can be beneficial, especially if a practitioner does not feel confident about a certain action or strategy. Local organizations such as PRSA and the International Association of Business Communicators (IABC) are ideal starting places for creating this safety net.

Everyone loves the fun stuff, but being "your own boss" will not eliminate the need to do the "dirty work" of business, like budgeting, negotiating vendor contracts, and keeping an eye on your profit and loss statements. The independent consultant is going to be the one responsible for copying, invoicing, mailing, paying business taxes, and other seemingly mundane office work.

Additionally, public relations practitioners at firms, corporations, and nonprofits have an automatic advantage over a solo practitioner—the cachet that comes with that organization's reputation and performance. The consultant has to be comfortable with this bias and have confidence in his or her abilities to overcome it. As Hanson put it, "You're not going to get a lot of pats on the back in this line of work. And there's no corporate ladder to climb."

Finally, unreliable income is a disadvantage that often prevents practitioners from taking the leap to solo practice. The solo consultant needs to be prepared for the inevitable downturns and slow periods. During these lean times, the consultant needs a nest egg to fall back on, which means saving along the way. The consultant must also adapt with the market; standing on one's laurels is a death knell in today's rapidly changing business environment. The ego is also likely to take a hit during these downturns, so the consultant needs to have thick skin.[7]

CONSIDERATIONS FOR BECOMING A CONSULTANT

While being a consultant may seem like an attractive option to many public relations professionals, it is not necessarily the easiest professional path. There are a number of areas that public relations consultants must consider, regardless of whether they are employed by a firm, serve on staff for an organization, or act as an independent professional.

Experience and Niche: Consultants are often hired for their specific expertise within an industry or a particular type of issue. For example, some practitioners specialize in crisis communications, which could span industries, while other consultants might specialize in health communications, which is specific to companies and organizations operating in the health care sector. Think back on your professional experience, classes you have completed, and any professional certifications or trainings you have received. If these are focused on a particular industry or discipline, then you may have a niche already. If not, then consider shadowing experts in an industry, following them on social media, and/or attending professional development sessions or certificate programs that are focused in an area of interest to you.

Additionally, consider how saturated your area of interest might be with specialists. The music business, for example, has no shortage of public relations practitioners, so this industry will be harder to break into and find and retain clients in. Consider other areas of specialization that may not have as many professionals, and also keep a close eye on the trade publications (e.g., *PRWeek, PR News*, and *The Holmes Report*) to see what areas are predicted to grow in the coming years.

Finding Clients: Once you have found a specialization, you will need to explore ways of finding clients. Clients are the lifeblood of any consultancy, and a consultant without any clients will not survive very long. Your personal network can go a long way toward getting clients through referrals, but you first need to build that network. Your own skills as a public relations practitioner should be very helpful to you here.

One key way to build your network is to position yourself as an expert in your area. Seek out speaking opportunities that will help you reach your target audience, and look for presentation opportunities particularly at professional conferences. Large professional organizations including the IABC and PRSA have annual conferences, but they also have smaller regional conferences that will help you get in front of professionals in your area. Veteran consultant Les Rubenovitch also suggests approaching local colleges and universities as a way to get in front of large audiences of potential future clients:

> Call the dean of the faculty that's most relevant to your area of expertise and offer to do a no-charge "real-world" presentation to their graduating class. If they're not receptive, ask for suggestions for an alternative topic or perspective. Thank them, think about it for a few days and call back with a proposal along the lines of their suggestion.[8]

Similarly, writing bylined articles or thought pieces for trade publications can allow you to position yourself as an expert to even larger audiences. You may also think about volunteering with your local or national professional organizations to help industry decision makers become familiar with you. Monitoring requests for proposals databases and freelance sites for ads can also be helpful, but you may be competing against hundreds of other consultants for those gigs. Having a strong, professional online presence is also critical.

Lastly, keep in mind that happy clients are very likely to refer you to others or hire you for additional projects, so perform well for your clients, and they will advocate on your behalf.

Maintaining Clients and Managing Expectations: While finding clients is crucially important for a consultant, maintaining existing clients is equally important. While you may get along great with your clients and feel like you have a great relationship with them, keep in mind that this is still a business relationship, and you need to fulfill your obligations and prove your value to the client organization.

Part of fulfilling your obligations means making sure that you meet any and all deadlines you have agreed upon and having a transparent and honest relationship with your clients. Trust is key in the consultant–client dynamic, and clients need to know you are being authentic and transparent with them. This includes declining a project that you believe will not benefit the client or will be impossible to complete in the time frame you have been given. If you communicate these concerns to the client with a thorough rationale and an alternative solution, your contact will see you as honest and proactive. As Darren Dahl with *Inc.* noted, many times it is better to listen to clients than to talk to them.[9] Clients are looking for thoughtful counsel about whatever situation the company is facing, and by taking the time to listen, you will be able to craft a strategic response that genuinely addresses the executives' concerns. Listening carefully also helps you anticipate ways you can demonstrate your vision of a long-term collaboration.

Additionally, ensuring you have regular contact with clients through consistent meetings will help establish a rapport with them and give you an opportunity to discuss any issues or concerns you may have. Aside from regular meetings, try to establish some touch points with your clients so they will know their company is still top-of-mind for you. For example, forwarding along some articles that may be of interest to your clients, while not time intensive for you, will still let them know you have a keen interest in their organization. Similarly, make time to meet your clients in-person on a regular basis. While phone calls and virtual meetings are great ways to keep in touch, in-person meetings will allow clients to get to know you on a more personal level and help establish a good rapport.

Keep in mind that no matter how happy a client is with you, there may come times during your relationship that the company will search for a new consultant or adviser. While your client contacts may be the ones to interact with you regularly, they likely will work with a host of other decision makers within the company, who may determine that the organization needs a new perspective or that a consultant is no longer necessary. While you should always strive to maintain a positive client relationship, make sure you plan for the day your client is no longer your client.

SUMMARY

Whether your career goes the route of an on-staff public relations practitioner, an agency practitioner, or a solo practitioner, using these basic approaches to public relations consulting will allow you to start your career effectively. In many ways, these fundamental approaches relate to what Dale Carnegie observed in 1936: "There is one all-important law of human conduct. If we obey that law, we shall almost never get into trouble. . . . The law is this: Always make the other person feel important."[10] Carnegie stressed that, for this law to actually bear fruit, one must act out of a genuine interest for others. In other words, the ability to listen clearly for the client's concerns does not arise solely from the practitioner's prior experiences and technical abilities—it also comes from the counselor's authentic desire to help the client achieve constructive ends for the organization, for its stakeholders, and for society. Said public relations pathfinder Ivy Lee in 1928:

> This technical side of the publicity man's work coincides with his work as an ethical advisor. Eventually, corporations called the advisor in not merely to tell management what would be effective or pleasing to the public but what ought to be done in the interest of social good. In this sense, the advisor in public relations fulfills a social function and, in so far as he is upright and intelligent, performs a public service.[11]

REFERENCES

1. Turner, A. N. (1982, September). Consulting is more than giving advice. *Harvard Business Review.* Retrieved from https://hbr.org/1982/09/consulting-is-more-than-giving-advice

2. Broom, G., & Sha, B. (2013). *Cutlip and Center's effective public relations* (11th ed.). London, England: Pearson.

3. Ibid.

4. Rayburn, J., Hazleton, V., & Davis, K. J. (2008). Solo practitioner survey results: 2008. *Public Relations Society of America.* Retrieved from http://apps.prsa.org/SearchResults/view/2D-0011/0/Solo_Practitioner_Survey_Results_2008#.WiquOkqnGUk

5. Swim, K. (2008). Why public relations consulting? *SoloPRPro.com.* Retrieved from http://soloprpro.com/why-public-relations-consulting/

6. Hanson, A. (2011, September 20). The pros and cons of the solo PR life. *ACH Communications.* Retrieved from http://www.arikhanson.com/2011/09/20/the-pros-and-cons-of-the-solo-pr-life/

7. Ibid.

8. Get your consultant business going in 90 days. (2010, February 24). *CNN.* Retrieved from http://www.cnn.com/2010/LIVING/02/24/consultant.business.tips/index.html, para. 27.

9. Dahl, D. (2011, January 25). How to build better business relationships. *Inc.* Retrieved from https://www.inc.com/guides/201101/how-to-build-better-business-relationships.html

10. Carnegie, D. (1998). *How to win friends and influence people.* New York, NY: Gallery Books, p. 95. (Original work published in 1936)

11. Lee, I. (1928). *Mr. Lee's publicity book: A citizen's guide to public relations* (B. St. John, ed.). New York, NY: PRMuseum Press, pp. 355–356.

INDEX